Methods of

Effective Teaching and Course Management

for University and College Science Teachers

Eleanor D. Siebert
Mount St. Mary's College
Mario W. Caprio
Volunteer State Community College
Carri M. Lyda
Eastern Oregon University

KENDALL/HUNT PUBLISHING COMPANY
4050 Westmark Drive   Dubuque, Iowa 52002

Copyright © 1997 by Kendall/Hunt Publishing Company

ISBN 0-7872-3723-X

Printed in the United States of America
10 9 8 7 6 5 4 3 2 1

To Andrea's teachers

CONTENTS

III   *Introductory Courses and the Classroom*

IV   *Management Issues*

V   *Measures of Success*

Appendices

PREFACE

This book is intended to be a resource manual for science teachers at the undergraduate level who are looking for ways to become more effective teachers. It is written for new and adjunct professors, for teaching assistants and graduate students, and for long-time professors searching for new approaches to teaching.

There are many books that offer tips for teaching in higher education (see references), but this one focuses on the teaching of science. It is written by classroom teachers who are trained in a scientific discipline and who are scholars in the field of education and more specifically, science education. The book summarizes the changes occurring in pre-college education and speculates on the impact of those changes on undergraduate education. The authors offer tips on teaching today's wide diversity of students, insights garnered from research on learning, and discuss a few of the administrative details necessary for course coordination and management. The suggestions have worked for our authors, but every teaching situation is unique, and you will find some things will work better for you than others. We welcome your comments and suggestions for future use!

Why now?

Today's students are living in a period of rapid change, and they must be prepared to deal with, participate in and even promote change. This rapid change is due in large part to the rapid development in technology and to expanded access to that technology. Technology has heralded the Information Age, where the accumulation of information has increased exponentially. Traditionally, colleges and universities were the institutions where information was stored and dispensed, but now the consumer friendly "information superhighway" makes information readily available to people at many cognitive levels, to those with many and varied objectives, and to those with limited financial resources—often without the necessity of leaving a home or office. The fundamental role of higher education is shifting from that of giving out information to one where students must be taught how to access, evaluate, and utilize it. In science education we, too, still struggle to cope with and communicate the ever-increasing base of knowledge, but we must focus on the new principles that have emerged and on the process by which those principles are discovered. There is no sign that the accumulation and cataloging of information is slowing!

As is the case for scientific knowledge, our understanding about how to teach and how people learn has grown; and that growth has opened up, perhaps for the first time, the possibility that education can meet the challenge of science literacy for all. However if it is to do so, the teachers must have in their hands the finest and latest tools of their trade. Now they can have them, because now they exist, and we have tried to include as many of them as possible between the covers of this book.

Why bother?

As we enter the new millennium, the interplay between technology and science has helped produce instruments to probe more deeply into the previously "unseen" and unimagined—to the smallest levels of matter and at the same time to the largest levels toward the edge of the universe. These instruments help Society to pose new questions which the previous generation would not—indeed could not—conceive. The students we teach will face new problems and will solve those problems in new ways; we believe that the "habits of mind" utilized in scientific inquiry will remain valid and crucial.

Disappointingly, a recent report (Science and Engineering Indicators 1996) revealed that at present only 23 percent of persons in the United States understand the nature of scientific inquiry well enough to make informed judgments about the scientific basis of results reported in the news. Clearly, for the well-being of our future and that of our children, those of us in science education have a job to do! We believe that more effective undergraduate science teaching is an important key to change.

The Society for College Science Teachers

This publication has been coordinated by the *Society for College Science Teachers* (SCST), a society of professionals involved in science education at the undergraduate level. SCST provides a forum for interdisciplinary interaction among teachers of science at all institutions of higher education, with a primary goal the improvement in the teaching of college science courses. Individual contributors welcome questions, comments and suggestions; they are profiled in Appendix A.

Eleanor D. Siebert

Introduction

THE LEARNING-TEACHING PARTNERSHIP

The student is at the center of all learning.

This theme appears over and over throughout the book; it appears in different words and by different authors, but it is clear that learning requires the students to be actively involved in incorporating new information into their pre-existing knowledge base. As teachers, we cannot learn for students, but we can facilitate that learning by guiding them through a morass of information and by providing them with the tools for learning. The student and the teacher form an alliance in the learning process, and this introduction explores the roles of each partner necessary to a successful course experience.

The Learner's Role

Attitude. Learning is facilitated when the student wants or at least is willing to learn. Fortunately, at the college level students have made some choices that place them in your science course. For example, students choose an institution, a major or minor area of interest and—often with some assistance—their own course schedules. This self-determination usually is evidence of some interest in the course material and makes students more receptive to the course experience. The degree of self-determination, however, varies depending on the type of course (course for science majors, for related majors, for general studies, *etc.*), so that students in elective courses may value the course experience more than students in required courses. While students' attitudes are important and a positive attitude will facilitate learning (and your job of teaching), interest alone does not mean learning will occur or that it will occur easily. Other critical characteristics of successful learners include commitment, time management, learning skills, and good study environments.

Commitment. The student is an active participant in the learning process. At the very least this commitment is demonstrated in attending and participating in class, completing assignments and spending adequate time in preparation and achieving understanding of concepts. Without the student's commitment to learning course material, it is likely that you will not be able to ensure that learning occurs.

Time Management. Organizational and time management skills are essential for successful learners. Even for students who are enthusiastic (or receptive) to learning, only some will know to set priorities or will be aware of the effort and time required to be successful learners. Based on earlier educational experiences, for example, some students believe that the instructor is the dispenser of all important information; and that the students' primary and perhaps sole responsibility is to come to class where the instructor will shovel any necessary information into their heads. Successful students in my introductory science classes report that they spend on average *two to three hours outside of class for every hour spent in class.* This is not an easy time commitment for some students to make because of other demands on their time. Some of today's students hold two full-time jobs: they work 20-40 hours a week, while attending school full time. For many, heavy course loads, tuition, family responsibilities, and decreasing educational loan money make learning a lower priority than earning (money).

Learning Skills. An important learning skill often overlooked in science is the ability to read. Students need to be able to read the textbook critically and effectively. However, the percentage of students who do not buy the required textbooks (and, presumably, who do not read them) has grown rapidly in the past few years to average 25-40 percent nationwide. (Gilbert 1996) Some resistance to buying the text occurs because of the enormous expense involved, but others may not buy the text because the lecture (which accounts for more than 75 percent of all undergraduate education according to Gilbert) tells them what they "need" to know. Effective reading requires that students reflect on the words and extend the concepts beyond the specific cases presented. They grapple with concepts, often discussing them with classmates, and they practice applications. For some of my readers, just knowing the words or the definitions seems sufficient to them—but it is likely that these students will not succeed even if they read the text over and over. Essential learning skills such as reading are often referred to as *cognitive* skills.

Learning Assistance. When concepts and applications do not come easily to students, they should persist—but not to the point of complete frustration. Students should recognize when help is needed—and then seek it! Learning assistance is always available from the instructor during certain hours outside of class, or from electronic communication. Often the most valuable assistance will come from other students who have successfully mastered the material or raised questions. Such collaboration among class members can be encouraged by the instructor (see Chapter 2). Also some institutions have learning resource centers staffed by professional tutors. Students need to be aware of the entire learning support system available to them, and to *seek help when needed.*

Study Environment. Students more or less choose where they will study, and some choices are more conducive to learning than others. The most effective study environment will vary because some study time should involve group work, while at other times it may be more beneficial for students to study individually. Study should be focused, and students who have children or those who live at home may find it difficult to set aside extended periods of time when they are not disturbed. For students in such circumstances, it may be critical that they arrange to study outside the home.

Successful students generally have in common these five practical habits; they:
1. *Read* course materials;
2. *Attend class* regularly;
3. *Spend time* out-of-class time to "study"
   - time to read (and reread) notes and text,
   - time to reflect on the material to gain an understanding,
   - time to extend knowledge beyond the specific cases presented, and
   - time to apply information in problem solving;
4. *Persevere* until the concepts are grasped; and
5. *Seek help* when needed.

While these points may seem straightforward to an instructor, they may not be so obvious to students. Over the years, with the increase in factual information, the reluctance to read, and the lack of time to reflect and practice applications, my role as teacher has acquired a new dimension: that of teaching students how to become independent and active learners.

The Teacher's Role

The role of the learner has been couched in terms of attitude, commitment, time management, learning skills, and study environment. As a partner in the learning process, then, a part of the teacher's role should be to support students in these areas where possible. For example, teachers should model the attributes of a learner by demonstrating commitment to the course. Show students that you take the course and them seriously by articulating clear course objectives, coming to class prepared, and having a pleasant attitude. Be aware of and concerned with class progress and demonstrate openness and respect for students. Model time management skills by setting priorities that allow you to honor office hours and to provide timely feedback to students.

Today's teacher serves as a learning guide—one who facilitates learning. In the area of learning skills, probably the single most important thing for instructors to do is to recognize and address the cognitive level of incoming students who may need to acquire skills for successful learning. Important study skills surely include critical reading, reflection, and practice in application of principles, each of which is covered in referenced chapters.

Critical reading. Many students do not read the book because it is difficult for them—pre-college reading skill level may result when English is not their primary language outside of the classroom, or they do not practice reading. It is important at the beginning of a course to make certain that students are able to read the text book critically, differentiating between evidence and resulting principles. Class exercises designed to have the students draw the important points from the narrative by outlining or writing summaries are useful. Chapters 2 and 12, among others, include detail on teaching and assessing student reading.

Reflection. After reading the assigned text material, students may then wonder what to do with the remaining hours they are "supposed" to study. Many do not understand the concept and value of reflective thinking—of considering fundamentally how we *know* what the text has presented as fact, how the text materials apply beyond the specific cases presented or beyond the course—in short, many do not come to a full understanding and personal acceptance of the concepts. A few questions that deal with conceptual understanding in the classroom and then on tests generally spur students into solidifying their understanding and into expanding their thinking. Chapter 3 on Enhancing Critical Thinking will give you guidance in this area.

Application. In the sciences, it is important that students engage in problem solving, where the solutions require an application of concepts. Unfortunately, many text problems require little more than filling in a blank, definitions, or selecting an equation, plugging in the numbers and numerically solving for an answer. This type of activity not only fails to engage the student, but it fails to teach the importance of integrating concepts in creative problem solving. Chapter 3 will also give examples of problems that require critical thinking in developing solutions.

It is important that students (and teachers) understand the collaborative nature of the learning process. Effective teachers strive to create a community of learners in the classroom and out. Such a community not only requires active participants, but it requires cooperation and teamwork. Intense competition among students for grades generally discourages teamwork and deprives students of an important learning resource—their peers. The community ethos requires that the instructor also be a part of the community, demonstrating an interest in student learning and progress. Outside of the classroom, today's support system includes office hours for one-on-one or small group consultation, sufficient and timely feedback to students through appropriate assessment, and sometimes the use of supplementary course material and teaching assistants. Several chapters in the units on *The Art of Teaching* and those in the unit on *Introductory Courses and The Classroom* present suggestions and proven approaches to providing support techniques.

Many students have a background significantly different from their teachers. As teachers, we have little knowledge and influence over much of what our students face, but we must be sensitive to these constraints in order to humanize and to facilitate learning. Aside from communicating the nature of scientific inquiry and an essential body of facts to our students, successful teachers need to

- Expect and teach students to be active learners;
- Reinforce or teach basic study skills in the context of course content;
- Contribute to a learning support system both inside and out of class; and
- Be sensitive to individual needs of students.

Diversity and Equity in the Classroom
A special word about individual needs follows, but for more guidance in this area, please see Chapter 14. Increasing diversity in the classroom brings a broader and richer experience and perspective to the classroom, but it also brings an increasing number of special needs. Students vary in background preparation, in learning styles, in cultural background, in learning experiences, and in a host of other ways. Each student has a

unique set of references when they come to your class: some misconceptions that you will need to ferret out (Chapters 2, 9); some well-developed ways of learning that you will need to build on (Chapters 1, 2); and a personal background created, for example, by culture and gender that will give each a special way of understanding and acting (Chapters 1, 14). While as teachers we cannot walk in every student's shoes, we can give the individual due respect and hopefully find the means to help each student to reach and to maximize potential, and to contribute to the community. This accepting attitude—which assures equity, inclusivity and fairness in the learning process—encourages students and may do more than anything else in increasing their desire to learn.

Acknowledging Partnering Roles and Responsibilities

Often after the first examination or first formal evaluation (*i.e.,* grade) in the course, I encourage the class—both students and myself—to reflect on how well we are working together in learning. One technique is to devote a few minutes of class time for open exchange. First I ask students to complete a study inventory—perhaps by filling out a form similar to that illustrated in Table 1. The inventory is answered anonymously but is collected. This form guides the students to look at how they study; and shows me in what areas they need additional guidance. Note, too, that the study inventory invites students to offer comments on how the instructor might be more effective in utilizing class time. After the class has participated in the inventory, I usually spend a few minutes with them reflecting on results. A part of that discussion includes what past students have told me works for them—two to three hours study outside of class for every one hour in class; two readings of text material—once before the material is covered in class and another during the week the material is covered in class; and the bulk of the time doing homework or suggested exercises. Some individual work is beneficial for most students. When working on a question that the student cannot answer, it is important to emphasize that he or she work long enough on a problem or question to understand what the stumbling blocks are, but not to the point of total frustration; students tell me this takes about 20-30 minutes per question at a maximum. Again, it is important that the responsibilities of both the students and the instructor be examined.

Table 1
Sample of Study Inventory

Name of Course: _____ Score on First Examination: ___

Average number of hours per week studying this course
    group work: _____ homework assignments: _____
    reading text: _____ studying notes: _____
    suggested exercises: _____ other: _____

                        TOTAL: _____

Number of times you read chapter in text:
        Before it is covered in class: _____
        During week material is covered: _____
        Just before examination: _____
                 TOTAL: _____

Number of times per week you attend class (on average): _____

What do you do when you cannot answer questions about the course or about the homework?

If you were the instructor, how would you use class time more effectively?

Comments?

    The study inventory has an added benefit. Students will often come to ask how to perform better in the course (*i.e.*, get a better grade); unfortunately, I don't have *the* answer. But a quick study inventory will show how much time outside of class the student spends on the course. Some students relate they study over ten hours a week on average;

however, the study inventory dissects that time spent. If virtually all the time is spent in group work or very little time is spent in working suggested homework problems, any suggestions I might make will be more relevant

Is It Worth It? [1]

In the abstract, we believe that science teachers, particularly at the undergraduate level, are poised to educate a generation of people who understand the nature of scientific inquiry and who understand the broad dimensions of political debate in the context of the science involved. Surely there could be no more important work! But the reality is that teaching is hard work—and all of us have wondered on some days whether our lives should be better spent in other activities. So many misconceptions persist in students' minds, so many anxieties about science go unresolved, and so many students consider science "their worst subject"—despite our most lucid explanations and creative activities designed to reveal the beauty of science to them. But every so often you know that the passion and love of science that you experience, the curious-ness of nature and the excitement of discovery that captured you has been recognized. Students reveal that the most important characteristics of successful teachers are their interest in and enthusiasm for the subject. (Feldman 1989). Enthusiastic teachers stimulate the interest of students in the course and its subject matter:

Enthusiasm is contagious—so be sure to use it!

References

Feldman, K. (1989) Instructional Effectiveness of College Teachers as Judged by Teachers Themselves, Current and Former Students, Colleagues, Administrators, and External (Neutral) Observers, *Research in Higher Education*, Vol. 30.

Gilbert, S. (1996) Making the Most of a Slow Revolution, *Change*, March/April.

---

[1] YES!

I

How People Learn

Introduction

HOW PEOPLE LEARN

For years, education muddled along, an infant social science, but it has slowly and deliberately been gathering its data and growing its principles. Today, education stands firmly on a strong foundation from the cognitive sciences and supported by an enormous research base in teaching. We have based this book on that research, and it is here—in Unit I—where those basic supports are revealed and where we discuss some of their more global implications.

Now better than ever before, we know How People Learn, and knowing that is the sine qua non of good teaching. It is here, in Chapter 1, for it is symbolically and cognitively the portal we must all pass through on our way to making a real difference in the classroom.

In Chapter 2, we see the application of the lessons of Chapter 1 to classroom teaching. As a teaching method, we know that collaborative techniques have the power to tap into how people learn best; but how do we make it work in the classroom? You'll find some concrete answers to that question here.

Critical thinking is a term that is thrown about by most teachers at one time or another, but what is it? And, equally important, how can you use the best of what we know about how people learn to integrate this important topic into every course you teach? Chapter 3 is a primer on teaching critical thinking skills.

The "Coordination of Learning Experiences," Chapter 4, talks about connecting your course with the larger program of which it is a part. But, beyond that, it provides some hints at helping students create a synergy between it and other courses they take outside your discipline, and to help them make connections between your course topics and the larger world. The ability to connect learning in one area to their own, larger cognitive structures is a defining characteristic of independent learners, and creating independent learners is a significant goal of all teaching.

Most college teachers think the National Science Education Standards apply only to K-12 teachers and students, but that is not the case. In Chapter 5, the Director of the National Science Education Standards Project provides an overview of what the Standards are (and what the are not) and talks about their significance for college science teachers.

Finally, with the information revolution upon us, there is the emergence of information literacy as a basic academic skill. Its position in this unit, along with these other fundamental considerations, underscores its importance to education. Because of the rapid accumulation of new knowledge in science, the hard fought acquisition of scientific literacy in students will decay too soon if information literacy does not grow along with it. You will learn more about this important topic in Chapter 6.

William H. Leonard

Chapter 1

HOW DO COLLEGE STUDENTS LEARN SCIENCE?

This chapter begins with a definition of science and outlines what scientific knowledge may be most appropriate for college students. It reviews some important characteristics of our student audience, what research on learning suggests are the most productive ways to teach and how these relate to the process of constructivist learning. A theory of college science instruction based on active learning is proposed, and ways that effective student learning can be implemented are suggested.

What is Scientific Knowledge?

One can find many definitions of science. The literal "to know about..." implies also "to learn about...." Although traditional views of scientific disciplines usually include the natural (physical, biological, earth and space) sciences, science can potentially apply to almost any discipline of study, including education. Typical science departments in higher education include biology, chemistry, physics, geology or earth sciences, and frequently mathematics. Universities containing colleges of agriculture, medicine or allied-health have diverse departments in applied sciences. The content within all these disciplines is what we have come to know as scientific knowledge. Knowledge represents the "noun" dimension of science. It is made up of a loose progression of observations, facts, hypotheses and theories. Theories are really the "meat" of science, because they are attempts to provide cause and effect explanations of natural phenomena. This is true in spite of the popular misconception that theories and hunches are one and the same. Most people with an undergraduate major in any science can state some of the major theories in their field. Therefore the most historically recognized component of science has been the accumulated knowledge about the natural world.

Scientific advocacy groups such as the American Association for the Advancement of Science, the National Science Foundation, and the National Academy of Sciences have for the past few decades recognized the need for non-scientists to become scientifically literate. They have emphasized that science is also a verb. Contemporary descriptions of the verb dimension of natural science are given in *The National Science Education Standards* (NRC 1995), *Benchmarks for Science Literacy* (AAAS 1993) and its predecessor *Science for All Americans* (AAAS 1990). The thinking processes historically used by scientists have high utility for the average citizen who is trying to participate or to survive in a technological society. Being able to make accurate observations, predictions, collect and organize data and make inferences are among the most basic of such skills. But to be aware as a consumer and competitive professionally, our citizens must also be able to define and operationalize variables, hypothesize the relationship between independent and dependent variables, control for variables, and make rational associations between them. These scientific thinking processes are an essential component to any citizen of the world of science.

The liberal art of science as a way of knowing—or the nature of science—can be viewed as a third dimension of science and is also emphasized in the above references as well as in *The Liberal Art of Science* (AAAS 1990). Science has characteristics which make it unique. Some of these include a desire to interrogate nature, to be curious and inquiring, intellectually honest, skeptical and open to new ideas. One of the most basic characteristics of science is that scientific knowledge is tentative and that current scientific knowledge should, in fact, always be questioned. Finally, scientific knowledge should be open and shared with all persons. The very nature of science is probably the reason why many scientific ideas come under the attack by segments of our society whose dogma is threatened by the scientific enterprise.

What Scientific Knowledge is Most Useful to College Students?

Since scientific knowledge is growing exponentially and the time available to teach science is nearly constant, it is widely recognized that not all science can be taught to an individual at any level of education. The *Benchmarks for Science Literacy* (AAAS 1993) and the *National Science Education Standards* (NRC 1995) have made a major contribution in identifying what understandings about science are essential for every person who graduates from high school. But, being strong advocates of science, the AAAS and NRC have set some very ambitious goals for K-12 science education. Many science educators and scientists believe that perhaps a more realistic goal for the near future would be to have high school graduates meeting most of the AAAS and NRC goals and college graduates meeting all of these goals. Accomplishing this would be a major step forward in national scientific literacy. One only has to be reminded of recent interview studies of college graduates in which serious misconceptions are revealed such as "summer is caused by the earth being closer to the sun," "the age of the earth is much closer to being 5,000 years than 5,000,000,000 years old", and "evolution means that man came from monkeys." College science educators should feel successful if non-science majors could demonstrate proficiency in the nature of science, science process skills, and scientific concepts as identified in *Benchmarks for Science Literacy*.

Finally, it can be argued that scientific content (such as concepts and theories), scientific thinking skills, and understanding the nature of science are inseparable. All three of these dimensions of science are functionally scientific knowledge, and they should be taught together. Postsecondary science courses have historically placed far too much emphasis on only the content of science. Worse yet is that college science courses have been notorious for an overemphasis on the factual component of content knowledge at the expense of promoting students' deep understanding of concepts, theories and principles. The result is that our students, for the most part, simply do not understand science (Bracey 1991; Shamos 1995). We need a more balanced distribution of content, thinking skills and understanding of the nature of science.

What Do We Know About the Learning Capabilities of College Students?

One important factor in learning college science is the ability to process and understand abstractions. Much of scientific knowledge consists of abstract ideas. Important concepts such as natural selection, plate tectonics, equilibrium, conservation of energy and ions are very abstract. These are much different from concepts which can be experienced and processed directly such as the cell, heat, force and a rock. One of the most significant contributions to education by Jean Piaget was the recognition that an individual's ability to reason and understand concepts becomes more developed as that person matures into adulthood (Inhelder and Piaget, 1958; Piaget 1970). The vast majority of children and young adolescents are said to be *concrete thinkers;* that is, they must see, touch, or hear something to begin to understand it. Some adolescents and most adults possess the ability to process and understand abstractions without direct sensory experiences and are therefore called *formal thinkers.* As for most life processes, the mental development from concrete to formal thinking is gradual. Thus we have a continuum of potential development from concrete operational in children to formal operations in adults. We now believe that most adolescents and young adults tend to flip between concrete and formal reasoning modes, a condition termed *transitional.*

There have been a number of estimates of the percentages of persons at various age groups which are primarily concrete, transitional and formal. A population of college students selected at random in our country is estimated to be at most 50% formal thinkers (Lawson 1990, 1992, 1993). Unfortunately, this ratio is also apparently true of our adult population in general. The difference is that a larger proportion of college students tend to eventually become formal as adults compared to overall adult population. These stages of reasoning even have been studied by college major (Lawson, as before). It should come as no surprise that most college students who self-select into science and engineering majors tend to be mostly formal thinkers. After all, if a student cannot deal with abstract concepts in introductory chemistry and introductory calculus, he or she will probably not be inclined to select, let alone continue, as a science major.

But what about the majority of college students representing our non-majors? Although perhaps up to 50% of them are formal thinkers, a large proportion (probably about half) are transitional and some (perhaps up to 25%) are even concrete thinkers (Lawson, as before). This poses a serious challenge for the large-enrollment science course in which students are exposed to ten to thirty (perhaps even more) abstract concepts per lecture.

What Do We Know About Learning?

One thing we do know is that the vast majority of college students are not successfully learning science. "The present way we teach undergraduate science at colleges and universities almost everywhere simply does not stimulate active learning" (Lord 1994). The dominant lecture method just does not seem to be doing the job (Leonard 1992). Angelo has shown that college students remember only 20% of what they hear from a traditional lecture (1990). Our students entering and leaving high school are not scoring well on tests that measure understanding of science (and mathematics) relative to other developed countries, and this appears to continue through college (National Center for Education Statistics, 1997). Moreover, college science courses are equally notorious for poor teaching (Lord 1994; Seymour 1995). It has been suggested that one major reason for this lack of success of lecture methods is that students do not have the opportunities to expend much energy thinking about what is being discussed in a traditional lecture presentation. On the other hand, a truly interactive lecture, interactive group learning, or an experiential learning setting such as laboratory or field work, provide opportunities for students to process, interpret and internalize the concepts they experience. The literature contains many testimonials and experimental research studies which support the idea that meaningful learning is tied to experience (Bodner 1986; Leonard 1989 a and b; Angelo 1990; Lorsch and Tobin, 1992; Bybee 1993; Caprio 1994; Lawson 1990, 1992, 1993; Lord 1994; Roth 1994; Seymour 1995). Cannon (in press) has suggested that a lack of appropriate learning strategies (especially student-centered methods) is the largest variable contributing to attrition in science majors.

A learning approach called *constructivism* is receiving much attention in the literature. Frequently cited as the source of this term, von Glasserfeld (1987) states that "Constructivism is a theory which asserts that knowledge is not primarily received, but actively built and that the function of cognition is adaptive and serves the organization of the experiential world." Rooted in Piagetian thought, information processing and concept mapping, constructivism assumes that learners build upon prior experiences. The learner has a neural network which organizes and relates previously-learned knowledge. New knowledge is constructed by the learner out of new experiences. "Constructivists hold that learning is an interpretive process, as new information is given meaning in terms of the student's prior knowledge. Each learner actively constructs and reconstructs his or her understanding rather than receiving it from a more authoritative source such as a teacher or textbook" (Roth 1994).

Constructivist learning can be compared or contrasted to an *objectivist* approach in which knowledge is viewed as something which can be imparted. Objectivists like to use the lecture approach because they believe that they can open up the student's head, pour in knowledge, close the student's head and then have the student take a test. Caprio (1994) believes that "The objectivist teacher rewards students when their understanding is more or less the same as that of the instructor." This is a very dangerous learning approach when viewed in terms of how scientists themselves discover new knowledge. The objectivist approach is also popular among university administrators interested in the lowest possible cost to get a student through a course.

Constructivist learning also has garnered much support in the literature ranging from philosophical discussions, testimonials by instructors who have seen constructivism work successfully with their students, and experimental studies showing higher student performance in constructivist learning environments (Bodner 1986; von Glasserfeld 1987; Lawson 1988; Braathen and Hewson, 1988; Tobin 1990; Leonard 1991; Glynn, Yeany and Britton, 1991; Pressley, Harris and Marks, 1992; Lawson 1990, 1992, 1993; Lorsbach and Tobin, 1992; Bybee 1993; Leonard and Penick, 1993; Caprio 1994; Lord 1994; Seymour, 1995; Leonard and Penick, 1998; and Cannon, in press). Lord has suggested that having students work in collaborative groups is central to a constructivist learning environment because it provides opportunities for students to clarify their understandings. Constructivism warrants serious consideration in college science teaching. It is becoming clearer to many college science faculty that constructivist approaches facilitate producing meaningful understanding of science. The strong support in the literature for constructivism is probably why both the *National Science Education Standards* and the *Benchmarks for Science Literacy* essentially endorse constructivist approaches to learning.

What Do We Know About Individual Learning Styles?
There is also much evidence that students learn in different ways. The term *learning styles* has been used extensively in the literature to describe the possible means by which an individual student may best learn. Some research supports that individuals prefer to learn through one or more of the different senses (Jung 1970). Concrete learners rely more on touch, taste, smell and more intuitive and abstract learners prefer hearing and sight.

Several measurement instruments to assess individual learning styles have been developed. These, of course, vary according to the definition of learning styles. One classic instrument is the Meyers-Briggs (1958) which measures four bipolar descriptors based upon personality type: introversion *v.* extroversion, sensing *v.* intuitive, thinking *v.* feeling and judging *v.* perceiving. Another, more recently developed instrument by Krause (1996) was a variation of one used by Hansen, Silver and Strong (Silver and Hansen, 1981) which places less emphasis on introversion *v.* extroversion. It uses the variables sensing (S), feeling (F), intuitive (I), and thinking (T). For example, sensory learners (Ss) depend on experiences taken in through their senses; intuitive learners (Is) benefit from discussions of abstractions; feeling learners (Fs) tend to relate what they learn to their own personal and/or societal values; thinking learners (Ts) benefit most from a logical progression of organized and related concepts.

There is some evidence to suggest that the vast majority of learners do not sort entirely into any one of the above categories but instead into four bipolar combinations of two of these categories (Silver and Hansen, 1981; Krause 1996). Thus, ST learners need a highly organized and quiet environment, work best alone, memorize well, benefit from repetitious drill and practice and do well on recall exams. Krause (1996) believes that ST's are the classic student for which American schools have been structured. The SF is a verbal learner, is highly interpersonal and benefits from stories and examples. Cooperative learning works well for SF's. ST and SF learners are a large proportion of entering college freshmen. They are highly constructivist because they build abstractions through progressive concrete experiences.

IT learners search for logic and patterns of understanding. Since it is beneficial for them to see the whole picture of where specific knowledge fits, advance organizers such as concept maps are helpful. Being global and deductive learners, they do not memorize well but can handle abstract theories. IF learners tend to learn from metaphors, do well in social contexts such as cooperative learning, yet are very creative. Krause (1996) believes that IF learners are the most endangered in traditional American schools.

There is much debate in the literature on learning styles, primarily because of the different ways in which learning styles are categorized. There is some evidence to indicate that learning is most effective if a student is provided information about his or her unique learning style preference and is then provided instruction which takes into account that particular style (Krause 1996). It has been suggested that most instructors teach using their own preferred learning style and ignore the fact that most of the students in their class learn better in other ways. Given that there do seem to be style preferences in the way individuals learn, instructors may be well advised to first recognize this, and then try to diversify the teaching methods they use in order to accommodate the learning needs of a diverse student population.

A Theory of College Science Instruction

Although the field of education has long been criticized for not having substantial research-based theories, there has been significant work about the learning process during the past two decades. Education is emerging as a science in its own right and does have an embryonic theoretical base, for which recent developments in cognitive psychology and effective teaching have made a major contribution.

Perhaps the most embracing theory in science education today is *active learning*. It is becoming clearer in educational research that learners who are actively engaged in the learning process are the most successful. Experienced teachers have an intuitive feel that if a student is directly involved (physically, emotionally, and mentally) with the concepts or skills to be learned, the student will have a deeper understanding of and retain that understanding longer than if the learning experience is passive. This is one reason why the lecture, although superficially expedient, is not a very effective teaching strategy, even for college students. This is also why the inquiry strategy, for example, is so productive in learning concepts and processes. A theory of active learning has a considerable research base. Nearly all the citations in the bibliography of this chapter provide direct research or observational support of active learning or support active learning philosophically. Among all of the research reports on constructivism or other aspects of active learning in the literature, none were found in which an objectivist learning approach, such as lecture, produced more learning than a more student-active approach. *Based on this body of evidence, a theory of effective teaching should be based on active learning.*

Any good theory will have one or more sets of empirical observations which support it, and there are at least five supporting sets of observations found in the research on active learning. Although the essence of these has been discussed earlier in this chapter, the following five hypotheses represent areas of inquiry which provide significant support for a theory of active learning.

1. Abstract concepts are learned relatively easily only by individuals who are formal thinkers. The vast majority of learners in our secondary schools and perhaps as many as half of the students entering college are not formal thinkers. This presents special challenges to college science instructors who do not recognize this and who introduce science concepts only in abstract terms and only with passive teaching methods.

2. Learners who are concrete or transitional thinkers will benefit most from concrete learning experiences prior to successfully understanding abstract science concepts; that is, lectures and readings of an abstract nature should follow, rather than precede, an engaging activity (such as a laboratory investigation) related to the concepts to be learned. It appears that all but the most motivated students learn very little that is meaningful from lecture and textual reading alone. This hypothesis suggests that a productive learning sequence is probably (a) orientation, (b) hands-on investigation, (c) discussion, perhaps a little lecture, then (d) reading and working problems. It has been suggested by Lawson (1992) that transitional and possibly even concrete learners can learn formal concepts provided that a progression of appropriate concrete to formal instruction is provided.

3. Each individual learner must continuously reconstruct knowledge about scientific concepts as they are provided with new experiences. Most knowledge, if it is to be applied, cannot simply be imparted (poured into a student's head). Learners must interact with and reconstruct the concepts for themselves. Not all of this needs to be with concrete objects, but there should be meaningful interaction between the learner and the science concepts the learner is to understand.

4. Learners will attempt to connect new conceptual development to their existing cognitive framework. These connections can be alterations (improvements) on existing concepts or entirely new concepts. Unfortunately, these alterations can also be misconceptions. This hypothesis suggests that providing the student with a conceptual framework and advance organizers which fit onto their existing network will allow the student to relate what is being learned into what is already known. If the connection is successful, that knowledge is more easily retrievable, is more lasting, and is able to be more meaningfully applied in other contexts. The more a concept is explored, the more likely is the learning to be successful and the more likely misconceptions will be identified and rejected.

5. Individual students learn in different ways. Whether their preferred method of learning is developmentally-based, physiologically-based or personality-based, all students in a given class probably do not learn best through a single approach. Instructors need to accommodate the many ways in which different students learn by being sensitive to learning styles and by using different approaches.

What More Can College Science Teachers Do?

Active learning has long been a part of some high school biology curricula, and it is being incorporated as the major instructional theory and philosophy of many new secondary science curricula (Leonard and

Penick, 1988; BSCS 1997; *Active Physics*, in press; *EarthComm*, in development). Active learning is also emerging in mathematics, language arts, and social studies curricula because it makes learning interesting to teacher and student alike and provides learning based upon experiences to which students can make relevant connections to their real world. The college science community should examine these constructivist and standards-based curricula as possible models for future college science textbooks.

Suggestions for implementing constructivist learning environments in college science courses are now appearing regularly in the literature. Suggestions for asking questions in large enrollment lecture courses in order to promote inquiry have been given (Leonard 1992). This "reverse-lecture" approach was found to be more interesting to students than the old-fashioned lecture because there is an element of mystery as well as more active student participation in the learning process. The interaction between instructor and student provides students time to adequately process concepts. As mentioned above, Lawson (1992) has suggested some specific ways to "push" previously transitional and concrete thinkers into understanding formal concepts when given a progression of concrete to formal experiences with the concepts. The notion that formal operations are somewhat experiential and contextual has important implications for college science instruction. More college science curricula which are able to do this need to be explored and developed.

Lord (1994) tells how he uses Bybee's (1993) 5E constructivist model (engage, explore, explain, elaborate and evaluate) to improve student interaction in large group biology courses. Caprio (1994) describes how he lectured less and gave students more responsibility outside of class for their own learning. Leonard (1989) made suggestions for accommodating different student learning styles by using visuals and objects and for making abstractions more concrete to students in large-enrollment classes. Cannon (in press) suggests assessing the student perception of the extent to which a classroom environment is consistent with constructivist epistemology. He has developed an instrument which can help teachers to reflect on and, perhaps, reshape their teaching practice. Bybee and McInerney (1995) recommend that colleges and universities implement national standards and benchmarks both in their courses for non-majors and in their teacher preparation programs; in addition, they recommend that colleges and universities use appropriate, research-based pedagogy for these audiences. These recommendations include science department programs used to train teaching assistants.

The Laboratory Provides a Special Opportunity

The college science laboratory classroom or field experience is an obvious place to achieve a constructivist learning environment. It is also the best setting for students to learn scientific thinking skills and the characteristics of science. Here is an opportunity to provide students concrete experiences with abstract science concepts prior to their being further developed in lecture. One problem with many current laboratory activities is that they do not use constructivist approaches themselves. So-called "cookbook" laboratory manuals frequently present the abstract concept at the beginning of the exercise and then ask students to perform "experiments" to verify the concept. This is entirely the reverse of a constructivist approach and becomes meaningless to many students.

Methods to "uncookbook" traditional laboratory investigations are available (Leonard 1991) so that students can discover the concept for themselves by having direct, hands-on experience with it, followed by discussion and expression of the concept. The approach includes providing students with:

1. a question to explore,
2. knowledge of the materials and other resources available, including time,
3. a minimum set of general instructions to guide exploration—few enough so the student does not get bogged down in simply following directions to the point where they lose sight of both the question and the concept (although specialized technique instructions are fine),
4. a request to make predictions or construct hypotheses,
5. an opportunity to work in collaborative groups,
6. a requirement to collect data,
7. a set of questions which allows students to interpret and infer the desired concepts from their data, and
8. an opportunity to discuss in class among themselves and with the instructor the interpretation of their results.

The questions (see 7 above) lead naturally to a discussion. Three kinds of questions are helpful. First, ask students to summarize the data and examine the data for patterns or regularities. Then, ask questions which require that inferences be made from the data. Questions asking for support or rejection of hypotheses are appropriate here. Finally, ask extrapolation questions or ones which suggest generalizations and implications. This gradual and hierarchical process of thinking through the data facilitates conceptualization. The questions can be verbal but are probably more effective if written on a student handout. The instructor should place continuous emphasis on *"Where is the evidence for that inference?"*

It is very tempting for the instructor to tell the student how to carry out the investigation, but this practice needs to be resisted. Give the student help in other than technical procedures only when you feel they are becoming frustrated to the point that is unlikely they will be able to determine a reasonable plan on their own. Coach and coax them without giving it all away. Remember, the object is to give the student the opportunity to think. This means thinking about connections between the major concepts of the course, the goals in a given laboratory investigation, and the use of science process skills.

So, How Do College Students Learn Science?

This chapter argues that, because of the characteristics of the majority of students taking our science courses, *an active learning environment is the most appropriate mode of instruction.* A theory of active learning for college science instruction seems to be well supported. As for most scientific theories, active learning is bound to be discussed, further researched and modified. Hopefully, these activities will shed further light on how college students learn. There appears to be enough research support for constructivist methodologies at the college level to warrant their use. How much time you decide to spend on passive *versus* active learning in your classroom is up to you. You should at least try some of the suggestions given and see how the results fit into your own reconstruction of how college students best learn science.

References

• American Association for the Advancement of Science. (1990) *The Liberal Art of Science.* Washington, D.C.

American Association for the Advancement of Science. (1993) *Benchmarks for Science Literacy.* New York: Oxford University Press.

American Association of Physics Teachers. (in press) *Active Physics.* The Learning Corporation.

Angelo, T.A. (1990) *Learning in the classroom (phase I).* A report from the Lawrence Hall of Science, University of California, Berkeley, CA

• Bodner, G.M. (1986) Constructivism: A theory of knowledge. *Journal of Chemical Education. 63,* 873-878.

Braathen, P.C. and Hewson, P.W. (1988) A case study of prior knowledge, learning approach and conceptual change in an introductory college chemistry tutorial program. ERIC Accession # ED292687.

Bracey, G. (1991) The big lie about U.S. education. *Phi Delta Kappan, 73,* 104-117.

• Biological Sciences Curriculum Study (BSCS). (1993) *Developing Biological Literacy.* Boulder, CO: Biological Sciences Curriculum Study.

Biological Sciences Curriculum Study (BSCS). (1997) *Biological Sciences: An Ecological Approach,* 8th Edition. Dubuque, IA: Kendall/Hunt Publishing Co.

Biological Sciences Curriculum Study (BSCS). (1997) *Biological Sciences: A Human Approach,* 8th Edition. Dubuque, IA: Kendall/Hunt Publishing Co.

• Bybee, R. (1993) An instructional model for science education. In *Developing Biological Literacy.* Colorado Spring, CO: Biological Sciences Curriculum Study.

Bybee, R. and McInerney, J. (1995) *Redesigning the Science Curriculum.* Colorado Springs, CO: BSCS.

• Cannon, J. (in press) Further Validation of the Constructivist Learning Environment in College Science Courses. *Journal of College Science Teaching.*

• Caprio, M.W. (1994) Easing into constructivism. *Journal of College Science Teaching, XXIII,* 210-212.

• Glynn, S.M., Yeany, R.H. and Britton, B.K. (1991) A constructive view of learning science. In S.M. Glynn *et al,* (Eds.), *The Psychology of Learning Science* (pp. 3-20). Hillsdale, NJ: Lawrence Erlbaum Associates.

Jung, C.G. (1970) *Analytical Psychology, its theory and practice.* New York: Vintage Books (original work published in 1936).

Krause, L.B. (1996) *An Investigation of Learning Styles in General Chemistry Students.* Ph.D. Dissertation, Clemson University, Clemson, SC.

Lawson, A.E. (1988) A Better Way to Teach Biology. *American Biology Teacher,* 50, 266-273.

Lawson, A.E. (1990) An inquiry approach to non-majors biology. *Journal of College Science Teaching, 20,* 340-346.

‧Lawson, A.E. (1992) The development of reasoning among college biology students: A review of research. *Journal of College Science Teaching, 22,* 338-344.

Lawson, A.E. (1993) At what levels of education is the teaching of thinking effective? *Theory into Practice, 32,* 170-178.

Leonard, W.H. (1988) What Research Says about Biology Laboratory Instruction. *American Biology Teacher,* 50, 303-306.

Leonard, W.H. (1989) Ten years of research on science laboratory instruction at the college level. *Journal of College Science Teaching,* 18, 303-306.

Leonard, W.H. (1989) Using inquiry laboratory strategies in college science courses. *Research matters ...... to the science teacher,* 24, 1-2. National Association for Research in Science Teaching.

Leonard, W. (1989) Problems with large group instruction: What can we do? Paper to the Society of College Science Teachers. NSTA National Convention in Seattle.

‧ Leonard, W.H. (1991) Uncookbooking your laboratory investigations. *Journal of College Science Teaching,* XXI, 84-87 (Nov).

Leonard, W. (1992) Lecturing using inquiry. Paper to the Society for College Science Teaching. National Science Teachers National Convention in Boston.

Leonard, W.H. and Penick, J.E. (1993) What's important in selecting a biology text? *American Biology Teacher, 55,* 14-19.

Leonard, W. and Penick. J. (1998) *Biology: A Community Context.* Cincinnati, OH: South-Western Educational Publishing/ITP.

Lord, T. (1994) Using constructivism to enhance student learning in college biology. *Journal of College Science Teaching,* 23, 346-348.

Lorsbach, A. and Tobin, K. (1992) Research Matters ....To the science teacher: Constructivism as a referent for science teaching. *Narst Monograph,* 5, 21-27. National Association for Research in Science Teaching.

Meyers, I. and McCaulley, M. (1958) Manual: *A Guide to the Development and Use of the Myers-Briggs Type Indicator.* Palo Alto, CA: Consulting Psychologists Press.

National Center for Educational Statistics. (1997) *A study of eight-grade mathematics and science teaching, learning, curriculum and achievement in international context.* Washington, D.C.: U.S. Department of Education.

National Research Council. (1996) *National Science Education Standards.* Washington, D.C.: National Academy Press.

Novak, J. (1991) Clarify with concept maps. *Science Teacher, 58,* 44-49.

Piaget, J. and Inhelder, B. (1952) *The growth of logical thinking from childhood to adolescence.* Paris: Basic Books, Inc.

Piaget, J. (1970) *Structuralism.* New York: Harper and Row.

Pressley, M., Harris, R.K., and Marks, M.B. (1992) But good strategy instructors are constructivists. *Educational Psychology Review, 4,* 3-31.

Roth, Wolff-Michael. (1994) Experimenting in a constructivist high school physics laboratory. *Journal of Research in Science Teaching, 31* (2):189-223.

Rutherford, F. J. and Algren, A. (1990) *Science for All Americans.* New York: Oxford University Press.

Seymour, E. (1995) Revisiting the problem iceberg: Science, mathematics and engineering students still chilled out. *Journal of College Science Teaching, 24,* 392-400.

Shamos, M. (1995) *The myth of scientific literacy.* New Jersey: Rutgers University Press.

Silver, H. and Hansen, J.R. (1981) *Teaching Styles and Strategies.* Moorestown, NJ: Hanson Silver Strong and Associates, Inc.

Tobin, K. (1990) Research on science laboratory activities: In pursuit of better questions and answers to improve learning. *School Science and Mathematics. 90,* 403-418.

- von Glasserfeld, E. (1987) Learning as a constructive activity. In C. Janvier (ed.), *Problems of representation in the teaching and learning of mathematics.* Hillsdale, JN: Lawrence Erlbaum Associates

Thomas R. Lord

Chapter 2

COLLABORATIVE LEARNING

> *An undergraduate once asked his favorite science professor why she used collaborative learning instead of lecture to teach her classes. "With collaborative learning" answered the professor, "all the students use their minds when they discuss information together. With lecture the information usually passes from the notes of the instructor to the notes of the learner without passing through the minds of either one!"*

Students handle the challenge of learning in different ways. Some ignore course content until right before an exam; some regularly read class notes and the assigned book chapters during the semester; while others review the course information after each class. But, according to learning theorists, the most common way students learn is by sharing their understanding of the course materials with each other (Bosworth and Hamilton, 1994). In addition to discussing the course information, peers also assist each other with projects, work together on assignments, compile and analyze course data, and complain about their courses and professors.

Peer collaboration has always been a valued way of acquiring knowledge. Our earliest ancestors learned how to stalk and capture prey from each other, and ancient farmers taught each other how to tend their crops and select the healthiest plants for the next generation. As human populations increased, people discovered the benefits of becoming experts in a single line of work and specialization developed. The skills of a job were learned or apprenticed, not in schools, but from others in the trade. History records that the students of early philosophers gathered around their prophets and discussed, analyzed and questioned new knowledge together with the master. With increased interest in learning came academies, centers for scholarly inquiry where students and professors shared their knowledge and enlightened ideas. Early scholars weren't worried about covering their discipline's content *for* their eager students; their role was to uncover the content *with* their students.

Why Collaborate?

Gathering together to discuss matters with colleagues is an important aspect of acquiring knowledge. Students make sense of what they are presented by attempting to associate it with what they already know. Once information is properly assimilated in the learner's mind, he or she can make predictions about outcomes and effectively explain information to others. Small group discussions encourage the confirmation of information. During the interactive process explainers test the fit of their understanding with what they already know, and listeners question and challenge their own ideas about the information while trying to understand what their colleagues are saying (von Glasersfeld 1989).

Knowledge, therefore, cannot be acquired passively by the learner. In order to learn, students must expend energy in the thinking process and not simply be present during the class. Small group collaboration forces students to think for themselves with little or no input from the teacher. During the collaborative learning process, mental energies are expended by everyone, both explainers and listeners.

It is not uncommon for beginning teachers to note that they have learned more about their subject the first year of teaching than they did all the years they were undergraduates. This is because new teachers are forced to organize the subject matter in their minds so that it can be clearly presented to their students. Good teachers do not read their notes to their classes; instead they create learning experiences that trigger new knowledge in the minds of their students. Teaching what one knows about a topic to others is one of the major ways long-term learning takes place (Yager 1991).

Different Forms of Collaborative Learning

Over the years collaborative learning has taken many forms and names. For decades science teachers have utilized *group learning* in their class (usually the laboratory) where small teams of 2 to 4 students follow written or verbal procedures for a exercise or inquiry. The directions for the exercise are clearly defined, straightforward and often illustrated (such exercises are often described as a "cookbook" lesson). There is little incentive for the students to explore or create new investigations, and expected results are pretty much guaranteed if the group follows the procedures correctly. With group learning, collaboration occurs only during the performance of the task; interpretation of the results and write-up of the activity are usually done by individual class members.

A less common but more effective collaborative learning experience occurs when we provide small groups of students with initial directions or details but do not give them a road map to the answer. In this form of collaboration, the students in each team share the challenge of discovering the solution. Competition between students so often seen in self-directed learning is replaced by cooperation and teamwork. With *cooperative learning*, students unite in a group and work as a team to generate a single answer that summarizes the team conclusions. Three components apparent with this form of instruction that are not seen with general group learning are *positive interdependence* (total involvement of all the members in the task), *individual accountability* (each student is responsible for learning the materials), and *enhancement of interpersonal skills* (students encourage and teach each other).

The most effective and least common form of collaborative learning in science classes occurs when teams are presented with challenging tasks without instruction on how to accomplish them. In high level collaborative learning, the instructor becomes the creator of thought-provoking learning tasks rather than the verbal disseminator of content that students are supposed to store for later use. Instead of lecturing, the teacher's job is to provide students with ideas and experiences that will cause them to construct new knowledge on their personal conceptual framework or on understandings they already hold. In this situation, the constructivist philosophy is blended with cooperative learning in what has been called *collaborative constructivism* (Lord 1994). Students not only share their ideas about the subject, but they decide on the best plan to solve the dilemma. Each group collects and organizes its ideas, forms a common hypothesis, and develops a means to answer the question. This includes deciding what procedures will be followed (experimental design), what the data they collect suggest (interpretation of findings), and the best way to report the outcome of their effort (dissemination of results). Collaborative constructivism utilizes the positive qualities of cooperative learning (interdependence, accountability, interpersonal enhancement) to their highest degree. As students in a group work through the challenging task, each member makes his or her own connections with what he or she already understands. This is top level teaching for it gets each student involved in the active construction of new personal knowledge.

Collaborative Learning in Large Classes

Collaborative learning is not reserved for small classes. New methods of classroom instruction have emerged in recent years in which student teams have been used successfully with class enrollments of 200 or more. In all cases the students in large classes must be separated into small groups early in the semester. This is best accomplished by directing each student to an assigned desk on the first day (a seat number on the course syllabus works well). Teams are established with two members sitting directly in front of the other two members of the group.

In one collaborative learning method that has been successful with large groups, the professor directs the class for some of the period and students direct the learning for the rest of the time. During the professor led, whole-class discussion portion of the class, students face the front of the room in a rather traditional setup. When this style of instruction is utilized, it is usually done with as little teacher lecture and as much class participation as possible (usually in question-discussion fashion). During the student-centered portion of the class, students in the odd-numbered rows face their team-mates in even-numbered rows. In these small heterogeneous groups, the students work through thought-provoking scenarios, critical thinking questions, or they construct concept maps on information given by the instructor. Approximately half to three-quarters of the class time is generally spent in this student-centered collaborative fashion while the other half or quarter is spent in teacher-led, whole-class discussions. Studies on such a plan find that students typically show higher achievement and productivity, become more supportive and considerate of each other and show greater psychological health, social competence and self-esteem. (Haring-Smith 1993; Lorsbach and Tobin, 1993; McKeachie 1994)

Resistance to Collaborative Learning

Despite what the research shows about the benefits of using collaborative learning, the vast majority of college science instructors still conduct their entire class in a teacher-directed fashion. One of the reasons given by professors for using instructor-directed methods instead of student-centered collaborative methods is the belief that the teaching style they presently use is effective in getting the essentials across to students. A science professor I know reads his lessons directly from his notes to his students class after class for the entire period. When he comes to an important fact or word during his delivery, he may turn to the chalk board and jot it down to suggest to his students that it is something they will see again on the test. And most of his students "prove" they have learned the material by passing the tests which have been created directly from the lectures! Studies have shown that most of what is remembered from this type of teaching is forgotten soon after the grades are determined (Perkins 1993). Many professors who resist student-centered teaching add that students prefer to be given the facts they are expected to know for the tests and not be forced to sort them out from "irrelevant" content found in journals and text readings. For these instructors, despite the passive nature of students in the learning process, lecture is the most efficient way to teach at the college level.

Yet some college science teachers would be willing to adopt more student centered forms of instruction if they could be sure it would lead to greater student learning. Many of these educators, however, have misgivings about student-to-student instruction because they have tried using collaborative teaching methods, such as cooperative learning, in the past. Some say they returned to teacher-directed instruction because their students needed more direction and could not stay on task with the method. Other instructors have tried student-centered teaching practices in past years but have gone back to a teacher-centered format because they could not cover all the science content to which they were accustomed. Still others believe that collaborative learning works in the arts, humanities and the social studies, but it is too open-ended to work in science which deals with precise and abstract concepts. Almost all of these instructors support the contention that students learn science best by themselves and not in collaboration with others.

Science in the real world, however, is not done individually. Scientists constantly converse with each other, exploring and debating their ideas and work plans. Teams of scientists work together to devise ways to prove ideas; scientists share findings and discuss results with others in their profession; and they encourage colleagues to duplicate their experimental design and evaluate their data. Why should the teaching and learning of science be done individually when science itself is not done that way?

Problems Experienced With Collaborative Learning

The reasons given by science instructors for not using collaborative techniques in their classes are often well founded. First, it must be pointed out that some students do succeed in teacher-directed, lecture settings. These are typically students who read, write and memorize well and who are competitive and goal oriented. Students in this category tend to succeed no matter what instructional method is used by the teacher.

Many students who take science, however, have a difficult time learning through memorization. Non-rote learners greatly benefit from student-centered activities since they discover for themselves the information in the lesson and apply the content to real world events. Furthermore, it is not just the non-rote learners that benefit from student-directed classes. Gamson (1993) found that learning in even the most gifted students is enhanced when students discover with their colleagues the important aspects of a lesson.

Collaborative learning enhances the lesson in another way. The student-centered approach forces instructors to appraise what is most important in the lesson for students to understand and to remove superfluous content from the syllabus. Many instructors continuously add new material to their lessons, but only marginally eliminate the older, "standard" content; as a result, the amount of subject matter in their courses has increased appreciably over time. This places an undue burden on the learner that often leads to frustration and disenchantment with the course.

Several research studies, however, have found that up to a third of the content in a traditionally taught science class can be eliminated without sacrificing the students' understanding of the subject (Mayer-Smith and Moon, 1993). By eliminating superfluous and repetitious content from traditionally-taught science classes, the teacher has the time to include beneficial collaborative learning activities. These activities might include constructing concept maps (visual flow charts representing concepts and their relationships; Novak and Gowin, 1991; Ault 1985); analyzing scenarios posed by the instructor; and interpreting charts, graphs and diagrams. Therefore, by reducing the breadth of coverage in science courses, a greater depth and understanding of the subject can take place.

Collaborative Learning Activities That Will Cause Problems

Well-designed and correctly-managed collaborative learning science activities will always enhance student learning. The most common reason that collaborative learning activities fail is that they have not been constructed correctly. There are several types of activities that are not effective with student-centered learning. An activity that has members of a collaborative team do something that can easily be done by one person will usually doom a group learning experience. It is relatively common, for example, to ask student groups to copy a chart from their lab manual onto a sheet of paper. This type of activity is generally performed by just one member of the team and creates a poor learning situation for the others of the group.

Another problem activity that is often used in collaborative learning lessons in science is asking team members to do a task that has only one right answer. It is relatively common, for example, to have student groups label pre-drawn diagrams in a laboratory manual (*i.e.*: various body systems in a dissected cat or fetal pig). This activity may help a student learn the names of the organs, but it is not a productive collaborative learning experience.

Group work that requires students simply to memorize science information is another type of exercise that will eventually lead to failure. A climatology professor, for example, may assign student groups to memorize the symbols for various weather phenomena at the end of the text, or a professor of anatomy and physiology may ask students in collaborative teams to find the origins and insertions of muscles in their texts. While knowing the information may be important in the course, the activities are inappropriate for collaborative learning lessons and are generally seen as busy work by students.

Creating Collaborative Learning Activities That Really Work

There are many student-centered, science-related collaborative activities that lead to productive learning. I often use collaborative groups to answer questions in class. Five types of questions that are particularly useful are:

Questions with answers not directly found in the text. Such questions engage the students in the teams to come up with answers from their experiences, knowledge and beliefs. For example, rather than having groups label diagrams or drawings that are similar to ones in their text, have them invent a model that has parts that function in a manner similar to those in the text. Tell the students that they must use most of the terms in the text diagram and be ready to explain their answers. The teams may not be able to accomplish all aspects of the task, but they will work together and put creative, high-level thinking into their team effort.

Questions that require integrating knowledge of two or more factors to find the answer. This kind of activity provides an opportunity for several members to contribute. For example, many systems in science depend on several factors or cause several things to occur. Rather than telling students the factors, ask teams to predict things that will influence the outcome before they are presented with it (*i.e.*: ask students to come up with 8 factors that influence the rate of diffusion). Always ask the teams to come up with a high number of factors; the required large number increases the challenge and helps assure that all of the members will contribute to the answer.

Open-ended questions. Many science professors who utilize collaborative learning enjoy the spontaneous and impromptu nature of this form of interaction. For example, when teams are asked to come up with the twenty-five most important skills needed by settlers on a deserted island or the inhabitants of a colony on the moon, students vigorously interact and it is sometimes difficult for them to come to consensus. Queries that do not have specific answers allow students to bring up and support their own analysis, and they encourage all the members of a team to contribute to the group answer. Open-ended questions also work well with concept maps where student teams are challenged to develop a comprehensive grid showing cause and effect relationships of a scientific phenomenon. With concept maps, for example, student groups could be asked to develop grids of direct and indirect factors that influence the rate of a particular natural action (*i.e.:* acceleration, sedimentation, oxidation).

Questions that require interpretation. Asking student teams to decipher information from a chart or graph forces each member to manipulate data, observe relationships and predict trends. This process develops their deductive reasoning skills and enhances their ability to interpret information.

Questions that may be interpreted different ways. Directing student groups to come up with reasons why humans are starving in all countries of the world could lead to answers that include such things as politics, climate, economy, education, and natural disasters. The smorgasbord of answers provides for rich discussions and enhanced learning.

Managing Collaborative Learning Classes
Student-centered teaching requires a large amount of time to set up and manage. Since college instructors only see their students two or three times a week, the period for teaching is precious. Dedicated educators realize that valuable instruction time can be lost if careful planning does not precede the establishment of student teams and the distribution of group activities.

The management of the collaborative experience, however, need not be overwhelming. Establish student groups at the beginning of the semester and require the teams to sit together each class—even during teacher-directed activities. In this way time is not wasted initiating short group activities at various times during the class hour. An efficient way of getting the students into groups the first day is to write a different seat number on each course syllabus or schedule. As students enter the class for the first time, they obtain a descriptive plan of the course and locate the seat holding the same number as is on their syllabus. If the desks in the room are not individually identified, a seat diagram of the room can be placed on an overhead projector or numbers can be taped on the chairs before class. When the students find their new place in the room, they meet the class members they will work with for the semester (Lord 1997).

To further increase time efficiency, all materials needed by each group during the class can be placed in a large envelope for each team before the session. As students take their seats before the class meeting begins, a member of each team collects the group's envelope from the front of the room. The team answer sheets, short readings, information outlines, team quiz results, and even the day's activity questions and team quizzes (sealed in different small envelopes) are included in the group materials. When the instructor wants to have the class work on a team activity during class, a team member pulls an answer sheet and/or sealed question from the large envelope and the group works on it as a team. When a team reaches consensus on the response, someone in the group writes down the agreed-upon statement on one of the answer sheets provided in the envelope. As each team completes the question, the answer sheets are collected by the instructor. When all teams have completed the question, the teacher randomly selects one or two answer sheets and asks one of the team members to state their group's answer. The given answer is discussed by the class as a whole and corrections are suggested by classmates when needed. Following this event the professor may elaborate on the topic for a short time in a teacher-centered manner or introduce another group activity. This sequence is repeated several more times during the class period as learning is extended further and further into the topic. The teaching pattern can be thought of as a series of short readings, each followed by a period of discussion and analysis. During the class hour students pick up new information in 5 to 10 minute spurts of professor-directed instruction, each separated by 10 to 12 minutes of student-centered interaction.

One of the most interesting aspects of this form of collaborative learning in college science is that it allows for individual accountability and positive reinforcement at the conclusion of each class. With eight to ten minutes left in the class period, the instructor gives the teams several minutes to review the information learned in class that day. Then in the final 3 to 5 minutes, a colored ball (or a number) is randomly drawn from a hat (each group member has been assigned a color or number). When the ball is selected, the person having that color takes a short quiz on the day's material, and the rest of the class is excused. All members of the team present during the class receive the grade earned by their quiz taker. Because the students do not know which member of their team will be selected to take the quiz, they all review for it together. In this way all of the team members are held accountable for the information even though only one will take the quiz.

Sharing of the Grade in Collaborative Learning

A concern about grading collaborative activities is often expressed by some instructors and conscientious students. How can an instructor ensure that the work in the course is being shared equally by group members rather than being done by one or two students in the team? The answer is that one cannot be sure. In fact, the course work probably is not equally shared by everyone in the group. One of the most difficult challenges for teachers in all formats of instruction is to assess the level of learning of each student in the class. Instructors who utilize collaborative learning and collective exercises still need to evaluate students individually. Many instructors assess their students with tools similar to those traditionally used (*i.e.:* individual term papers, non-shared tests, *etc.*).

The question of equal sharing can be applied to any effort where teamwork is an important goal—whether it be on athletic teams as in basketball, academic teams as in debating, or performing teams as in drama productions. If everyone in the group contributes what they can, the whole team benefits. Similarly, if every person in a community does what they can in their neighborhood, the whole of that society benefits as well. The enhancement occurs despite the fact that some societal members contribute more than others to the effort. If neighborhoods only recognized and rewarded the most productive member in the community, many would-be supporters and contributors would become disinterested, resentful and turn away. With collaborative learning, the goal is to gain success through the combined or shared effort of each person. Because the individual members of teams begin at different levels of ability and knowledge, some members need more time and help in making a contribution. Through teamwork, those who know more learn as they teach their colleagues; those who know less at the beginning learn from their mentors. Everyone benefits as all participants learn from the experience.

As mentioned before, many instructors see grading as a problem with student-centered classes. A good way to avoid this dilemma is to base student grades on points earned during the semester; students earn points toward their grade both through their team contribution (*i.e.:* group answers on team questions, group quizzes, group homework and papers, group projects) and through their individual understanding of the material (*i.e.:* individual exams, individual project contributions, topic contributions to a term paper). Instructors determine what percentage of the final grade should be based on points earned through group work and what percentage should be based on the student's individual effort, although this breakdown should be made clear to the student at the beginning of the course.

Sometimes a single collaborative group activity may carry with it both group and individual assessments. Team projects, debates, term papers, and presentations can be scored both as one unit and/or individually, especially if the assignment includes a specific component for each member of the group to complete. Dual assessment of a project gives the student points for both the team collaboration as well each individual's contribution to the effort (and, therefore, how accountable each member is for the information). Instructors can weigh the two scores the same or differently depending on the workload of the assignment. For example, a professor of environmental science that I know assigns each student group a term paper on an environmental issue (*i.e.:* population growth). The professor stipulates that the paper must include four different aspects (*i.e.:* biotic impact, abiotic impact, economic impact and social impact) of the topic and requires that each member of the group be responsible for one of the portions. Students receive 100 points for the overall paper (team aspect) and 100 points (individual aspect) for their section of the assignment. This system encourages each member of a team, not only to do a good job on his or her section of the paper, but it motivates other members to help their less capable team mates to furnish high quality sections to the paper. In addition, this team plan allows other members in the group to critique all sections of the paper for errors and flow, and provides each student with a different sense of audience than if he or she were writing just for the instructor. If one of the group members fails to contribute to the project (or provides a half-hearted effort to it), the team's points can be determined without the negligent student's contribution. The neglectful student does not receive the points awarded to the team, and the team is not penalized for that member's lack of effort.

Another plan that works well when deciding grades for members of the team, is for the instructor to read the overall paper and assign a percent grade to it (say an 82%). The grade is then multiplied by the number of students in the group for the total number of points the team members get for the project (*e.g.*, for four students, the group receives 328 points). The instructor returns the project to the team with the comment that they can divide the points between them in the "fairest" manner. This places control of the grade for the effort in the hands of the students. They know how much time each member put into the project and generally reward the hardest worker on the project with more points than the laziest. The teams submit their individual member's points to the instructor with a rationale for their decision. If this procedure is utilized, it is helpful for the instructor to give the students a set of guidelines for evaluating the effort ahead of time (*i.e.:* to what extent did each person cooperate with others, exhibit competence, and demonstrate initiative). Alternatively, the team can come up with its own criteria for the evaluation and report it with a rationale. The method gives the instructor some insight into what went on within the group during the project. In addition, the method provides students with the experience of doing peer evaluations, which will eventually help them in the work place.

Conclusion

Science is full of excitement, mystery and wonder. It is a field that should easily stimulate young minds and spur student imagination. But for a large number of students, science courses just are not inspiring enthusiasm for the field. Instead of creating interest, taking a course in science for many undergraduates is an unwelcome and frightening experience. For a large number of our students, science courses are only taken to fulfill the college science graduation requirement.

Many students feel that science is a compilation of facts and figures that need to be memorized to pass the class. Rarely do they relate the facts and figures to their understanding of the real world or recognize that the process of learning science is the same as everything else they know. The problem is often compounded by science instructors whose teaching styles do little to alter this notion. For many instructors, the primary role of the college teacher is to describe the content students must know to pass the course as clearly and thoroughly as they can. They feel that once the facts and figures are memorized by the students, the understanding of meanings and relationships will automatically follow. A large number of professors see the challenge of college science teaching as holding the students' attention for as much of a lecture as possible.

But the challenge to college science instructors is not to deliver entertaining lectures; it is to construct thought-provoking scenarios, questions and puzzles that cause students to think about what they are learning. As students ponder what they are being taught, they build new insights based on their prior understanding and belief. Furthermore, not only do students need time to reflect on the challenges put before them, but they need time to discuss their ideas with other students in their classes. When this collaborative process begins in the classroom, it continues outside of class and becomes a valuable life-long skill. It is through such collaboration with peers that all people test their new understandings and correct their misinterpretations. As knowledge is gained, it is molded with the pre-existing insights held by the student. This is how knowledge grows in our minds, and it is what good science instruction is all about.

References

Ault, C. R. (1985) Concept Mapping as a study strategy in earth science, *Journal of College Science Teaching*, **15**: 38-44.

Bosworth, K and Hamilton, S.J. (1994) Collaborative learning: Underlying processes and effective techniques. *New directions for teaching and learning*, San Francisco: Jossey Bass.

Haring-Smith, T. (1993) *Learning together: An introduction to collaborative learning.* New York, Harper Collins College Publishers.

Lord, T. (1994) Using constructivism to enhance student learning in college biology. *Journal of College Science Teaching* **5**: 346-348.

Lord, T. (1997) A comparison between traditional and constructivist teaching in college biology, *Innovative Higher Education*, **21** (3): 197-216.

Lorsbach, A. and Tobin, K. (1993) Constructivism as a referent for science teaching, *NARST News*, **34**: 9-11.

Mayer-Smith, J. and Moon, B. (1993) Enhancing undergraduate student learning of cell biology: moving away from the lecture podium, presentation at the annual meeting of the National Association for Research in Science Teaching, Atlanta.

McKeachie, W. (1994) *Teaching tips: strategies, research and theory for college and university teachers,* 9th Ed , Boston; W.C. Heath.

Novak, K. and Gowin, B. (1984) *Learning How to Learn,* Cambridge University Press, New York.

Perkins, D. (1993) Teaching for understanding, *The American Educator,* **17**: 28-35.

• von Glasersfeld, E. (1989) Cognition, construction of knowledge, and teaching, *Syntheses,* **80**: 121-140.

• Yager R. (1991) The constructivist learning model: toward real reform in science education, *The Science Teacher,* **9**: 53-57.

Robert D. Allen
David J. Stroup

Chapter 3

ENHANCING CRITICAL THINKING

Several months ago, a biology faculty member at a large east coast university called us with a problem that students from his department were having. Many of their students intended to go to medical school, but their performance on the MCAT (Medical College Admissions Test) in their senior undergraduate year was unacceptable. He felt that these students knew a lot of biology, but they were unable to handle unfamiliar questions that required them to apply their knowledge in new situations to interpret, predict, evaluate, and draw conclusions—characteristics of many questions on the MCAT test. Although the students' memory and recall were impressive, their thinking skills were poorly developed.

Actually, this is a scenario that is found at many colleges and universities. The question to us in this case was whether a crash course on critical thinking would help his students improve their MCAT scores. Our response was that a crash course might help but that thinking skills require early and effective attention in teaching—especially since the consequences to college students are so serious.

Today there are powerful forces for change to improve students thinking skills. National agencies and professional associations have made strong recommendations to place much greater emphasis on thinking skills. For example, the National Science Foundation has released a report that emphatically recommends increased attention to critical thinking in undergraduate courses (NSF 1989). In another report, the National Advisory Group of Sigma Xi (1989) recommended the following:

The National Advisory Group was adamant that entry-level courses (in the sciences) should focus upon thinking, analysis, synthesis, critical reasoning and understanding and that the current emphasis on memorization of facts be minimized and, whenever possible, eliminated.

More recently, the *National Science Education Standards* developed by the National Research Council (1996) repeatedly emphasize inquiry skills. The teaching standards include that teachers of science should:

-Plan an inquiry-based science program for their students
-Create a setting for student work that is flexible and supportive
of student work
-Encourage and model the skills of scientific inquiry

And in content standards, students should:

- Develop abilities necessary to do scientific inquiry
- Develop understandings about scientific inquiry

Standardized tests, such as the MCAT, ACT, and tests from the Educational Testing Service, require students (and teachers) to utilize critical thinking skills at a fairly sophisticated level. The expectation is that these skills should be well developed and used to solve problems (Allen and Stroup, 1993).

For almost 20 years we have worked with a great many teachers on how to teach thinking skills. Almost all teachers express a sincere desire for their students to understand and to use information and concepts in new situations. They are keenly aware of the national recommendations and standardized test requirements. Yet, when one examines teaching practice and learning outcomes in the great majority of classrooms across the nation, achieving significant improvement in students' thinking skills has proven surprisingly difficult. Why, then, do difficulties persist; and is there any promise for improving the teaching of critical thinking? In our experience, there are logical reasons for these difficulties but they *can* be overcome and students *can* learn critical thinking skills with the appropriate techniques and materials. Our intent in this chapter is to provide you with insights, recommendations, suggestions, and source material that will greatly assist your efforts in this endeavor as a teacher.

Teacher Concerns

Teachers generally agree that they want their students to develop and practice critical thinking skills. These skills include the ability to evaluate and interpret experiments, draw conclusions from data, make predictions, and identify assumptions. From this point, however, teachers will take one of two distinctly different teaching strategies:

STRATEGY 1	STRATEGY 2
↓	↓
If students are deficient in these abilities, it is because they have incorrect or insufficient information.	If students are deficient in these abilities, it is because they have not had the opportunity to practice or apply these skills.
↓	↓
Techniques and presentations should be used that improve the correct recall of information by students.	Techniques and presentations should be developed that give students specific instruction and practice with critical thinking skills.
↓	↓
Improving recall and retention of correct information will lead students to demonstrate the desired abilities in critical thinking. Corollary: *The more information students can recall, the better their critical thinking.*	With appropriate instruction and practice, students' skill will improve. Corollary: *Without such practice, student skill will not improve.*

By far, the more common strategy that teachers seem to adopt is the one on the left, strategy 1. There are probably several reasons why this is so. On the whole, college science teachers have had little training or exposure to innovative teaching methods or the literature on teaching styles. They are likely to "teach the way they were taught" which is usually a traditional approach, or "let the textbook be the guide" which leads to strategy 1 because college textbooks focus on the transmission of large amounts of information.

Another factor may be that teachers have developed good thinking skills as they progressed through their undergraduate and graduate education. Perhaps new teachers tend to take skill development for granted as something that happens without conscious effort as more information is learned. However, this is clearly not true for the great majority of students.

Indeed, a great many teacher participants in our workshops indicate that they have always assumed that if students have all the correct information they need, then they will be able to automatically practice good thinking skills. Their experience with their students indicates that this is not the case, but in the absence of a better strategy they continue to provide increasing amounts of information with the hope that students will improve.

Another serious concern of teachers is covering the content in their courses. If too much time is spent on developing thinking skills, perhaps this will mean less time for content coverage. Teachers already are pressed to cover what they feel is the necessary information. Such feelings will naturally influence teachers to focus on content. There are two ways to deal with this concern. One is to simultaneously develop both critical thinking skills and content understanding, but this usually requires substantial changes in teaching style and approaches as discussed under "Effective Strategies" later in this chapter. A second is to deliberately decrease content. This is a more delicate issue and is the subject of considerable controversy. How much and what kinds of content should be included in different courses varies widely across departments and institutions, but there is growing concern that content is over-emphasized as evidenced by the position of Sigma Xi cited earlier (1989). In the absence of any clear guidance on this issue, and it is not likely that any will be forthcoming in the near future, teachers are left to decide for themselves or with their immediate colleagues on the best course of action.

Student Difficulties

In our experience, the greatest barrier to students' skill development is their perception that effective learning is characterized by the retention and recall of large amounts of information. Correct information and answers are obtained from the teacher and textbook, and their task is to remember this information. Unfortunately, this is a problem that is often reinforced by teachers who dispense right answers in class and expect the same back from students on their examinations. Students fail to recognize that critical thinking skills extend their abilities so that they can understand information at a deeper level, can apply concepts in new situations, and can solve new and unfamiliar problems. They fail to recognize that critical thinking is a skill that grows with practice, reflection and refinement—not just memorization.

This problem is not new. Arnold Arons (1976) has discussed this issue in detail and indicates that students and teachers should constantly examine questions such as: *"How do we know....? Why do we believe...? What is the evidence for...?"* He points out that:

"The great majority of our students have accepted these propositions (conclusions or 'facts' of science) on faith. They have almost never examined evidence or articulated in their own words any of the reasons that lead us to hold these views. They received them as end results from authority and pass them on to others in exactly the same manner. Eventually it does become necessary to take some end results of scientific inquiry on faith; we cannot develop extensive evidence on every single area we wish to study or interrelate. The students, however, have never discriminated between assertions such as 'scientists know that...' and instances where they have followed at least some of the evidence and understood how the particular result was validated and accepted. Before submerging them in further assertions of end results, it is essential to lead them to an understanding of the basis for some of our most fundamental and far reaching ideas."

Given Arons' views, it is not surprising that most students have poorly developed critical thinking skills. It logical to expect that these students will not attempt to solve new and unfamiliar problems or to extend their knowledge beyond what they "know." Rather, they will simply wait for the teacher or textbook (or some other authority) to provide the "answer." To some extent, this behavior is understandable. Students feel the teacher knows so much and they know so little. Yet students can and should begin developing the analytical skills that will allow them to use what they "know" in an intelligent and productive way. *How do we guide students to develop the necessary thinking skills?*

Effective Strategies

Instructional strategies to improve critical thinking skills can take several forms. In the classroom, for example, students can observe analyses demonstrated by the instructor. In our experience, the most effective demonstrations are structured in a form that Arons terms "Forwards Science" (doing science the way scientists do it); teachers start classes with observations, descriptions of experiments, or experimental results. Ask students for their observations, predictions, conclusions, interpretations, and assumptions. Use their responses as a springboard to develop the concepts. This approach has been described in detail (Allen and Stroup, 1993), and student responses and progress have indicated the effectiveness of the techniques.

In contrast, a more traditional approach typically emphasizes the detailed description of interpretations only. Experimental designs and results are seldom discussed and students are not asked for their observations, predictions, or assumptions.

The effectiveness of "Forwards Science" was vividly demonstrated to us while videotaping a demonstration tape for use in a workshop. We first presented a short lecture in a "Forwards Science" manner and then the same topic, using the same visuals and examples, in the traditional manner. Several undergraduate students volunteered to serve as a typical audience. When we finished the second tape, the students immediately spoke up and said, "We liked the first one better!" (the Forwards Science example). We asked why they felt this way and they replied, " In the first one we knew what you were talking about. But in the second one we didn't know what was going on". We were somewhat puzzled and pointed out that in the second demonstration they had already seen the content, tables, and graphs. How could they not understand the second presentation? They continued, however, to maintain that the Forwards Science approach was much more clear and understandable. While this is only one isolated instance, it was a vivid and honest response from the students. This response is both disturbing and revealing when it is recognized that textbooks are generally written in a format that reflects the second approach. On the other hand, textbooks are written to appeal to teachers, not students. *Why don't we listen to our students and use textbooks and teaching techniques that help them learn and make the learning process more effective?*

For most teachers, implementing a "Forwards Science" format is relatively simple. Start with concrete examples, experiments, and data. Start with relatively simple questions such as, *"What do you see (observe)? How would you explain (interpret) these data? What would you look for next (predict)?"* Moving to more complex concepts from this point makes a lot more sense to students. If our students' comments are any indication, your efforts will pay major dividends!

Written Exercises

Effective programs do exist that emphasize written exercises to provide practice with critical thinking skills. Statkiewicz and Allen (1983) have used multiple-choice exercises that require students to write clear and complete justifications to accept or reject each choice. The process of constructing, evaluating, and revising a written rationale for the choices provides students with extensive practice in developing lines of reasoning. Highly significant improvement was demonstrated by the students after several weeks practice with these exercises.

In another study by Tyser and Cerbin (1991), students read and analyze short articles from a newspaper or popular science magazine. The intent of these exercises is to guide them "to become proficient at writing logically persuasive responses to claims made about newspaper and science magazine articles." Student responses indicated significant improvement in critical thinking skills.

A similar approach is used by Rau (1991). Students read short articles, write brief summaries, and identify questions that could be pursued. The primary intent is to have students make and defend judgments. Every student is engaged in extensive writing practice and analysis.

All these reports of significant improvements in critical thinking skills strongly emphasize writing. These techniques may be most effective because they engage the student on a personal level that encourages them to reflect on their thinking and structure an argument in their own words. The written activities allow for individual, extended, and self-paced practice. As students review what they have written, revise their comments, and produce a finished product, they should become more aware of and more skilled at developing a well-structured line of reasoning. Moreover, the written responses provide ample material to the instructor for analysis of student work and progress.

As one example of an effective written exercise, consider the following that was used by Statkiewicz and Allen:

PROBLEM: A biochemist was studying an organism known to synthesize a red pigment from substance 'A' in the organism's diet. Furthermore, it was known that substance 'A' was first converted to substance 'B' by the action of an enzyme (E_1). Then substance 'B' was converted to the red pigment by the action of a second enzyme (E_2).

$$A \xrightarrow{E_1} B \xrightarrow{E_2} \text{Red Pigment}$$

The biochemist discovered a few mutant organisms that could produce the red pigment only when provided with compound 'B'. Which of the following would you most likely conclude about the mutant organisms?
1. They do not have the genetic information to produce the second enzyme (E_2).
2. The mutants are producing too much of the second enzyme (E_2).
3. They do not have the genetic information to produce the first enzyme (E_1).
4. They do not have the genetic information to produce either enzyme
5. Choices 2 and 4 are equally likely as the best conclusion.

The following is the kind of analysis expected from the students:

Analysis The mutant organisms differ from normal organisms by their inability to convert 'A' to 'B'. With food source 'B' red pigment is produced, but with food source `A' red pigment is not produced. Therefore, `A' cannot be converted to 'B'. The most likely explanation is that E_1 is missing.

1. If the organisms can convert 'B' to red pigment, then E_2 must be present. Therefore the organism must have information to synthesize E_2. Using this argument, choice 1 does not follow from information given in the problem. *Reject*

2. An excess amount of E_2 does not affect the conversion of `A' to `B'. If there is any effect it would be an acceleration of the conversion of 'B' to the red pigment, but there is no evidence that such an acceleration actually occurs. This statement does not account for the inability to convert 'A' to 'B'. *Reject*

3. If E_1 is not present, then 'A' could not be converted to 'B'. Lack of information to produce E_1 would obviously lead to the absence of E_1 and the inability of the mutant organisms to convert 'A' to the red pigment. *Best Choice*

4. If they did not have the information to produce either E_1 or E_2, then 'B' could not be converted to the red pigment. However, the mutant organisms can produce the red pigment when provided with 'B'. *Therefore, reject*

5. Both 2 and 4 have been rejected

A complete and persuasive written rationale to accept or reject each choice is expected from the student. The expected analysis is very difficult for students to write at first, but with several weeks practice most can achieve this level of competence. By writing, reviewing, and revising their written choices, the students engage in extensive critical thinking practice. Exercises can be used as out of class assignments and greatly extend students' practice. This is the primary way we use the exercises, and in about six to eight weeks significant improvement in problem solving can be detected in their responses.

The primary disadvantage is the instructor time required to grade and evaluate student written responses. Another disadvantage is that the time lag in providing feedback to students can be significant and seriously detract from the effectiveness of the feedback.

Computer Exercises

A relatively new development in effective strategies to teach critical thinking is the use of interactive computer exercises. Computers have the potential to relieve the demands on instructors and at the same time provide more rapid and effective practice for students. Until recently, computer assisted instruction was almost entirely devoted to simple presentation and drill and practice. Last year, however, we began working with a software package (IMMEX Author and IMMEX Analysis) that allows teacher authoring of interactive computer exercises and analysis of student problem-solving skills.

IMMEX Author can be used to create interactive computer exercises allowing students to access and explore a variety of data bases as they attempt to solve a problem. The activities of selecting appropriate data, rejecting inappropriate data, proposing and pursuing potential hypotheses, making observations and interpretations, evaluating experimental designs, and developing a line of reasoning incorporating data from a variety of sources that will ultimately lead to a valid and well-supported conclusion provide ample opportunity for students to practice critical thinking skills.

Perhaps more important are the capabilities of IMMEX Analysis. As a student works through a problem, each step is recorded. This information can be retrieved in the form of a pathway map showing the sequence of data sources examined by the student. The individual pathway maps can be used by the instructor to provide feedback to students. When a sizable number of maps is available from the same problem solved by different students, these can be analyzed using neural network software that can identify patterns of problem-solving strategies. As a powerful analytical tool, IMMEX Analysis provides possibilities previously unavailable to teachers.

In one study (Palacio-Cayetano 1997) biology students who work with IMMEX exercises demonstrated significantly improved critical thinking skills compared to students who received traditional instruction. These promising early results open new possibilities for critical thinking skill development.

Advice

If you implement the strategies we have described, we feel sure you can expect impressive progress by your students.

- *Be patient*-most of your students will initially struggle with the written exercises.

- *Be supportive*-most of your students will find, at least initially, critical thinking a frustrating endeavor.
- *Be persistent*-critical thinking is not something to be covered in the first week of class and then expected to be understood by the students.

Observation, interpretation, prediction, and assumptions are activities that should be examined every day as an integral part of science in every topic. Be alert to developments in computer assisted instruction. The increasing sophistication and capabilities of instructional software promise major advances in critical thinking instruction.

Do not underestimate the importance of your efforts! Improving students' critical thinking skills is a high-stakes endeavor. Our increasingly complex society relies on people with well-developed thinking skills. Their best opportunity to develop these skills is in your classes.

References

Allen, R.D. and Stroup, D.J. (1993) *Teaching Critical Thinking Skills in Biology*, Published by the National Association of Biology Teachers.

Arons, A.B. (1976) Cultivating the capacity for formal reasoning: Objectives and procedures in an introductory physical science course. *American Journal of Physics,* **44** (9), pp.834-838.

National Science Foundation, Directorate for Science and Engineering Education. (1989) *Report on the National Science Foundation Discipline workshops on Undergraduate Education.*

Palacio-Cayetano, J. (1997) *Problem-solving skills in high school biology: The effectiveness of the IMMEX problem-solving assessment software.* University of Southern California Dissertation.

Rau, A.D. (1991) Developing analytical reasoning and judgment skills in non-science majors. *Journal of College Science Teaching,* **21**(2), 97-99.

Sigma Xi, The Scientific Research Society. (1989) *An Explanation of the Nature and Quality of Undergraduate Education in Science, Mathematics, and Engineering.*

Statkiewicz, W.R. and Allen, R.D. (1983) Practice exercises to develop critical Thinking Skills, *Journal of College Science Teaching,* **12**, 262-266.

Tyser, R.W. and Cerbin, W.J. (1991) Critical thinking exercises for introductory biology courses. *Bioscience,* **41**(1), 41-46.

Eleanor D. Siebert

Chapter 4

COORDINATION OF LEARNING EXPERIENCES

The aim of a college education is to produce independent, life-long learners who can deal with a massive collection of facts—facts which often are subject to conflicting interpretations. Independent learning requires that a person connect concepts, organize thinking, recognize patterns and possess cognitive skills that will allow them to explore and expand ideas. Adult learners must know how to learn and must know how to utilize information given an intellectual base of ethical, social and scientific knowledge. They must know how to think, and how to think critically. The question is: how can college or university science courses produce such an adult learner?

Classroom experience of teachers and research on learning indicate that coordinated learning experiences will result in more effective learning, and nowhere is coordination of learning experiences more important than in the sciences (NSTA 1995). A coordinated curriculum presents a comprehensive and coherent framework of science concepts, reinforcing the connectedness and significance of all science in our lives. This premise is at the heart of the *National Science Education Standards* developed by the National Research Council of the National Academy of Sciences (NRC 1996; see Chapter 5) and in pre-college curriculum projects at the American Association for the Advancement of Science (AAAS 1993), the National Science Teachers Association (Scope, Sequence, and Coordination Project (NSTA 1990), and by other professional groups such as the American Chemical Society (ChemCom). In general, K-12 curricula are coordinated at the State level by the State Boards of Education, which have frequently endorsed a strategy such as that outlined in the California State Science Framework. The National Science Teachers Association holds the position that "coordination of curriculum from kindergarten *through undergraduate years* is essential for effective, meaningful and developmentally appropriate science education." (K-16 Coordination Position Statement, 1995; italics mine). However, there are few efforts currently in place to provide a continuum in science learning from the high school to college transition. Perhaps the best articulation effort is through the Advanced Placement Program at the Educational Testing Service, where high schools must coordinate with colleges to meet their expectations in providing courses for college credit. (SCST 1997)

It is difficult to provide a seamless transition in science courses at the high school-college level because students in a college/university introductory science course come from many schools, with varied academic backgrounds and interests. Some entering and re-entering college students have had their last previous science course anywhere from one to 10 years earlier; in some cases, students enrolling in your course may have had *no* science course in their secondary schooling. There is, too, a school of thought that argues that students making the transition from high school to college need to be readied to cope with change and non-linear ways of thinking. That is, a "seamless transition" may not be the best option to teach young adults the skills they will need to become scientifically literate citizens.

Nevertheless, whether or not there is close coordination between the high school and the college and university level science courses, sequential development and interlinking of concepts in the undergraduate curriculum continue to be essential to enabling students to gain a solid understanding of scientific concepts and develop an ability to use the scientific process. There are many aspects to coordinating learning experiences in introductory science courses at the undergraduate level; these include, for example, coordination within a course, within a program, and across programs at the undergraduate level. Coordination efforts require communication and cooperation among department members, with faculty of other departments, with high school teachers, with professional organizations and with business and industry representatives. In addition to content objectives, there are important goals of higher education and expectations of society which may need to be coordinated and integrated into your course objectives. Examples of such objectives transcending subject matter may include respect for human dignity, ethical standards, and community service.

What Can an Introductory Science Course Instructor Do to Ensure a Coherent and Well-coordinated Learning Experience?

* *Take time to plan your course.* Ideally you will begin planning your course and articulating your course objectives as much as three to six months before class begins. Occasionally new instructors are hired only weeks (days?) before the course begins, and this does pose a problem with careful planning—hopefully, in these situations the course you have been hired to teach is a course with which you are familiar so that your planning period need not be so extensive.

* *Know what the program and/or department expects students to learn from your course.* Talk to other members in your department and institution to ensure that students in your class will be exposed to essential information and that they develop increased problem-solving skills as they progress through advanced levels. Then, choose content and exercises to provide students with critical information and skills upon which subsequent courses will build. Examine your course content carefully and critically in the light of students' needs. A common failing of introductory courses is to try to cover too much material in one course. Many educators today find that some traditional topics are not essential to advanced courses or they are covered better in advanced courses. The current wisdom is that students are better served by covering fewer concepts better and in greater depth to achieve solid understanding than to speed up to survey topics at a superficial level.

* *Set course goals or objectives* for your classes that specify what learning should be achieved by the end of the course. These course objectives should be sensitive to the needs of the students, the program, and the institution. Many instructors articulate course outcomes in terms of the content to be covered (cognitive domain) as well as to the skills and attitudes to be developed (affective domain). The classic reference on educational objectives by Benjamin Bloom (1964). Although a specific classification of objectives into the two domains is not necessary and may not be useful for you, the important thing to

remember is that carefully coordinated course objectives will allow you to develop a continuum of concepts spiraling toward increasing complexity.

* *Become active in professional organizations* to ensure that your course outcomes are linked to outcomes expected in other institutions. These organizations are generally aware of and sensitive to the needs of the businesses and industries who will employ our students. Successful teachers communicate often with colleagues in professional organizations to determine national trends in content coverage as well as to discuss innovative and effective teaching strategies. Examples of professional organizations for science teachers are profiled in Appendix B.

* *Connect your course material across disciplines* as often as possible. Coordination efforts beyond the classroom and department need to include a horizontal thread. Many of the students in an introductory science course are majors in other science and non-science fields. These students need to see the importance of science to their areas of study. Talk to members of other departments to see what concepts students in other majors build on and how those concepts are introduced in their courses. For example, a quick glance at a biology textbook lets me know how to introduce solution behavior in chemistry so that both courses can reinforce these principles for students.

* *Permit students to build on their previous learning.* Talk to a sample of students taking your introductory course to determine what they have learned and how they have been taught. The transition between high school and higher education is generally the most disjunctive transition that students make in the K-16 formal education system. Teachers of college science courses need to be aware of their students' backgrounds, of course, and some introductory courses use an assessment test for appropriate course placement. Perhaps the real shock to entering college students is not so much in content expectations, but in the different teaching styles they encounter. The *National Science Education Standards* emphasize learning through inquiry; teachers of college and university science courses, who recognize the value, excitement (and frustrations) of scientific inquiry in their own work, are in a strong position to integrate the principles of the Standards into their own teaching. Why not

initiate a dialog between a science teacher in grades 10-12 in order to better understand student expectations?

* *Help students connect your course material with the "real" world.* Students need to be able to use the data of the discipline to come to a basic understanding of our world. There are some undergraduate curriculum projects—for example, *Chemistry in Context: Applying Chemistry to Society* (American Chemical Society, 1997), that centers its chemistry content and problems about genuine social issues. John Moore (1994) argues that "science teaching will always be incomplete unless it deals explicitly with the world of the student, explains the strengths and limitations of scientific procedures, provides ample information on the total dependence of human life on the living and nonliving worlds, unfolds the beauty and creativity of science, and helps the student live in this world with joy, understanding, appreciation, and sensitivity."

References

Bloom, Benjamin S. *et al.* (1964) (Eds) David McKay, *Taxonomy of Educational Objectives: The Classification of Educational Goals. Handbook 1: Cognitive Domain*, NY 1956; Krathwohl, David R. *et al.* (Eds), David McKay, *Handbook 2: Affective Domain*, NY.

Chemistry in Context: Applying Chemistry to Society, Second Ed. (1997) A project of the American Chemical Society, A. Truman Schwartz, Ed., Wm. C. Brown, Pub., Dubuque, IA.

Moore, John A. (1994) *Science Discoveries and Science Teaching: The Link*, The Society for College Science Teachers, Siebert, Eleanor and Estee, Charles (Eds).

National Science Education Standards. (1996) National Research Council of the National Academy of Sciences.

NSTA Position Statement (1995) *K-16 Coordination.*

NSTA (1990) *Scope, Sequence, and Coordination Project.* Aldridge, B., Principal Investigator.

Project 2061. (1993) *Benchmarks for Science Literacy*, American Association for the Advancement of Science, Oxford Univ. Press.

SCST Program and Abstracts, Vol 17 (1997) Heady, J.(ed).

Angelo Collins

Chapter 5

NATIONAL SCIENCE EDUCATION STANDARDS AND THE COLLEGE INSTRUCTOR

In 1996, the National Research Council released the National Science Education Standards (NRC 1996) describing a vision of science education which promotes scientific literacy for all students in grades K-12. Striving to address the concerns of numerous organizations and individuals concerned with the quality of science education in the U. S., almost five years were spent developing the Standards. The argument posed here is that college science instructors have an obligation to know of and carefully consider the Standards in the design and implementation of the college-level science classes they teach.

College science instructors have a responsibility to consider the Standards in the design and implementation of their courses for at least three reasons:

First, college science instructors are the primary providers of science instruction to prospective K-12 teachers of science. The images of science that teachers have are the result of the college science courses they have taken. If teachers believe that science is an accumulation of arcane terms and abstract mathematical formulae produced through the manipulation of complex instruments that have no impact on their everyday life, this is the image they will impart to their students. If teachers imagine science as the continuous development of understandings and abilities that allows us to describe, explain and predict natural phenomena, many of which are encountered daily, this is the image they will impart. College science instructors should know that the Standards mandate that teachers learn science in the ways they will teach it, by developing understanding through inquiry.

Second, the Standards describe the vision of what a scientifically literate person understands and is able to do. As college science instructors recognize that many of the students they teach, especially in the introductory, liberal studies courses, will not become professional scientists, the Standards provide guidance about what to teach and how to teach it.

Finally, the Standards influence the understanding and ability of the students that college science professors will encounter in their own classes. While it will be years before colleges will be inundated with students who have experienced a Standards-based science education program throughout their K-12 education, students from schools and districts that are implementing Standards-based instruction are entering colleges this year. College science teachers need to consider what their instruction will look like when students come to college having acquired their understanding of science through conducting inquiries on topics of interest to the student and importance to science rather than having memorized the definitions of bold faced terms in a textbook.

In this chapter, college-level science instructors will be introduced to the Standards through an overview that highlights five features of the document: its history; the focus on all students understanding science; the definition of science content; the inclusion of standards for content, teaching and assessment; and the inclusion of support standards.

In the *National Science Education Standards* the term *standard* means both a banner and a bar, a vision and criteria to measure progress toward that vision. Taken as a whole the Standards describe a vision of science education in which *all* students achieve understanding of important ideas about natural events and phenomena through inquiry. To attain this vision requires consideration of the science content, the science teaching, the science assessment, the science education program and the science education system. Considered separately, each standard provides a guide that can be used to measure progress toward the vision. The Standards implies that if all of the individual standards are not considered, the vision becomes extremely difficult, if not impossible, to attain.

History

To begin the story of the current reform in science education, recall that the 1989 Education Summit held by then-President Bush and the National Governors Association, proposed that: *By the year 2000, U.S. students will be first in the world in science and mathematics achievement.* (Goal 4) Influenced by the mathematics standards, *Curriculum and Evaluation Standards for School Mathematics* (National Council of Teachers of Mathematics [NCTM] 1989), national education standards in basic school subjects were recommended as a means for achieving this and other national education goals. In the Fall of 1991, the National Research Council (NRC) agreed to coordinate the development of Standards for the science education community.

The first period in the development of the Standards emphasized information gathering, discussion and debate. The initial work included studying science education standards from other countries, curriculum framework documents from those states which had developed them, and many existing reform documents. Four documents were submitted for public critique. Over two hundred presentations were made to hear concerns and opinions about national science education standards.

The second period of development moved from study, discussion, and presentation to capturing the ideas for science education standards in writing. Review continued during this second period, but it was targeted review. As each section was written it was reviewed by knowledgeable persons who had not been engaged in the preparation or writing task. For example, when the physics section was completed, five National Academy of Science members who are physicists were asked to review the section. When all sections had been written, reviewed and rewritten, they were bound into a single document and reviewed by representatives of major science education organizations.

After this targeted review and subsequent rewrite, in December, 1994, thirty thousand copies of the *National Science Education Standards (Draft)* (NRC 1994) were distributed for a three-month period of national review. Over 250 groups of teachers, scientists, administrators, educational specialists, policy makers and others reviewed this draft as well as over a thousand individuals who submitted questionnaires. All the reviews were studied carefully for consistent criticisms. The document released in December, 1995 represents an iterative series of successive approximations produced through cycles of review and rewrite involving thousands of people. The involvement of many persons in the development of the Standards is one of its strengths.

Science Understanding for All Students

All Students. The Standards focus on all students understanding science, with equal emphasis on *all students* and on *understanding.* The first principle of the Standards is that

> *All students, regardless of age, gender, cultural or ethnic background, disabilities, aspirations or interest and motivation in science should have the opportunity to attain high levels of scientific literacy.* (p. 20)

The goals for science education provide the reasons that understanding science is important for *all students*. First, understanding natural phenomena is rewarding in and of itself as this understanding helps stimulate and satisfy basic human curiosity. Understanding scientific principles and processes is useful in making personal decisions as well as when participating in public debate on the increasing number of social issues that have scientific components. Informed personal and public decision making is a right and a responsibility for all citizens. Finally, science is important in maintaining economic productivity in a world in which science and technology play increasing roles.

Understanding. Equally important in the vision of science education described by the Standards is the emphasis on understanding. Understanding implies a breadth and depth of knowledge about the facts, concepts, laws and theories that describe, explain and predict natural phenomena. Understanding, however, goes beyond knowledge in that this rich organized body of knowledge is attained through the processes of scientific inquiry. Understanding also requires relating different aspects of science knowledge to one another and to knowledge of other non-science topics. Understanding presupposes a complex structure of knowledge and ability that is useful, not only in answering questions about natural phenomena, but also in addressing concerns beyond a laboratory or classroom that have a science component. Finally, understanding implies the ability to reflect on what is known, how it is known, and the value of that knowledge. Scientific literacy is the product of understanding science.

Definition of Science Content

Another feature of the *National Science Education Standards* is the manner in which science content is designated. The Standards does not define a national curriculum. Curriculum is the structure, organization, balance and presentation of science content. There are many possible curricula for the fundamental science content identified in the Standards. In the Standards, science content is considered fundamental if it:

> ...*represents a central event or phenomenon in the natural world; represents a central scientific idea and organizing principle; has rich explanatory power; guides fruitful investigations; is applicable to situations and contexts common to everyday experiences; can be linked to meaningful learning experiences; is developmentally appropriate at the specified grade level.* (p. 109)

The Content Standards begin with unifying concepts and process of science: systems, order and organization; evidence, models and explanation; constancy, change and measurement; evolution and equilibrium; and form and function. These unifying concepts and processes are important in all science disciplines and for students at all grade levels.

The remainder of the science content standards, organized by grade levels K-4, 5-8 and 9-12, begin with inquiry, followed by science subject matter. The final three categories of Content Standards focus on human, contextual aspects of science: science and technology, science in personal and social perspectives, and the history and nature of science.

Inquiry Inquiry is more than the familiar processes of science. Inquiry includes these processes used in conjunction with well-structured science subject matter knowledge, reasoning ability, and utility in the application of science understanding to a variety of problem settings. Inquiry implies facility in asking questions about nature, conducting investigations using appropriate tools and techniques, constructing and analyzing explanations, and communicating arguments.

The Content Standards begin with inquiry because it is the foundation of the other science content standards. Scientists' practice and students' understanding and ability in science are both grounded in the experience of inquiry.

Subject Matter   The next categories of Science Content Standards are the Science Subject Matter Standards—the facts, laws, concepts and theories about nature. Organized by the traditional science disciplines of physical science, life science and Earth and space science, the subject matter standards present major fundamental ideas in science. Focusing on ideas that are fundamental to science and recognizing that achieving understanding through inquiry of these ideas is a time-intensive activity, many science topics currently in text books are not in the Subject Matter Standards. Students in grades 9-12 are expected to develop understanding of the following ideas:

In *Physical Science* students attain understanding of structure of atoms, structure and property of matter, chemical reactions, conservation of energy, and interaction of energy and matter.

In *Life Science* students attain understanding of the cell, molecular basis of heredity, biological evolution, interdependence of organisms, matter, energy and organization in living systems, and behavior of organisms.

In *Earth and Space Science* students attain understanding of energy in the earth system, geochemical cycles, origin and evolution of the earth system, and origin and evolution of the universe.

Human Aspects   Science and technology are closely related. While the former is concerned with answers to questions about natural phenomena, the latter is concerned with solving human problems and meeting human needs. In the Standards, Science Content Standards include the abilities of technological design: identifying a problem, proposing a solution, implementing the solution, evaluating the product or design, including a cost-benefit analysis, and communicating the problem and its solution. The Science and Technology Standards intentionally parallel the Science as Inquiry Standards.

Because science occurs in a human, social context, science influences and is influenced by events beyond the laboratory. As defined in the Standards on Science in Personal and Social Perspectives, science is essential in understanding personal and community health issues, human population growth, natural resource management and environmental quality, and natural and human-induced hazards. Science is done by people who abide by rules of evidence, rituals, and mores that regulate the conduct of science. The Standards on the History and Nature of Science highlight that science is a human endeavor, done by men and women with diverse interests and abilities engaged in a variety of tasks; that scientists evaluate the procedures, evidence, and reasoning about their own work and the work of other scientists in public forums; and that science has played and continues to play an important role in human history.

These later Content Standards assume facility in inquiry and understanding of subject matter and transcend boundaries between science disciplines. The Standards prohibit one from claiming that students have achieved understanding of scientific ideas unless and until the students are able to apply these ideas to situations in the world beyond the science classroom.

Content, Teaching and Assessment

A fourth feature of the *National Science Education Standards* is the inclusion of standards for content, teaching and assessment in a single volume. Content, teaching and assessment can be compared to three legs on which the vision of scientific literacy for all rests. If one leg is missing, the vision will be unable to stand. The inclusion of all three elements in the Standards reinforces both the importance of each and their interdependence on each other. In addition to the Content Standards described above, there are Standards for Teaching and Standards for Assessment.

Teaching The Teaching Standards do not propose a single method of instruction. Rather, they require that teachers select, adapt and design instructional practices that promote student understanding and application of major ideas in science through inquiry. The Teaching Standards require that teachers plan and implement an inquiry-based science program, focus and support inquiries as they interact with students, encourage and model skills of inquiry themselves, and structure classroom time so that students can engage in extended inquiries. Since inquiry includes communicating ideas and arguments in science, the Teaching Standards encourage teachers of science to build learning communities which promote collaboration among students and provide opportunities for students to engage in discourse about science. In addition to redefining typical tasks of teaching, the Standards call for teachers to become active members in the school community, working with their colleagues and the administrators to plan a coordinated school program that includes science, to plan and implement professional development activities, and to engage in research that promotes student learning.

Assessment The Assessment Standards do not prescribe specifications for a national science test. Rather they present a set of principles that guide quality assessment practices both in the classroom and in externally mandated and designed assessments. For example, the variety of achievement data collected should focus on the science content that is most important for all students to learn. Because assessment practices provide the operational definition of science content, all of the outcomes of learning science must be assessed. The Assessment Standards suggest it is often impossible to separate the assessment task from the instructional activity. They also demand that the assessment of student achievement be coupled with the opportunities students have had to learn. They call for assessments that are consistent with the decisions they will inform, are fair and are of high technical quality.

Support Standards

Although teachers and the classrooms in which they teach are central to the vision called for by the Standards, teachers cannot accomplish the transformation alone. Therefore, the Standards include three sets of what might be called support standards: the Professional Development of Teachers of Science, the Science Program and the Science Education System.

Professional Development The Standards for the Professional Development of Teachers of Science speak to college science instructors because these Standards describe how teachers come to learn science, learn to teach science, and become life long learners. These Standards demand that teachers come to understand science in ways similar to the ways they are expected to teach it, through inquiry. This understanding may be in a course in which important scientific ideas are embedded in instruction about how these ideas have come to be accepted by the scientific community. Teachers also might learn science through a summer apprenticeship in a research lab where they participate in data production, organization, analysis, and discussion.

Program The Program Standards call for a science program that is consistent within and across grade levels, that employs a variety of curriculum patterns that are appropriate for the students and the geographic area, and that emphasizes the relationships between science and mathematics and among the other school disciplines. In order to affect such a science program, adequate resources—qualified personnel, time, space, and materials—must be provided to teachers by the school and district. All students must have equitable access to these resources. And the school community must be structured to support reform efforts.

System The Science System Standards provide criteria to policy makers and others for creating mechanisms to consistently provide resources in an equitable manner to promote the vision of the Standards. Consistency demands coordination and cooperation about curriculum, teaching and assessment across and between federal, state, district, and school levels. This consistency may require changes in policy or in resource allocation. While constantly evaluating changes in science education policies for intended and unintended outcomes, these policies must be sustained.

Conclusion

The Standards do not provide guidelines for implementation. Further, the implementation will require time and resources, and we are impatient to see immediate results. Since the implementation calls for many changes in practice and in the system, it is too easy to place responsibility for action on someone else. Also, it is naive to infer that inquiry and application can be laid on top of the current subject matter and that there will be sufficient opportunities for students to develop understanding.

Standards for science content, science teaching, assessment of science achievement and opportunity to learn, the professional development of teachers of science, the science program and the science education system provide a set of lenses to look at a vision of science education that is different from current practice. From any perspective, the challenge is complex and is influenced by each of the other perspectives. Yet each lens provides a meaningful perspective to consider implementation of the *National Science Education Standards*. College science instructors have an important role to play in that implementation.

Angelo Collins

References

NCTM (National Council of Teachers of Mathematics). (1989) *Curriculum and evaluation standards for school mathematics.* Reston, VA National Council of Teachers of Mathematics.

NRC (National Research Council). (December 1994) *National Science Education Standards (Draft)*, National Research Council. Washington, D.C.

NRC (National Research Council). (1996) *National Science Education Standards.* National Academy Press, Washington, D.C.

Louise Kelly
Mario W. Caprio

Chapter 6

INFORMATION LITERACY

We already have crossed the threshold into an information revolution that is bound to have at least the impact of the agricultural and industrial revolutions we've experienced in our less recent history. The way information is processed, stored, and accessed is changing almost as rapidly as its volume is growing. Since it is not really possible to teach the students all they will need to know about our subjects (for the simple reason that much of what they need to know has not yet been discovered), **scientific literacy without information literacy is doomed to early obsolescence.**

In order to learn, students must know how to access, evaluate and utilize information. Information literacy refers to the skills and knowledge required to locate information and to evaluate and use it appropriately. It is becoming a basic learning tool, not unlike reading, writing, and the quantitative disciplines have been. As is the case for the other basic academic skills, its practice enhances all courses of study, and its mastery is essential if life-long learning is to be a reality. Knowing the way around your school's library is a start. Being able to use the catalog to find books; print and computerized indexes to find journal articles; reference books to find specific information; and the Internet to find other research materials are a few of the skills required of a student who is doing research. But the various information sources (books, articles, indexes) and electronic information systems (online bibliographic and full/text databases, Internet) are going to vary from library to library, so the student needs to understand the concepts behind the organization of knowledge and the processes used to locate information.

61

As is the case for the natural sciences, information science has a specialized subject matter of its own. Of course we expect college science teachers to be information literate; it would be hard to imagine them completing their advanced course work if they weren't. But it takes more than knowing how to do something for one's self in order to be able to teach it to others. The problem is that students do need to be able to access scientific information for their science courses and for their lives in a scientific age, but their science teachers neither have the background in this specialized area, nor do they have the time, to teach it effectively. On the other side, librarians have the skills to teach about the research process, but they know it is done best when the students come to them motivated by questions important to their courses. The obvious solution is collaborative teaching. Clearly, this is an area where a science instructor and a librarian can be a powerful instructional team to help students construct this important academic skill.

Teachers and librarians can and should share the responsibility for teaching students to locate, evaluate, and use information. When the science teacher thinks of the research process in these larger terms, research is not just a means to an end; it is an end in itself. Instructors who are sensitive to this issue can incorporate information literacy in their course outlines as one of the objectives. Here is an example from a course outline of a science literacy course:

> Students will be able to use an academic library to locate information relative to this course, evaluate it for suitability, and use it appropriately in class assignments.

The remainder of this chapter will set out several objectives of information literacy (see Table) and discuss how a classroom teacher and a librarian can help students achieve them.

Objectives of Information Literacy

1. Refine and Focus the Topic. Students frequently come to the library to research topics that are too broad. The first stage of research involves the process of narrowing down a topic so the final product of the research (the presentation, paper, *etc.*) will have sufficient depth. This is difficult to do if the student does not already have some knowledge of the subject. Generally speaking, students in introductory courses do not know enough about their research topic. So the first step, then, in the research process is for them to find general background information. Dictionaries for definitions, and general encyclopedias or subject-specific encyclopedias like *The McGraw-Hill Encyclopedia of Science and Technology*, or *Magill's Survey of Science* are useful in providing an overview of a topic.

It may be tempting for the instructor to focus the project so specifically that the student can skip doing this and avoid some of the frustration it offers. This would further the ends of the science subject matter portion of the assignment, but obviating this step in the process will make the library experience less valuable to the goal of enhancing information literacy.

The more natural and rooted in reality the research topics are, the better students will exercise and develop skills that will be useful in the real world. Topics that naturally develop from classroom discussions or students' questions, as well as topics students generate themselves, will have a challenging rawness to them and will require the full range of processing.

Students will soon learn, or you may want to guide them in this direction, that by rephrasing their topic as a question, or as a series of questions, they will arrive at a sharper focus more quickly. In the reality of the process, however, it is probably the librarian part of this teaching team that will talk to the student about these sorts of details during their one-to-one conversations in the library.

General Information Literacy Objectives   *Students will be able to:*
1. Refine and focus their topic of research
2. Develop a search strategy
3. Locate the information they require
4. Evaluate the information they discover
5. Organize the information to suit their needs

2. Develop a Search Strategy. The information-literate person does not approach all research topics in the same way. Beginning students, however, will have a way of doing library research that they may have learned in lower grades or may have invented *de novo*. Some rush first to the catalog, to find books; others almost never use the catalog, preferring

CD-ROM indexes. These are the students who come back to you and say: "Can I change topics? There's nothing in the library on mine."

The research strategy is a logical approach to the project. It generally begins with a search for the most general sources and moves to the more specific. Just how specific their research will get will depend on the nature of the assignment you give the students. For the most part, beginning students do not think in terms of having a strategy. They go to the library to "look for stuff on my topic." Of course they will be able to think strategically—it isn't difficult—but first someone needs to tell them about it. (See *Information Literacy Workshop* below.)

Having some strategy is important to efficient research, but having a rich strategy is better. Knowing which tools to use and in which order they serve best is immediately dependent on first knowing what is in the toolbox. For example, journals, books, the Internet: these are places where information resides; the corresponding tools for finding that information are the indexes, the catalog, and the Internet search engines. There is no question that the easiest way to learn about these tools is in a workshop specifically designed to suit your students' needs.

How will you know if your students are using an effective strategy? You will see the final product, of course, but there is a better way. You can have them keep a library log where, each time they go to the library to work on this project, they jot down the date, the amount of time they spent there, and describe the research tools they used and the relative effectiveness for their topic. Afterwards, you can collect the logs and review them with the librarian to be able to give students some feedback, which they may be able to use to improve future researches. Some instructors grade the logs with respect to the degree that they represent coherent strategies.

3. Locate the Information. If the strategy is the plan, then this objective is the execution. Fortunately, though, even if students have been utilizing faulty strategies, they have likely been gathering some experience with the actual mechanisms of locating the sources. They may have used the wrong index and used it in ineffective sequence, but they still know how to use the index. One can hope.

Students seem to have the least difficulty with this part of the process, from the point of view of the classroom teacher. However, the librarians will bear the brunt of this burden. They will be there when the students are struggling to "figure out" the microfiche reader, the online catalog, the organization of the *General Science Index,* or the difference between "keyword" and subject searching in electronic indexes. But, in the end, time and practice ultimately lead to acquisition of this objective.

4. Evaluate the information. When you evaluate the bibliographic portion of the student's project, you will have an opportunity to comment on the sources they have used. To get some idea about how well they are discriminating between the usefulness of available sources, you might want to ask your students to submit to you a list of *sources omitted*, as well as the more usually required list of works cited.

When deciding whether or not to use a source, the students must evaluate it as to its timeliness, level of scholarship, and presence of bias. They must also consider its authority and the reliability of the author and publisher. If you plan a library workshop experience for your students, some of the following points will likely be brought up by the librarian presenting the session. You may also find yourself jotting some of them in the margins of papers you are correcting.

➤Timeliness of information is relatively easy to establish by determining the date of publication.
➤Determining the authority and reliability of the author and publisher often leads to information on the accuracy and reliability of the information presented, as well as to the level of scholarship.
➤Students can find biographical information about the author in the book itself or in reference sources such as *Contemporary Authors, Who's Who*, or the *National Faculty Directory*.
➤Book reviews are a good source of information on the quality, reliability, and accuracy of the information found in books. Students can locate them through *Book Review Digest* and *Book Review Index*.
➤Who published the book is a good indication of its quality. (Instructors will have to help students learn about the better known publishers in their fields.)
➤Popular magazines, such as *Time, Newsweek, U.S. News and World Report*, and *Science Digest* contain articles written by journalists for the general public.
➤Journal articles are written by experts in the field and are intended for other experts. They are generally reviewed for accuracy and reliability by specialists in the field before they are published.
➤Students must also examine sources of information for bias. For example, they must understand that a book or article written about creationism by a Christian fundamentalist author would not be likely to offer a balanced view of human origins.

65

Evaluating information found on Internet sites is not as easy as evaluating print sources. Many students believe they can find everything they need on the Internet and that all of it is accurate and reliable; but they need to be told that there are no standards or guidelines concerning what can and cannot be put on the Internet, nor is the information found there usually verified by reviewers. Anyone can put anything on the 'net.

Evaluating Internet Resources is Difficult
Usually no publisher
Dates are ambiguous
No standards are enforced
Rarely is an author's name provided
Anyone can put anything on the Internet

The same guidelines applied to evaluating books and periodicals also need to be applied to Internet sites, but this is often difficult to do. Rarely is the author provided, so a student cannot seek biographical information to determine if he or she is an authority on the subject. The publisher is usually nonexistent. The dates which appear on a site may be the date the information was first written, the date it was uploaded, or the date the page was last revised. There is usually no indication of what the dates mean, so determining the timeliness of the information is difficult.

Students need to pay attention to the origins of the pages. Is it a college or university? These pages are considered to be relatively reliable. Or, is it an organization that might be for or against a particular issue? If so, the student needs to be especially alert for bias. Is it an individual's opinion? If this is the case, the site may not be an appropriate source for research. A student can often determine from the suffix of the site address what type of source it is: *edu* denotes an educational institution; *gov*, a governmental unit; *org*, an organization; *com*, a business.

5. Organize the Information. From the perspective of information literacy, the student needs to learn how to integrate the sources into the larger project. But this skill really hybridizes with a similar objective of scientific literacy (see Chapter 7) and of communications in general.

To help students achieve this end, some instructors have found that making model projects available can guide the student in the direction of the goal. Copies of writing projects, videotapes or audiotapes of presentations can be on reserve in the library for this purpose.

Directing students to the appropriate campus learning center might be especially helpful. The writing center can coach students on organizational issues for written work, and the math learning center will assist them with quantitative topics that are part of the final project.

Library Assignments

Science instructors can help students learn the importance of information literacy by assigning projects requiring research. But it is important to note that this is not something just to tack on to a course. To say that information literacy is the topic "this week" is to miss the point of its significance. Accessing, evaluating and utilizing information is a thread that runs through all academic work. Accessing science information needs to be an ongoing activity in introductory science courses. During the semester students tend to use their textbooks as the primary—and sometimes the only—reference source for the subject matter. Once they are out of school, however, there likely will be no book handy for the kinds of science information they will need. Frequent trips to the library can build the skill and confidence they will need to become independent learners.

Before making any library assignment it is always a good idea to contact a college librarian to learn what resources are available. Students become very frustrated when the information they need for an assignment is not in the library.

Students usually respond to these assignments more positively if they are allowed to choose their own topics or if the topics evolve naturally from classroom discussions or questions students have about the coursework. These projects can be as simple or as elaborate as the instructor wants to make them, but they need not be enormous to be useful. It is probably more important that they be frequent. Some examples of library assignments follow:

1. Students are divided into groups. Each group selects a course-related problem, such as destruction of the rain forest, and performs extensive library research on the topic. The purpose is to develop a proposal for action, perhaps, for change or for improvement. The students need to take into account the political, social, and economic implications of the proposal. The final product may be a class presentation or a paper. Students should include a bibliography of sources used. The instructor may require a certain number of books, articles, Internet sites, *etc.* to be used and when grading the final product should comment on the appropriateness of the sources cited.

2. Before a new topic is introduced in class, the instructor assigns a student or group of students to find general information on the subject and present this to the class. The length of the presentation will determine the amount of information they will need. The instructor may have to assign the number of sources and/or the types of sources (encyclopedias, reference books, articles, Internet sites). The students turn in a bibliography of sources used for the report. You may have to refer them to a style manual (*e.g., Publication Manual of the American Psychological Association,* or the *MLA Handbook for Writers of Research Papers,* for the bibliographic form. This exercise couples nicely with the use of end-of-chapter questions to introduce new course material (see Chapter 9).

3. Students can review an assigned number of scientific periodicals and identify the purpose, target audience, and level of scholarship. They will be able to determine these criteria by reviewing the tables of contents, skimming the articles, looking for authors' credentials, and by examining bibliographies. They can also check for a review of these periodicals in *Magazines for Libraries* by Bill Katz. This sort of overview can be especially useful for science majors who need to become familiar with the professional literature early in their program.

4. You can have students use an index to periodicals, such as *General Science Index* or *Academic Abstracts* or other appropriate print, CD-ROM or online indexes subscribed to by your library to locate one article relevant to the course material you are discussing in class at the time. Instructors may assign the project several times a semester and require the students to copy the article and cite it in correct bibliographic form and note the index they used to locate it. Instructors may also assign students to find appropriate Internet sites and to cite them. This couples preparation for class with a research experience.

5. Require students to create an annotated bibliography of sources found in the library on a topic of his or her own choosing but approved by the instructor. The student lists appropriate books, articles, reference books, and Internet sites pertaining to the topic and writes a few sentences describing the content of the resources. Students take projects more seriously when they have a wider purpose than merely being ends in themselves. The bibliographies compiled by these students can be collected in a loose-leaf binder and placed on reserve for use by other library patrons.

6. Have students communicate with other students at other institutions on the Internet. For example, they can publish their work (Nadelson 1997) or enter discussions on critical issues. (Alexander *et al.* 1997).

There are many Internet sites dealing with library research instruction. A site at Tufts University may be of interest to biology teachers; after entering the address, click on "Library Research":

http:www.tufts.edu/as/biology/classes/bio14/biology14.html

Library Orientation Tours
Librarians will orient students to the library and instruct them on the use of the available research tools. If the instructor wishes, the librarian will emphasize resources in a particular subject area. In these orientation tours, students learn about library computer services, course reserves, photocopiers, study rooms, interlibrary loan, *etc.* Information Literacy Workshops can go considerably beyond the basic tour.

Information Literacy Workshops
This activity works best when students have a research project to do. Because of the specific nature of this activity, you will need to discuss the project with the librarian well in advance and will need to provide a list of the subjects the students will be researching. Depending on the policy at your school, these arrangements may need to be scheduled a few weeks in advance. Be sure to allow sufficient lead time.

On the day of the workshop, you meet with your students at the library for a short talk by the librarian with whom you are working. The session is brief and focuses sharply on the principles of refining and limiting research topics, developing research strategies, locating materials, and evaluating sources: the general objectives of information literacy. The

69

Kelly and Caprio

lecture will be tailored to your students' specific topics, and the librarian will prepare a Research Guide handout for them if you request it.

Immediately afterwards, in the time remaining, the students begin their research, with their teacher and the librarian there to coach them through the early stages of it.

Conclusion

Independent learners must be able to access information, evaluate it and use it appropriately. In other words, a citizen who is scientifically literate must be information literate. By working together, science teachers and librarians can assist today's students to acquire the skills necessary to become life-long learners.

References

Alexander, Richard and Robertson, Bill. (1997) Critical Issues Forum. *The Science Teacher* 64: 26.

Association of College and Research Libraries/Bibliographic Instruction Services Task Force on the Model Statement of Objectives. (1987) "Model Statement of Objectives for Academic Bibliographic Instruction." *C&RL News.*

Breivik, Patricia Senn. (1996) "Information Literacy: When Computers Aren't Enough." *Learning and Leading with Technology* 23: 65-67.

Daragan, Patricia and Stevens, Gwendolyn. (1996) "Developing Lifelong Learners: an Integrative and Developmental Approach to Information Literacy." *Research Strategies* 14: 68-81.

Farber, E. I. and Penhale, S. J. (1995) "Using Poster Sessions in Introductory Science Courses: an Example at Earlham." *Research Strategies* 13:55-59.

Fernandez, G. (1996) "Education Express: Librarians and Teachers in Partnership." *Florida Libraries* 39 : 9.

Gibson, C. (1995) "Critical Thinking: Implications for Instruction." *RQ* 35: 27-35.

Jacobson, Trudi E. (1991) "A Bibliographic Instruction Program for College Biology Students." *American Biology Teacher* 53.5: 298-300.

Mark, Beth. (1995) "Teaching Anxious Students Skills for the Electronic Library." *College Teaching* 43.1: 28-31.

McNally, M. J. and Kuhlthau, D. C. (1994) "Information Search Process in Science Education." *The Reference Librarian* 44 : 53-60.

Nadelson, Louis (1997) "Online Assignments." *The Science Teacher*, 64: 23-25.

Penhale, Sara J. and Stratton, Wilmer J. (1994) "Online Searching Assignments in a Chemistry Course for Nonscience Majors." *Journal of Chemical Education* 71.3 : 227.

Shapiro, Jeremy J. and Hughes, Shelley K. (1996) "Information Literacy as a Liberal Art." *Educom Review* 31.2. Online. Internet., 24 March 1997. http://www.educom.edu/web/pubs/review/reviewArticles/31231.html.

U.S. Department of Education. OERI.(1995) *National Assessment of College Student Learning: Identifying College Graduates' Essential Skills in Writing, Speech and Listening, and Critical Thinking: Final Report* Washington, DC : US GPO.

Young, V. E. and Ackerson, L. G. (1995) "Evaluation of Student Research Paper Bibliographies." *Research Strategies* 13: 80-93.

II

The Art of Teaching

Introduction

THE ART OF TEACHING

A powerful lever for the improvement of all of science education is to first improve the quality of undergraduate science teaching, especially the teaching of introductory science courses. These are the courses that the K-12 teachers must take, and strengthening their grasp of science and scientific literacy, and motivating positive attitudes toward science in them, means that their students will reap the benefits. This unit provides some background information on a few of the basic tenets of education as they apply to science teaching.

Chapter 7 offers the position statement published by the Society for College Science Teachers. This statement succinctly recaps some of the current thinking about the direction educational reforms are taking in science teaching. It heavily favors constructivism in education.

In Chapter 8, you will read about some personal and institutional approaches to the professional development of new teachers. Here the author describes practical ways to promote the development of college science teachers by providing a model of what is being done at a major "student-centered research university."

Interactive teaching deserves special attention, and while electronic technologies for it are very much in the forefront, there are many active learning strategies that are extremely effective and that would be clearly classified as low-tech. Chapter 9 describes some of these techniques in enough practical detail to allow the teacher to almost bring them directly into the classroom from the pages of this book..

Chapter 10 addresses motivation. Lack of motivation and students' unwillingness to strongly commit to studying science, especially the non-science majors, is a perennial problem and has a demoralizing effect on teachers of these courses. Students, however, never really enroll in a class because they want to be bored or want to fail it. Sometimes, though, the enthusiasm drains away and attending the class meetings can become the low point of everyone's day. Knowing some motivational techniques can empower students to learn, greatly enhance teaching effectiveness, and make your work more satisfying..

An understanding of the relationship between science, technology, and society is an attribute most science teachers would agree ought to characterize students who have successfully completed an introductory collegiate science course. Whole courses—indeed, entire programs—are devoted to this theme, but it is also a part of all our courses. Chapter 11 addresses this issue and talks about integrating science discoveries into science teaching.

The last chapter in this unit, Chapter 12, turns to assessment. Examinations are assessment tools, but assessment is much more than just testing. Once we decide what our course outcomes are to be, we need to develop a means to accurately measure how well we and our students accomplish them. Course objectives that are not paired with specific assessment strategies lack the rigor expected of modern educational practice. It is for that reason that you will find information here about writing course objectives and goals along with the various assessment techniques that you can use to measure their acquisition. You will also find that assessment, when used properly, can be a powerful learning tool.

Science teachers must be scientists, of course; but they must also be teachers. These scientists who teach do more than study the world, they change it—that is a special trust, and its practice deserves special attention. This Unit is about things that teachers can do to really make a difference.

Chapter 7

INTRODUCTORY COLLEGE-LEVEL SCIENCE COURSES

SOCIETY FOR COLLEGE SCIENCE TEACHERS POSITION STATEMENT[*]

The Society for College Science Teachers takes the position that the major goals of introductory college science courses are to contribute to the scientific literacy and the critical thinking capability of all college students and to provide a conceptual base for subsequent courses taken in the disciplines. The Society defines science literacy as the knowledge and understanding of a) the nature and role of scientific knowledge and process, b) the major principles and concepts that transcend the various sciences, c) the relationship of science to technology, and d) the applications of science to the individual and society.

THIS POSITION PAPER FIRST APPEARED IN *THE JOURNAL OF COLLEGE SCIENCE TEACHING*, SEPT-OCT, 1993. REPRINTED HERE WITH PERMISSION OF THE SOCIETY FOR COLLEGE SCIENCE TEACHERS.

Characteristics of an Exemplary Course
Content and Processes

An exemplary introductory science course should primarily serve the above goals. It should feature a carefully articulated sequence of topics that overtly illustrates, in a context of scientific inquiry, connections between concepts and principles germane to a course of study. The content and processes should not be all inclusive, rather they should represent the essential scientific information and skills of which students should become aware to function as scientifically literate and critically thinking adults. Accordingly, courses should emphasize the methodologies and logic used by scientifically literate people to investigate the world. Interdisciplinary connections between issues and principles of science, technology and society should be made where appropriate. The Society supports interdisciplinary courses as a means to achieve these goals.

Laboratory Experiences

Laboratory experiences should be related to and integrated with the conceptual flow of every science course. Laboratory activities should feature experimental procedures that require students to think about, select, generate, test, and evaluate the effectiveness of hypotheses and the scope of their results. The laboratory should be considered an opportunity either for discovery or for students to extend and refine their existing conceptual framework. Field experiences should be included where appropriate.

Format

Introductory course content should be presented in a format that promotes critical thinking, higher order cognitive skills, and a capacity for problem solving and decision making. Students should be given opportunities to work collaboratively on meaningful tasks, the completion of which requires intellectual rigor based on in-depth understanding of essential content in its relevant contextual framework.

Teaching Strategies

Teaching strategies should reflect established best practices as articulated in the research literature, particularly those of the cognitive sciences. Accordingly, instructional practice should diagnose and attend to students' learning styles as well as prior knowledge and alternative conceptions. Instruction should foster the nature of the thinking required to acquire and integrate both procedural and declarative knowledge. Additionally, opportunities should be made available for students, in both individual and collaborative settings, to extend and refine their knowledge and evaluative thinking capacity.

Assessment

Assessment of student performance should be matched with predetermined goals in terms of anticipated student outcomes. Both cognitive and process gains, particularly those associated with higher order cognitive skills should be appropriately appraised. Alternative means of assessment should be developed and used for those outcomes that cannot be evaluated by traditional means.

Student Outcomes

Upon completion of any introductory science course, at a minimum, every student should know and be able to do the following:

• Use the language and concepts of science appropriately and effectively in written and oral communication.

• Use the methodologies and models of science to select, define, solve and evaluate problems independently and collaboratively.

• Adequately design, conduct, communicate, and evaluate relatively basic but meaningful experiments.

• Make scientifically based decisions and solve problems drawing on concepts and experiences from relevant areas.

• Evaluate critically: evidence, interpretations, results and solutions related to the course content within a real life context.

• Explain scientifically related knowledge claims as products of a scientific inquiry process that, while diverse in scope, conforms to the principles of logical reasoning.

• Demonstrate research skills necessary to access needed data to support scientific inquiry.

• Ask meaningful questions about real world scientific issues and conundrums.

About the Position Paper

In this position statement, the Society for College Science Teachers (SCST) sets out basic goals for introductory science courses in a very simple and direct manner. These are: scientific literacy, critical thinking capability of all college students, and to provide a conceptual base for subsequent courses. And it succinctly defines *scientific literacy*. At the end of the piece, we find a set of expected student outcomes. These further specify the goals of the opening paragraph. What SCST has *not* done here is to write the assessment techniques to measure the achievement of these outcomes. They did not do it because they could not.

The Society for College Science Teachers is an interdisciplinary professional society. Their position statement needed to address all the sciences, but assessment must be much more specific. In Chapter 12, you will find suggestions whereby you can design your own assessment activities. The information there, coupled with your knowledge of your own discipline and the stated outcomes of your own course, will enable you to create the assessment tools you will need for your students.

Besides stating goals and enumerating outcomes, the Position Paper does something else that is very important: it clarifies where the intellectual activity we call teaching falls among the academic disciplines. It might have been a stronger paper had it done this more explicitly, but that it does do this at all is a triumph.

Consider this statement from the paper:

> Teaching strategies should reflect established best practices as articulated in the research literature, *particularly those of the cognitive sciences*. Accordingly, instructional practice should diagnose and attend to *students' learning styles* as well as prior knowledge and *alternative conceptions* [emphasis mine].

This is, clearly, the language of the social sciences. Education is a social science. There is no doubt about that, and science teachers—regardless of whatever the other discipline it is in which they claim expertise—are required to be competent, and preferably expert, in this area as well. Science teachers always wear these two hats. The best teachers know this and are proud of it.

80

Chapter 8

LEARNING TO TEACH

There is a growing national interest in improving the quality of undergraduate teaching. Major research universities have become increasingly concerned about undergraduate teaching. Although considerable effort has been devoted to K-12 science education reform, much less attention has been paid to the need for teaching reform at the undergraduate level. Model strategies and programs are needed that address the relevant issues.

Good teaching is not a genetic trait—it is a learned skill. This chapter provides a perspective and some practical suggestions about what might help to improve teaching in introductory science courses. The perspective is based upon the premise that an effective way to enhance undergraduate science education is to better prepare college science instructors to teach. Inadequate budgets, equipment, facilities, *etc.* are difficult problems for teachers as well as administrators; but it is critical to find new ways to help college science instructors become more effective teachers, even under these trying circumstances.

What Are Some Attributes of Effective College Science Teachers?

In my experience, effective teachers find ways to help their students learn. What really counts are meaningful interactions between a teacher and a student, and this can happen under all sorts of adverse conditions. Some of the important characteristics of an effective college science teacher include:

- an extensive knowledge of science content and process,
- good interpersonal skills,
- articulation and other communication skills,
- knowledge and application of educational research results, and
- a positive attitude toward teaching and students.

An effective college science teacher also needs an arsenal of resources, strategies, techniques, management skills, and administrative support. Desirable personal attributes include enthusiasm, a sense of humor, a caring attitude, a sense of fairness, positive values, analytical ability and good judgement.

How Can College Science Teachers Develop These Attributes?

We should start with the graduate education of future college science teachers. At many institutions, graduate students receive teaching assistantships in conjunction with their graduate studies in a science discipline. Many institutions offer a brief program of orientation and training to assist new teaching assistants (TA's) in becoming acquainted with the department and the facilities available. Some institutions even encourage new TA's to think about effective ways to teach, but most institutions offer little training for teaching. At Syracuse University we have developed an extensive program for preparing TA's to teach and to support and assist them in developing their teaching skills. This program is consistent with the University's aim of being widely recognized as a student-centered research university.

The TA program begins with an intensive orientation, followed by on-going activities to help new teachers develop teaching skills throughout the term of their contract. The program involves a mandatory week of orientation for new international TA's, followed by a week for all new TA's. This orientation includes a variety of faculty presentations, microteaching, discussions and tips about teaching. Graduate Teaching Associates serve as peer consultants for these sessions. International TA's receive special attention concerning English language skills and cultural orientation. They are required to participate in a special course and demonstrate an adequate level of English language proficiency in order to teach.

At the end of the general orientation meetings, TA's meet with their specific departments for an additional three days of orientation. In the Biology Department, this session focuses on specific duties of each TA and other departmental and course responsibilities. Experienced TA's help the new ones to prepare lesson plans and syllabi. Most new TA's in biology are assigned to my general biology course. They teach two recitation classes per week, supervise students for 4-6 hours in an autotutorial laboratory, proctor examinations, hold office hours and assist in a variety of other ways. Activities that support the development of the teaching skills of our TA's are provided throughout the course.

Features of a Model TA Program

The ongoing TA program in the Department of Biology at Syracuse which prepares and develops graduate students as effective college science teachers has several features. Participation in most of these activities is required for TA's, but there are additional development options for students who intend to pursue careers in academic institutions.

Content Meetings To be successful, each TA must have an extensive knowledge of introductory science content and process. At the beginning of the course, we hold weekly meetings for new TA's to review the content to be taught. We have fewer meetings as the semester progresses and as the TA's adjust to their teaching roles.

Mentoring by Teaching Associates Advanced, experienced TA's are appointed as Teaching Associates. Their role is to mentor new TA's, organize seminars for TA's, and generally help to improve the introductory biology course.

Peer Videotaping Each TA is required to videotape another TA at least once per semester. The observer then offers helpful advice to the TA who is videotaped. TA's view their videotape and do a self-analysis.

Resources A copy machine, video equipment, overhead projectors, 35-mm slide projectors, films, videotapes, a small library of biology books and demonstration specimens are available for exclusive use by TA's in the introductory biology course. We teach new TA's how to use all the equipment and encourage them to use it during the course.

Resource notebooks are also available. Each TA hands in a copy of any quizzes, handouts, special assignments, *etc.*, which are placed in a notebook accessible for reference by other TA's. We distribute teaching notes to the TA's periodically during each semester. These provide procedural information, content updates, and teaching tips. TA's also gain information about the course from the weekly course newsletter, *Bionews and Bioviews* (see Chapter 10).

Formative and Summative Evaluations After a few weeks of teaching, each of the TA's must ask students about positive features of their teaching and must solicit suggestions for improvement. They also collect general student comments about the rest of the course. By doing this early in the semester, there is still time to make adjustments based upon the feedback. The evaluation is confidential and only the TA sees it, except for the more general course review. Thus, the formative evaluation is non-threatening to the TA.

At the end of each semester, students evaluate the teaching assistant using an open-ended form. We categorize student comments as positive or negative and give a written teaching profile to each TA.

Classroom Observations Each TA is observed and critiqued at least once each semester. Most of the observations are done by students who are enrolled in science education methods courses, and they provide a written report to each TA observed.

Graduate Course on the Teaching of College Science This three-credit course (Bio/Sci 544) is offered each fall; it is open to any graduate student in the sciences. The main course objectives are to:
- increase skills in teaching college science
- develop greater self-awareness of teaching strengths and weaknesses
- increase awareness of issues in college science teaching
- develop expertise concerning a specific issue or topic in college science teaching
- develop skills in critiquing teaching
- develop skills in designing a course syllabus

Course experiences include:
- *reading and discussing relevant literature in the field.* Each student selects an issue in college science teaching, leads discussion about that issue and prepares a referenced paper.
- *peer teaching and self-analysis.* Each student prepares several brief lessons that are videotaped and critiqued, to identify teaching weaknesses and strengths.
- *observing teaching* done by the science faculty and teaching assistants. Each student writes an analysis of several observations, and we discuss these analyses in class.

- *writing examinations.* Each student learns about principles of test construction and prepares test items to be critiqued.
- *developing a syllabus.* Each student develops a syllabus and designs a college-level science course that he or she would like to teach in the future.
- *discussions of various teaching methods* at the college level, including lecturing, discussions, laboratory, and individualized instruction.
- *field trips* intended to acquaint students with various administrative and support services at the college level (*e.g.,* admissions, financial aid, student support services).

The grade for the course is based upon:
- a final exam on articles and class discussions and presentations
- evaluation of the referenced paper, syllabus, observations of teachers, class presentations, and assignments.

Special Topics Courses (Bio 200) Undergraduate students may take this two-credit course on a specialized topic in biology concurrently with introductory biology. It enables talented biology students to extend their study of beyond the core course, and explore the science in greater depth. These courses are designed and taught by Teaching Associates and advanced TA's. Thus, teaching a Bio 200 course serves as a reward to TA's for excellent teaching as they are relieved of other duties. (See Chapter 10 for more about Bio 200.)

Future Professoriate Program Outstanding TA's may choose to participate in this program leading to a *Certificate in University Teaching*. Initially, these TA's are appointed as Teaching Associates. As such, they mentor new TA's, plan seminars, and help with course improvements. In order to qualify for the certification, Teaching Associates in the Biology Department have to complete an independent, mentored teaching experience (usually the teaching of a Bio 200 course); satisfactorily complete the graduate course on the Teaching of College Science (Bio/Sci 544); and compile a teaching portfolio. If the portfolio is approved by the Department's faculty mentor committee, the *Certificate in University Teaching* is awarded with completion of the Ph.D.

Other Ways to Develop Teaching Effectiveness

Practical speaking experience, with feedback from the audience, is an important experience for prospective college science teachers. In some instances, Syracuse University Teaching Associates give talks about their research to high school teachers. And we are planning a program whereby Ph.D. students who are near completion of their degree will offer presentations about their research to the first-year students. This will enable graduate students to speak before a relatively non-threatening group, and first-year students can learn about cutting-edge research in the field from individuals closer to their age than most professors.

Reflective teaching and self-awareness is essential. The basic philosophy is that there is no single "best" way to teach. We want TA's to discover their own unique teaching strengths and weaknesses. Then they can move to expand their strengths and minimize their weaknesses. These developing college teachers must learn how to respond to student feedback as well as self-evaluation, make appropriate adjustments in their teaching strategies, and eventually develop their own effective style.

Networking and cooperative efforts are very useful for learning about teaching. We encourage TA's to work with each other, become involved in the University-wide program, and function as teaching colleagues in the Department. They are strongly encouraged to observe the teaching of other TA's and have workshop and seminar opportunities about teaching. For example, just as our TA's have workshops on electron microscopy and gel electrophoresis, they also attend organized seminars for teachers on the student athlete, learning disabilities, and writing grant proposals.

Effecting change is perhaps the most difficult part of improving teaching. It is particularly difficult to alter behaviors that have already become established. We find that even when TA's identify particular weaknesses they have great difficulty changing—it always requires considerable effort, encouragement and reinforcement. Most importantly, the TA has to be aware of the undesirable behavior and has to strongly dislike it in order to work toward change. Persistence of effort, practice, feedback, adjustment and more practice are critical elements for self-improvement.

Improving Teaching Skills of All Faculty

Although this chapter has focused on preparing and developing teaching assistants, we cannot ignore the need to improve the teaching skills of current faculty members. Increased demand for teaching accountability does not, in itself, solve the problem. To promote teaching excellence, current faculty members need opportunities and incentives to improve their teaching skills. Several features of our TA program demonstrate what can be done to assist college science instructors who want to improve their teaching.

Peer observations and critiques of teaching could prove useful.

Videotaping and self-analyses of the videotape could be made available to faculty on request. In one instance at Syracuse University, Teaching Associates videotaped biology faculty members, and then viewed and discussed the videotape and provided an anonymous, group critique to the faculty member.

Bring together those faculty who excel at teaching and are very concerned about making improvements. They can serve as leaders to influence others. At Syracuse University, selected faculty members who excel at teaching introductory courses have been designated as *Gateway Fellows*. These master teachers meet regularly and conduct luncheon seminars on teaching for other faculty and graduate students. They also collaborate in other ways to enhance teaching on campus.

Reward good teaching by recognizing outstanding teachers. Meredith Professorships of Excellence in Teaching have been established at Syracuse University. Recipients of this award receive $20,000 per year for three years, $5000 per year for professional development and $1,000 for group activities. Meredith professors must complete a project on some aspect of teaching or learning, teach a new course outside the department's regular offerings and work together to enhance teaching and learning. The Meredith Professors form a Meredith Symposium twice a semester to discuss the state of teaching at the University and to work collaboratively to improve teaching and learning. At some point during the three-year tenure, each Meredith Professor is expected to present a public lecture or seminar to share his or her activities with the community. As of 1997, seven Meredith Professorships have been awarded.

Administrative support can be a very significant factor in motivating faculty to improve teaching. Providing institutional grants for instructional improvements, requiring greater attention to assessment and accountability for teaching, offering resources and mentoring to faculty, establishing campus newsletters on teaching, organizing seminars and workshops on teaching, and finding ways to recognize and reward good teaching can be effective ways to affect professional development. Administrators must be persistent in promoting teaching. They should mobilize the talents of faculty who are good teachers to influence other faculty members.

Many different strategies and programs need to be instituted on a broad scale if we are to make improvements in college science teaching. College science faculty and administrators must encourage a nationwide focus on improving the quality of college science teachers, and hence improving the quality of undergraduate science education.

References

Allen, R.D. (1976) Effective training for teaching assistants. *The American Biology Teacher* 38:24-27.

Future Professoriate Project. (1995) The Graduate School, Syracuse University.

Lambert, L.M. and S.L. Tice. (1996) *University Teaching: A Guide for Graduate Students.* Syracuse University Press.

Lawrenz, F., P. Heller, R. Keith & K. Heller. (1992) Training the teaching assistant. *Journal of College Science Teaching* 22 (2): 106-109.

Lumsden, A.S. (1993) Training graduate students to teach. *The American Biology Teacher* 55 (4): 233-234.

McKeachie, W.J. (1994) *Teaching Tips: Strategies, Research and Theory for College and University Teachers.* D.C. Heath & Co.

Manteuffel, M.S. and R. Blum. (1979) A model for training biology teaching assistants. *The American Biology Teacher* 41 (8):476-480.

Smith, A.B. III. (1974) A model program for training teaching assistants. *Improving College and University Teaching* 22 (3): 198-200.

Chapter 9

INTERACTIVE CLASSROOM TECHNIQUES

*Think of something you learned years ago. Reach way back. It should be something you know that you know but do not use and reinforce frequently. I don't know what you picked, of course; but if it is an example of deeply rooted, long-term learning, it is easy to predict that you most likely learned it by actually doing it. For long-term learning, there is no contest: We learn what we do and, maybe, only what we do. Today we call learning by experience **Active Learning**.*

Lecturing is generally a passive process for students. A very strong message of the reform movement is that we can realize the most significant improvement in education by shifting from passive to active teaching and learning strategies. But lecturing is so entrenched that it is difficult for a teacher, whose own education may be deeply steeped in traditional methods, to instinctively know what to do in place of just talking at their students. This chapter offers some specific alternatives to the lecture method.

This is not to say that lecture presentations are not useful in some ways, and we may not want to totally abandon that approach, but we can replace some of their more mundane segments with more efficient, active learning strategies. *More efficient* here means better learning, not more

89

topics. I realize that getting students to become active learners in the classroom may mean that I will not be able to "cover" all the same items I could mention during a lecture. However, anyone who truly believes that *covering* a topic is the same as teaching it may have a worrisome gap in their early literary experience.[1]

This section contains some non-lecture classroom activities that can effectively help students construct an understanding of science concepts. They are ways to create an environment in which the students interact with the subject matter and with other learners; the teacher is present to guide them through the learning process. Constructivism in education relies heavily on collaborative methods and active involvement of the learner. But constructivism itself is not a method—it is an approach, a point of view of how to teach based on how people learn. You can find a thorough treatment of constructivism in Chapter 1 of this book, and in Chapter 2 you will find some of the more general principles of collaborative learning. *Collaborative methods support constructivism.*

The six teaching techniques in this chapter are examples from my ragbag of active learning classroom techniques. They do not come from some larger encyclopedia of collaborative methods; rather, they are teacher-generated classroom activities that fit the general model. I created them—and that is not to say that I was their inventor, except that perhaps I did re-invent them for myself—to be specific constructivist solutions to help me teach particular course concepts. They should be easily adaptable to any of the introductory science courses. You can, with only minor modification, almost take them into your classroom directly from these pages. But the real reason for including them here is to provide stepping stones for you to develop your own active learning techniques.

Some of the methods presented will seem like good ideas to you, and there will be others that appear to be odd or even inappropriate. You will want to try some from the first category, but I hope you will also try a few from the latter group; you may be pleasantly surprised at how your students respond. And logging some real-time experience with all of them will help you to construct your own knowledge about this part of the art of teaching.

The success of these techniques depends largely on our perception of just what the role of *teacher* is. Active learning strategies are student-centered; that is, they shift the responsibility for learning more toward the

---

[1] Andersen, Hans C., 1949. *The Emperor's New Clothes*, Houghton Mifflin, New York, NY.

students and are characterized by classrooms in which the students are very much involved with the subject matter throughout the session. In this setting, the teacher's role is not to be the fountain of knowledge but is that of a facilitator, to help point the way to learning. The teacher is also a resource for the students, but is only one of the resources available. There are books, electronic data bases, films, other students, other faculty, community sources—the list is long and confusing. Part of the teacher's role in the constructivist classroom is to work with the students, to minimize the confusion, show them how to navigate the resources, and offer a scholarly role model.

It may be trite to say that learning should be fun, but—in truth—it *is* fun. However, it is not the kind of fun most students will have learned to appreciate, and it will take a gifted hand to lead them to the point where they can feel the joy of it. Helping students to discover the joy of learning—that is part of what teachers do, too.

Some teachers are at center stage all the time. When you sit in their classes you see their students communicate virtually all the course business directly to them. The teacher fields all the questions, and discussion—if any—flows between individual students and the teacher. But there is usually little to discuss in these somewhat autocratic class meetings; "discussions" often run as monologues, with the student's only active role being that of note-taker. When I used to teach this way my lectures kept becoming more polished, impressed faculty and administrative observers, and earned me promotions. Strangely, though, no matter how pretty those lectures became, my students did not seem to learn the subject any better than they did when I was a first-year teacher. But when I moved toward a more student-centered approach and eased into constructivism, their performance took a significant upward swing (Caprio 1994).

These constructivist techniques require that students be organized into groups, and you can read more about group structure in Chapter 2. We establish groups on the first day of class, and we set the agenda for their first meeting before they leave. That agenda will reflect their first group assignment. In addition to the subject matter it embodies, that first assignment also serves to galvanize the group in response to an outside challenge. You will want to ensure that the group members can agree on a common out-of-class meeting time for at least a one-hour meeting per week, and that they exchange telephone numbers. It takes about twenty minutes to get the collaborative student groups established.

And, on that first day, I find it extremely effective to provide the usual course introduction along with a brief primer on constructivism and collaborative learning for the students. When students understand something about the process, and that it is based on sound principles of cognitive science, they are more willing to enter into the teaching and learning partnership. We want students to assume more responsibility for their own learning, and it seems reasonable to expect they would want to know the nature of the commitment they are making.

Table 1 lists some of the successful collaborative techniques that I use; descriptions of each activity follow.

End-of-Chapter Questions

You've finished a topic (or a review of one), and you have about twenty minutes remaining in the session. Here is a way to introduce the next chapter so the students will be well prepared for a thorough treatment of it at the next class meeting. Give the new chapter as a reading assignment. Then you might say something like, "This is a challenging read; let me orient you to it before you get started." Give a quick overview of the chapter, telling about the parts of it you find especially intriguing. Use the visuals (*e.g.,* overhead transparencies may be provided by the publisher) to look at some of the illustrations with the students, and point out the ones you think they will find most helpful. If there are any particularly confusing passages in the text, forewarn them. It helps if the students have their books, so they can make notes directly in the margin as you familiarize them with the reading. This would also be a good time to point out references in the library on this topic that they might find helpful. Here the teacher is acting as the guide to the textbook, smoothing the way for the learners.

Next, I have them turn to the end of the chapter, to the review questions, and ask the groups to select the questions (from among the ones I pick) on which they would like to work and present to the class at the next meeting. I usually find I have to add a few questions of my own that are important to my version of the course. I volunteer for some of the questions too.

If this is your first time using this activity with your students, be sure they understand that this is an important assignment: they are responsible for explaining the substance of the questions to their colleagues, so everyone's grades will partly depend on how well they do their job. Student assignments must be perceived as important. Having important things to do is a powerful motivator; no one can get very excited about doing trivial tasks.

Table 1 **Some Classroom Activities for Collaborative Groups**	
End-of-chapter questions	This uses the last few minutes of a class meeting to introduce the next topic and to have students come to the next class with a substantial start on it.
Verifying Notes	If I stop a complicated lecture part-way through so the students can compare and correct notes, I can teach more effectively after the respite.
Developing Questions for the Instructor	Students often need help to formulate questions. Making time for them to collaborate on this process during a lecture can enhance comprehension.
Review Questions	Coaching collaborative groups as they develop review and exam questions helps them to understand what is important to the field of study.
Group Presentations	A collaborative group presentation involves the group working closely with the instructor to assume full responsibility for a course topic.
Interpreting Diagrams	Collaborative groups can attack complex diagrams to learn the subject matter and to further develop this important learning skill.

Offer to help. If students need resource materials such as overhead transparencies or videotapes, or if they want some coaching on the subject matter, they should be able to call on you. Give them the name of a librarian who will be able to direct them to reference material on this topic. This expressed concern that they have all the tools for the job makes it abundantly clear that you expect superb work. Depending on the sophistication of the groups, you may have to give more or less direction. Some groups will need more preparation time than others, and they will need different amounts of out-of-class coaching.

Close the session by giving the groups a few minutes to confer. They need to set their out-of-class meeting time and place, and they will probably want to divide up the task. If it is the beginning of the term, remind them that their meeting will be more productive if everyone reads the chapter before attending. To insure that everyone in the group will be prepared on all the group's questions, you can establish the policy that the instructor will randomly select the speaker from the group for each of the questions.

The next class meeting starts with the students in their groups, taking a few minutes to plan the logistics of their presentations. I move among the groups, answering last-minute questions and offering advice. For the presentations, I am a member of every group. With some groups I need to do more talking than with others. The rest of the class takes notes and asks questions as each panel presents its segment of the chapter. The questions they ask and the answers to them can develop into rich discussions of the subject matter.

An interesting continuation immediately after a group's presentation is to give the listening groups a chance to confer and to compare notes, and I assign a member of the presenting group as a consultant to each of them. I move from one group to another while this conference proceeds, assisting as necessary. This final summary conference seems to be especially valuable for building confidence in science-anxious students, but I rarely have the time to do it, except for the neediest classes.

When the students complete the chapter questions in the book I give them my own review questions from which exam questions may be derived. The groups are urged to work on them at their very next out-of-class meeting, and I reserve a few minutes at the beginning of the next class session to answer their questions.

These activities where students prepare, present, discuss, and review the questions result in "teaching" the chapter.

How should you grade the students for this work? Chapter 12 addresses assessment in a broader context, and Chapter 2 deals with issues of evaluating group work. Here though I'd like to raise a more basic point: before asking *how* to grade student work in the collaborative setting, ask *if* it needs to be evaluated at all. Group work may just be the way of doing the business of learning; it is not a special project, but simply routine work. One could argue that it may even reinforce the student-centered nature of the approach if the work is *not* graded.

Verifying Notes

"Drinking from the firehose" has been a much used metaphor to describe the daunting problem that students in introductory science courses have coping with the sheer volume of information those courses contain. The fact is that despite our best efforts, after the first eight minutes of a lecture class less than 15% of the students are paying attention to what is being said at any particular moment (Angelo 1991). There is some value to stopping the flow of information occasionally to recharge the batteries that power the attention mechanisms, but only if it is possible to do something in the interval that will be of value to the business at hand.

An activity that can be mixed with some of the other cooperative learning strategies offered here is a brief (5 minute) hiatus from the lecture to verify notes. Try this after a particularly detailed topic, one that challenges even the best note takers. *Just stop.* Tell the students to form groups of three or four with those nearest to them and to compare notes. If you have been lecturing for a quarter of an hour, this respite need not be more than five minutes, if that. If I quickly wander among the groups while this is happening, I inevitably learn where I have been less than clear and find ways of improving my presentation of this topic the next time the opportunity arises.

In returning to the lecture, it would be appropriate to begin by asking if there are any questions. There will be. Some will be points of clarification—which you might want to reflect to the class as a whole, to learn if your presentation was at fault or if the lapse was only on the part of the questioner. There will also be questions that probe deeper into the topic. These will be the direct consequence of the students having had time to process the subject matter with their colleagues. The questions coming from the note verification session will make it quite clear that the time has not been wasted. And when the lecture resumes, the attention level will be higher than it would have been had the instructor deftly raced into the void; and it will be possible to proceed on a more sophisticated level with this, now, better prepared audience.

Developing Questions for the Instructor

It has happened all too often: I have just finished a truly elegant explanation of an absolutely exquisite phenomenon, complete with projected illustrations, and it is better than any description in any textbook or anything I have ever read anywhere; but instead of smugly satisfied faces glowing with the new knowledge I have just imparted, there are blank stares.

"Are there any questions?" It seems only polite to ask, under the circumstances.

No answer. Just more stares and counterfeit smiles. Finally, a hand goes up and its owner breaks the silence with the long awaited question: "Do we have to know this for the test?" If they don't understand it, why don't they ask the questions they need answered?!

When the subject matter gets complicated students frequently do not ask the right questions at the right time because they usually cannot. I think part of the reason is that the topic is new to them, and they are not yet quick enough or agile enough with it to construct queries in a form they would not be embarrassed to speak before a room full of their peers. They may, in fact, be silently toiling on their question's sentence structure, but by the time it is formulated the moment is lost and the lecture is moving on to the next point, which—if understanding it depends on comprehending the previous item—will be lost too. The more tightly crafted, the more economical and terse, and the more direct and unswerving the logical chain of a lecture, then the easier it is to lose the whole point of it by missing just a single link.

Now, when the confusion is at its peak, take a break from the lecture and have the students meet in their groups to formulate the questions they need answered in order to grasp the subject. When you do this they will: compare notes on the lecture you just gave, fill in gaps in those notes, develop questions which they will never ask because they are answered by another group member, and they will re-explain the topic to one another in terms they can understand.

As you move from group to group, you will see learning taking place, and what you could not do with your slick lecture will be happening like magic. Ease them over some rough points. Listen for phrases like, *"yeah, I get that part of it, but what I don't understand is ..."* Those are the questions in the raw, and you can coach their emergence. Set a time limit, if you wish, by which each group will have one question. I find that when I ask students to write their questions, they work with better focus, are more time-efficient, and produce better questions. When they hand me their questions (on index cards) I can sometimes quickly arrange them to become the outline of a brief lecture that will incorporate the answers and continue to move the class forward.

Review Questions

Getting students to the point of taking responsibility for their own education is part of what we want to achieve. For college students, most of whom are about to leave formal schooling forever, this had better happen soon if life-long learning is to become a reality for them. One way to get students to "buy into" the education process is to make them more than just passive partners in it. And nothing could be more convincing that they truly are part of the process than if they could play a role in the assessment of their own learning. They have been doing this informally and unofficially for most of their academic careers by trying to figure out what the instructor is going to ask on the next exam. And for just as long, their teachers have been telling them that trying to second guess the instructor is not a good study technique. Perhaps we ought to rethink this.

Put another way: trying to figure out what will be on the exam is an attempt to determine what a person would have to be able to do in order to demonstrate mastery of the subject matter, and certainly there is nothing wrong with that. *The problem is attitudinal.* If we can turn the students away from the attitude of "psyching out the instructor" and toward a quest for understanding what academic achievement entails in our areas, they would be able to learn more of the more significant information, because they would know what it is. Students would develop a more realistic appreciation of the science.

A way of helping this to happen is to involve the students in writing review questions before an exam, and—if you are really willing to break with tradition—having them contribute examination questions, too. I had better explain myself more thoroughly.

First, regarding groups writing review questions: this works well as an out-of-class group activity. Indeed, students do a certain amount of it anyway before exams, and it helps somewhat when their teacher sanctions it, encourages it, and coaches them on it. The effect is that what was only somewhat helpful becomes an invaluable study aid. With the teacher involved, students develop their review questions more than a day or two before an exam; if the teacher is going to see the questions, they also will be more carefully crafted; and the teacher will be able to help them rank their questions in order of importance to the course and to the discipline.

You might find yourself saying things like: "Yes, all biologists can explain adaptive radiation, but very few have memorized the scientific names of Darwin's finches;" and, "No, Dave, at this point it would probably be better to spend your time doing something else besides memorizing the atomic masses of all the elements."

When the groups give me their completed review questions I make a complete set available for all students. Other instructors who have students write review questions require questions on the previous lecture at the beginning of every meeting; others ask for them a week before an examination.

I also invite groups to submit questions for exams. I advise them that it is really my job to make up the exams and that their questions will probably be rewritten, combined with other questions, or be revised to eliminate ambiguities. The exam questions they submit are just more review questions with which they can work, but they have more importance and receive more attention if they believe the questions may actually appear on the exam. You will probably find, as I have, that students rarely ever write a question not already considered by the instructor.

The nature of the test does not really change because of this activity, but the grades improve. I am not sure whether that happens just because it causes the students to study more, especially in a group setting, or whether the question writing itself is responsible. It would be interesting to compare how students fare with instructor-made review questions *vis-à-vis* their own. The former would encourage and guide their study, as would the latter, but would by-pass the intellectual process of developing the questions.

Group Presentations

Group presentations need not be major project reports and can be quite informal; but, if they are to work at all, they must not be trivial. People are at their best when they have something important to do, and college students can easily spot instructor-contrived busy work. A group presentation needs to be meaningful and integral to the course if it is to have the desired motivational effect and significantly impact learning. If the instructor repeats everything students offer, even if it is one or two meetings later, it is clear to them that their contribution was not valued. And, if unique material is presented by a student but no one reacts to it or has questions about it, no one bothers taking notes while the student is talking, and the contributed subject matter is never included in assessment (the students' definition of what is "important" in the course), it is clear to everyone that the effort had little practical purpose. The cardinal rule is: student presentations—whether they are done by individuals or groups— must be significant. If not, despite the fine grade they may receive in the short run, they eventually devalue the presenter. No one really feels better about themselves after jumping through someone else's hoops, no matter how well they did it or how much they were paid.

Relying on a student group to present course material can be risky, and we must do all we can to reduce that risk, but we can't entirely eliminate it. There is, of course, the question of whether the risk is worth the benefit. You must decide that for yourself, but I have a *caveat* to offer.

The first time you try this you will likely have less than satisfactory results. It is complicated. Making it work to the extent that the students grow so much in the subject that they can actually teach it effectively is asking them to come a very long way in a very short time. The second time you try it you will have learned from the mistakes of your first round. It is probably only after two or three attempts that you would actually be evaluating the efficacy of the method and not the ability of the instructor to manage it.

Are there some general guidelines that can help it work? Yes, of course.

The topic must be small enough to be manageable in a reasonable amount of time. The students must access the information, process it for understanding, and organize it for presentation. When I have to do that for a presentation to my peers I find it enormously time consuming (much more so than if I am preparing to speak to students). And in my case, the skills for accessing, processing, and presenting scientific topics are well-practiced. These skills are still in early developmental stages for most students.

Students will do best if they are working with a subject they find interesting. We can form the collaborative groups by having students join the subject group of their choice.

Students will need the instructor's coaching outside of class if their product is to be able to carry the course in this area. In addition to some guidance with the subject matter, they will need some support with the presentation techniques. They will look to you as the acknowledged expert for both of these. And your purpose is to help them to be as successful as possible. The instructor must be part of the research team, as a resource person, and he or she must be part of the presentation team, but must not overshadow it.

One of the things that happens in this close teacher-student association is bond formation through common interest and interdependency. Connection between teachers and students outside of the traditional classroom setting is known to be a powerful motivator for success.

As an instructor works with a group, helping it to prepare the presentation, he or she is really preparing the "lecture." With this method, though, the student groups are a kind of teaching resource, much the same as audiovisual materials or a lecture demonstration. A slide that you might have used, if you were the only one who was going to speak, now might be shown as part of the group's presentation. As the plan takes form, you will see where the handles are for the other curriculum items you want to tie into the subject.

At the class meeting the instructor will not be center stage; others will be speaking, and that means the teacher will have less control of all that happens. This demands greater adaptability and more thinking on one's feet. The instructor needs to be able to listen accurately and to react appropriately to items that may come up which are not necessarily in the lecture notes. Teachers using this technique must have a much firmer grip on their subject matter than when presenting a monologue. The teacher's reward for the more intense commitment will be the knowledge that the students are similarly involved—there is spontaneity and excitement in these sessions that no monologue can arouse, and the evidence of more effective teaching and learning will appear on exams. *And, it is fun.*

Interpreting Diagrams

Publishers spend enormous amounts of time and money on elaborate art work for textbooks. As the illustrations have become more and more sophisticated, the promise that a picture would be worth a thousand words has become an understatement. Despite the visual orientation of this "TV-generation" some of the graphics contain too much information for students to manage. We can appreciate the elegance of them; but, for us, they are just other renditions of subjects we already know quite well.

Part of what I like to see happen in the classroom is students getting some grasp of the relevant textbook illustrations. I do use the visual aids (*e.g.*, overhead transparencies or computer software) provided by the publisher. That way I can clarify the illustration while I am explaining the subject matter through it. Then, when the students leave they have with them a drawing they can understand, and it is perfectly matched to the narrative in their text.

Another way of using the visuals is not to talk about them, but to ask questions that will lead the students into them and into an understanding of the subject. For example, virtually every biology textbook has a single, and extremely complex illustration of transcription and translation in protein synthesis. This diagram will have another hundred words or so in its caption; and, as if trying to get as much information compacted as much as possible, the caption will include some of the most complex sentences in the text. Working in groups and guided by the instructor's questions, students will be able to learn a great deal from the diagram, not the least of which is how to interpret diagrams.

When students look at diagrams they see a holistic image, the way we see a television screen. The color and form bring the illustration together (that's what artists do), but the processes it depicts are parts of the whole, and to understand the processes they must be seen as parts. We, who already know about the parts, see the fluidity of the piece as a triumph of integration, but most students are not quite ready for that yet. That is where the instructor's questions apply; they will fragment the whole into its manageable parts. *What part of the diagram is illustrating transcription? What is the product of transcription? What starting materials are required by it? What is the RNA polymerase doing? Where is transcription taking place in the cell? What purpose does transcription serve?*

The questions might be on the chalkboard and the instructor will probably be most useful moving from group to group helping where necessary. Then a brief lecture, five or ten minutes should be more than enough time, to summarize the answers to these questions before going on to the next part of the diagram and your questions about it.

The dissection of the diagram may take an hour to do, but the students will leave with an understanding of the subject and with a diagram, in the text, they can really use. Collaborative learning in the analysis of diagrams is a superb teaching technique. One warning note: it may be necessary to remind the students to take notes; they become involved in constructing the understanding and sometimes forget to write. If you do have a little time left at the end of the hour, you may want to combine this technique with the note verification exercise.

101

Mario W. Caprio

References

Angelo, T. A. (1991) *Learning in the Classroom* (Phase I), a Report from the Lawrence Hall of Science. University of California, Berkeley, CA.

Caprio, M. W. (1994) "Easing into Constructivism," *The Journal of College Science Teaching*, Feb, 1994.

Lord, Thomas. (1994) Using Constructivism to Enhance Student Learning in College Biology, *The Journal of College Science Teaching*, May, 1994.

Marvin Druger

Chapter 10

MOTIVATING THE UNMOTIVATED

*"These students simply don't want to learn.   It's frustrating.
What can I do about it?"*

This comment is often heard from teachers throughout the nation, and it identifies a critical issue in science education. Elementary school students seem naturally inclined toward science, but this interest tends to wane as they progress into their junior high school and high school years. In college, students are usually "required" to take a science course, and many non-science majors do so reluctantly. Thus, the introductory college science course for non-science majors provides an excellent opportunity for motivating students toward science. If we can motivate these students, they will learn science by themselves.

I have taught introductory college biology for about 40 years, mostly at Syracuse University. My introductory course enrolls a mixture of potential biology majors and non-majors, and fulfills a science requirement. A major goal of this course has always been to motivate students and help them become self-learners. I want students to enjoy learning about the world and to develop the knowledge base and the desire to learn more. I also want them to gain self-confidence about learning biology and reflect upon their individual strengths and weaknesses and how they relate to the living world as individuals. *How can such goals be accomplished? How can we motivate the unmotivated in science?*

103

In this chapter, I will suggest some approaches for your consideration. These suggestions reflect my many years of teaching experience. You may not agree with all of them, but I hope they will stimulate you to think more about the need to motivate students to learn (science) and to develop new perspectives.

Some Motivational Techniques

Establish clear goals and convey them to the students. Include the goal of self-motivation. We don't want students to be unsure of our intentions. Simply informing them of what we want them to accomplish sets the tone and directs their learning. Then, be sure to reinforce and reiterate these goals throughout the course.

Encourage class attendance. It's difficult to motivate students to learn if they are not in class. I emphasize to students that they are in class for the experiences, and not for the information. If attendance was just to gain information, they could simply read a book at home. I want my students to experience the class; I remind them that we learn from everything we do, and everything that we do becomes part of what we are. Even if a lecturer is terrible, students learn something...perhaps that they would never teach that way themselves. A student once pointed out that: "If I'm experiencing your class, then I'm missing another experience." That's true, but students have to prioritize their choices of experiences. If the alternative choice is doing the laundry, that can wait.

I also mention that if students miss the course experiences, they'll never know what they missed. Getting the notes is not sufficient. I want students to experience everything in the course, and take advantage of all opportunities to learn. However, if we expect students to experience all classes, it is our obligation as teachers to make sure that the experience is worthwhile. We have to prepare each class session thoroughly and try to make it motivational. My intention for each class session is to have students reflect on some aspect of the session and leave saying, *"I never thought about it that way before."*

Focus on interesting, meaningful learning experiences. The question I always ask is: "If I were a student in the class, what would I want to learn and why?" It's often difficult to answer this question, but reflecting upon it may help in planning what and how we teach. Those items that truly represent meaningful learning capture the students' attention. Once learning science becomes an enjoyable habit, students may learn science for the sake of learning.

Teach unusually. Students remember the unique events. This does not mean that we have to stand on our heads and do somersaults in class. Simply think of some unusual twists to teaching the subject that would capture the attention and interest of students. Demonstrations are often effective in this regard. For example, when discussing the history of microscopy, I dramatically reveal an exact replica of one of Leeuwenhoek's microscopes and let students handle it. When discussing mitosis and meiosis, I become a dividing cell and demonstrate the movements of large, cardboard chromosomes on my chest and in my pants belt. When discussing the uniqueness of every sexually-reproducing individual, I display a Drosophila fly in a vial on the overhead projector, and then release it to fly on to its own destiny.

Sometimes, teaching unusually may simply involve being dramatic and telling a story. Everyone loves a good story, and dramatization of relevant subject matter can be an effective motivator for students.

Make learning fun. Although learning science can be a serious business, it can also be fun and enjoyable. If scientists didn't enjoy science, would they choose to do it? A few years ago, even the National Science Foundation produced "Science is Fun" pins. I believe that students will learn more if they enjoy the learning experience. Having fun with learning may well enhance motivation and achievement.

Praise students (when deserved). Praise can be a very powerful motivator. I recall how my 10th grade geometry teacher motivated me through praise. He asked, "Is anyone able to do that difficult homework problem?" I raised my hand. "Marvin," he said, "Would you do that problem on the board?" I wrote the answer on the board. The teacher then exclaimed in a deep, vibrant voice, "Good job!" That comment still rings in my ears. I instantly became highly motivated to do more geometry problems and to learn more about the subject. How often do we, as teachers, praise our students for their accomplishments? Not enough, I'm sure.

Personalize instruction. Make students realize that you are there to help them learn. Students can become motivated when they feel that someone

105

really cares about their learning. Anything that teachers can do to demonstrate that they really care will have a positive influence on motivation. This may be as simple as holding an extra review session, or extra office hours, or special calling hours before exams, or having lunch with small groups of students. Students respond positively to knowing that the teacher is willing to take that extra step to help them learn.

Be a model. Sometimes the least motivated students become interested in the subject merely because they observe the intense interest of the teacher. If we display great enthusiasm about the subject, students may follow suit. We should convey to the student that we think about science; we should model the critical analyses and thinking processes that we would like our students to display. We should also keep in mind that our behavior as teachers will influence student perceptions about scientists.

Give students an identity bigger than themselves. It is important to accomplish a "we are in this together" feeling in the class. I refer to my biology course as *Adventures in Life.* The course is intended to extend beyond the mere acquisition of subject matter. The course experiences are designed to relate the subject matter to a larger context about living, in general, including self-awareness and personal growth and relations of the individual to the world of life. A constant theme is a focus on individuality. As a unique individual, each student has to find his or her strengths and weaknesses, capitalize on the strengths, overcome the weaknesses, and contribute to society in his or her lifespan. Thus, each student has a bigger goal in the course than simply learning content and processes in biology.

Specific Course Features

Over the years, I have developed a core of special course features that are designed to motivate students and get them involved in learning about life. The introductory college biology course at Syracuse University is a two-semester survey course enrolling about 600 students. The core of the course is taught through an autotutorial laboratory, lectures by the course professor, recitations by graduate teaching assistants, and special projects. And we have also added many enhancements to provide motivation. Any teacher can effectively utilize many of these enhancements in his or her own introductory science course.

Helpful Hints This detailed syllabus explains all aspects of the course, including goals, requirements, reading assignments, policies, philosophy, grading procedures, *etc.* When students know your expectations and philosophy, they feel more comfortable in the course and can be motivated simply by understanding *your* motives.

Bionews and Bioviews This is a course newsletter produced weekly; it contains tips for exams, biological information tidbits, relevant news items, gossip, information about learning opportunities on campus, *etc.* One regular feature is "What's Going On?" This outlines everything that is happening in the course. This newsletter helps ensure that all students know what's going on at all times. It helps set an informal, positive tone for the course and helps make students feel part of the bigger picture.

Staff Directory and Open Office Hours We give students a complete listing of the teaching staff, including office hours, telephone numbers, and e-mail addresses; and they are urged to contact us whenever a problem arises. This directory lets students know that we care about their learning, and that staff and faculty are available to help.

Personally, I hold open office hours, and students are encouraged to contact me at any time when advice is needed. My experience has indicated that students often cannot see me during specified office hours because of their class conflicts. Open office hours demonstrate to students that they are our business, and that we really do care about them and want to help them learn.

Conference Days Conference days can also be a positive feature. Set aside certain half-days, and ask students to sign up for a 15-minute appointment.

Suggestion Box A suggestion box and open mailboxes for each member of the teaching staff are available in the lab. Students are encouraged to submit anonymous comments. Each comment is read, and significant ones are responded to in the *Bionews* or in class.

Merely having a suggestion box is not sufficient to get comments. A positive incentive is to personally distribute comment cards to students in lab during the early part of the course, and ask them to write their comments and drop it into the suggestion box outside the lab door. Once students actually use the suggestion box, notes appear regularly.

Bio-Creativity Contest Students submit something creative about life. This can be a poem, essay, short story, poster, project, model, photograph, *etc.* Those who do a good job can earn ten points toward their final grade. Many students enter this contest and produce extremely creative entries. My favorites include a pig made from garbage collected in a residence hall, a carrying case sewn into the shape of a pig, a microscope made of hard candies glued together, and a water color rendition of a pig in heaven with a caption saying "Dissect frogs." This contest can be highly motivating to students, and it made me realize how infrequently we ask them to use their creative talents.

Other course contests have proven to be effective motivators. For example, we have had the name-the-pig contest (the winner being *Porkus unfortunatus*); a name-the-turtle contest (the winner being *Aristurtle gonad*); and a fly-counting contest, to guess at how many Drosophila flies would be caught in the fly-bottle trap by the end of the week of working with fruit flies.

Bio-Lunches Students are asked to drop four names and a phone number into the suggestion box. I call the number and arrange for a bio-lunch with the students in the residence hall dining center of their choice. We discuss the topics of their choice. This personal meeting in small groups provides me with feedback about the course, helps establish good rapport with students and can be a good motivator.

Grading and Exam Procedures Grades and examinations always provide motivation for students. If they know what is expected, and that they will be justly rewarded for their achievements, they respond in a favorable manner. I specify grading and exam procedures in great detail in *Helpful Hints* (see above). We establish course grades on the basis of three major exams and reports, papers, and quizzes done in recitation classes. The three major exams are worth 420 points and the recitation is worth 190 points. At the end of each semester, the graduate teaching assistants calculate the percentage of the possible 610 point total earned by each student. Every student who earns 90% of the points will receive an A; below 50% will result in an F. The main consideration in giving an A is determining if the student has done excellent work; B is awarded for good work; C is considered average; appropriate pluses and minuses are included. Students are not competing against each other, but against the course content. The TA's are asked to consider any special circumstances, and I meet one-on-one with each of them to decide upon a final grade for each student. Thus, each student receives individual consideration when assigning final grades.

We hold exams in the evenings to assure that students have ample time. We want to know how much the student knows, not how fast they can answer the questions. We hold review sessions before major exams; place previous exams on reserve in the library; add bonus questions to the basic exams; and make answer keys available immediately after the tests. The *biophone* is in operation the night before major exams (*i.e.*, we encourage students to call the biology staff or the course professor to get answers to last-minute questions or to get psychological reassurance).

Bio-Answer Show This is a closed circuit TV program that is aired on campus after major exams. I review the exam and the answers. After going over the exam, I draw names at random from a fishbowl of introductory biology student names and then award prizes which have been donated by local merchants. University Union Television (UUTV), a group of undergraduates studying for a career in TV or radio, produces the show.

"A" Letters and Certificates. Students who earn an "A" in the first semester of introductory biology are sent a letter of congratulations and encouragement. If they earn an "A" both semesters, they receive a congratulatory letter and a wallet-sized certificate of excellence. Such tokens of recognition can be good motivators.

Benefit-of-the-Doubt Credit Students are awarded benefit-of-the-doubt credit for attending a variety of special lectures and learning opportunities throughout the semester. For example, we have a *Frontiers of Science Lecture Series* in which outstanding scientists discuss recent scientific developments and stimulate discussion about the social, ethical and moral implications of these discoveries. Students write their names on tickets and hand these in after the session. We keep the tickets on file and refer to them at the end of the semester during the grading session. If students are on a grade borderline and have attended and participated regularly in these special events, they are given the *benefit-of-the-doubt*. Students seem to respond very well to this approach, and we get many attending these special lectures. Once they do attend a special session, perhaps for benefit-of-the-doubt credit, they often enjoy the experience and become self-motivated to attend future sessions for their own sake.

Bio-Feast At the end of the Fall semester, I organize a class dinner in a residence hall dining center. TA's in the course, the staff, and selected biology faculty are invited. In past years, we have had a live band; a special dinner; "mystery" guests, such as the University mascot and the Chancellor; and door prizes. After dinner, I hold a review session for the last exam of the semester. The Bio-feast has been well-attended in past years, and it helps generate good morale, rapport, and learning. It gives students a *group feeling* that helps promote motivation.

Cooperative Research Project In the Spring semester, we organize the students into teams of 2 to 4 individuals. Each team designs a research project involving plants. The plan is modified in consultation with a TA, and then approved. Students then spend the rest of the semester on the project and produce a final report. All members of a team get the same grade on the report. Designing and working cooperatively on a project provides good motivation.

Fetal Pig dissection During the Spring semester, students complete the dissection of a fetal pig. Those who may have ethical or moral objections to the dissection are dealt with on an individual basis, and an alternative assignment is provided, when appropriate. Otherwise, students can share specimens, work with friends or parents; but at the end of the semester, they must appear for a *pig interview* with their TA. The TA gives an oral, hands-on assessment of the dissection and requisite knowledge to each student, individually. At this interview, TA's are also asked to chat with the student about his or her career goals, academic performance, and other relevant issues. Thus, every student in introductory biology must have a one-on-one, personal conversation with a TA at least once during the year. This procedure helps provide good rapport, and helps assure that TA's have a personal acquaintance with each student.

Biology 200 Special Topics Students who earn a B or better in the first semester of introductory biology can apply for enrollment in a special, two-credit biology course, taken concurrently with the second semester biology. This course focuses on a specialty area, such as molecular genetics, ecology, or cell biology, *etc.*, and is taught by an advanced graduate student. Bio 200 provides in-depth insights and some laboratory graduate student. Bio 200 provides in-depth insights and some laboratory experience in specialized areas of interest. The course structure enables motivated students to extend their involvement in biology beyond the basic survey course. It also provides our best graduate students with an opportunity to develop and teach a course in their field of specialization. I teach one of these special courses for students with an interest in teaching. This small group also provides me with feedback about the larger introductory biology course.

Enrichment Section In the second semester, we arrange opportunities for students who did poorly in the first semester to improve their learning in the second semester. A special Enrichment Section taught by an experienced graduate student is offered to them. This section meets twice a week, and students get tutoring, extra handouts, and individualized help. Students who earn a C, or lower, in the first semester are eligible to apply for the Enrichment Section. This has proven to be very effective.

Optional Class on Wednesdays This provides teachers an opportunity to interact more with interested students, supplement the regular lectures, show films, have special guest presentations, and extend the core content.

Conclusion

In summary, this *Adventures in Life* approach in introductory biology uses many different strategies to motivate students and accomplish course goals. We try to provide an exciting range of experiences for students, and thus enrich their lives, their biological knowledge, their understanding of themselves, and their perspective on life. We want to have a significant, lasting, and positive impact on students. If we succeed in our efforts, the light bulbs in students' heads will be tightened and will glow brightly. That's the sign of a truly self-motivated learner. Let's do all we can to help students tighten those light bulbs!

References

Caprio, M. W. (1993) Teaching Seems More Complicated than I First Thought. *Journal of College Science Teaching,* **22**: 218-20.

Caprio, M. W. (1993) Cooperative Learning—The Jewel among Motivational Teaching Techniques. *Journal of College Science Teaching,* **22:** 279-81.

Coppola, Brian P. (1995) Progress in Practice: Using Concepts from Motivational and Self-Regulated Learning Research to Improve Chemistry Instruction. *New Directions for Teaching and Learning*; pp 87-96.

McCombs, Barbara L. (1996) *Understanding the Keys to Motivation to Learn*, The Mid-continent Regional Educational Laboratory, Internet address: http://www.mcrel.org/products/noteworthy/barbaram.html.

Ridley, D.S. (1991) Reflective self-awareness: A basic motivational process. *Journal of Experimental Education*, **60**(1): 31-48.

Rogers, C. (1983) *Freedom to Learn for the Eighties.* Columbus: Charles E. Merrill Publishing Co.

Weiner, B. (1979) A Theory of Motivation for Some Classroom Experiences. *Journal of Educational Psychology*, **71**: 3-25.

Wlodkowski, R.J. (1985) *Enhancing Adult Motivation to Learn: a Guide to Improving Instruction and Increasing Learner Achievement.* San Francisco: Jossey-Bass Publishers.

Eleanor D. Siebert

Chapter 11

LINKING SCIENCE DISCOVERIES TO TEACHING

We live in a world dominated by science and technology, and a broad understanding of these fields is required by our citizenry. In order to have an effective labor force, to sustain ever-diminishing resources, and to make wise social and political decisions, a knowledge of science is important. But the application of science to human concerns is generally in the realm of technology. The application of science to human concerns is not obvious to most students in introductory science courses; teachers must show the connection.

In teaching, most of us utilize technology in some way. It may be through computer-based applications, instrumentation in the laboratory, or through other audiovisual resource materials. Many of us, however, do not make the *explicit* connection for our students between science discoveries and how these have impacted our lives. In fact, the distinction between science and technology has become quite blurred; science discoveries enable developments in technology which, in turn, enable science discoveries; these discoveries, in turn, enable greater technological advancement; which, in turn, lead to.... Science, technology and society are so intertwined and relevant to us all that this connection between science and technology should be made in almost every introductory science course. John A. Moore has been a strong voice in detailing the need for a scientifically literate citizenry and in decrying the failure of the educational system in meeting that goal (Moore 1993). He writes that "we habitually short change our students, and hence our future, when we fail to show how the data and procedures of science can be of great import in solving many human problems." (Moore 1994)

Table 1

Highlights in 50 Years of Science and Technology

1950-59	Oral contraceptives developed in 1952
	More transuranium elements synthesized
	Hydrogen bomb tested
	Smoking linked to lung cancer
	Salk and Sabin polio vaccinations began
	Structure of insulin determined
	Space age began as Sputniks were launched and the US established NASA
	Double helix structure of DNA, by Watson and Crick
1960-69	LASERS were developed
	A version of DNA is synthesized
	Space exploration expands with landings on the moon
	Astronomers report the existence of quasars and pulsars
	Subatomic particles continue to be discovered
	Earth scientists propose the theory of Plate Tectonics
	Integrated circuits developed
	Fiber optics developed
1970-79	First supercomputer (Cray)
	Pacemakers become common
	Pioneer 10 launched; farthest launch when retired in 1997
	Cloning bits of DNA
	First test tube baby born
	Aerosol propellants reported to damage stratospheric ozone
	String theory developed
1980-89	Video cameras
	Interferon produced
	Scanning Tunneling Microscope invented
	Reusable space shuttle flights
	First artificial chromosome created
	Technique of genetic finger printing discovered
	First permanent space station (*Mir*) launched
	First Positron Emission Tomography (PET) image produced
1990-	Mapping of human chromosomes and the Human Genome Project
	Gene replacement therapy
	Gamma knife (LASER) surgery developed
	Structure to electron proposed
	First mammals cloned

To be continued!

Impacting the Way We Live

The twentieth century is unparalleled by any previous century for scientific activity, and it is likely that scientific progress in the twenty-first century will continue to accelerate. Many of the discoveries have profoundly changed our understanding of nature and the way we live, and many of the discoveries have promoted advances in technology that change the questions we ask and the way we answer those questions. The timeline shown in Table 1 highlights only a few of these discoveries and some of the technological developments enabled by science.

Scientific discoveries and events of the past few decades which have dramatically affected the public are perhaps most significant in medicine, communications, and the entertainment field. The medical field has become more science-oriented and aided by technological developments so that people can live longer and healthier than in the past. In a literal sense, society's heartbeats can be regulated by the use of Pacemakers, which became much more common in the 1970's. Some diseases such as polio have been virtually eradicated through immunization programs in the 1950's; and other diseases, such as diabetes, have been brought under wide-spread control by chemical treatment, in this case made possible by the discovery of the structure of insulin in the 1950's. Noninvasive medical diagnoses utilize X-rays and Magnetic Resonance techniques coupled to computers for imaging (CAT and MRI scans); these techniques are direct outgrowths of scientific discoveries of X-rays and of the magnetic properties of nuclei. Many cancers have been detected and controlled using radiation and/or nuclear medicine; and LASERs (developed in the early 1960's) have expanded the field of noninvasive treatment in surgery. The basis of life illuminated by the double helix structure of DNA proposed by Watson and Crick in the 1950's has given new understanding of genetics—and *in vitro* fertilization (1970's), diagnosis of inherited diseases and genetic fingerprinting (1980's) have resulted. The mapping of human chromosomes and the Human Genome Project and gene replacement therapy are areas of active (and expensive) research today.

Both the communication and the entertainment fields of today utilize technological developments enabled by discoveries in science. For example, prior to the middle of this century almost no one had been exposed to television—a medium which is found in almost every home today. Musical synthesizers have replaced backup musical groups and films utilize animation and other special effects made possible by the use of computers. These technologies sprang from the development of the transistor (1947) and integrated circuits of the 1960's. Though research in modern optical fiber technology dates back only to the 1960's, it has brought about changes that have reshaped and restructured the entire telecommunications industry. Networks of computers run the telephones and transportation systems vital to the functioning of our society. The transmission of information using optical fibers has increased both the amount of information and the speed with which information can be transmitted. In fact, the citizenry might be said to be drowning in a sea of endless information which has been cataloged and is accessible as a result of computer technology.

Impacting What We Teach

Such scientific discoveries and technological developments have not only affected the public, but they have impacted the teaching of science at the undergraduate level—they have influenced what is being taught, as well as how science is being taught. Computer technology, for example, which is an outgrowth of discoveries made almost fifty years ago, has dramatically changed many aspects of our lives, including that of the college professor. One of the jobs of science educators at the introductory college/university level is to ensure that our students have a knowledge of fundamental over-arching scientific concepts; in fact, in earlier decades of this century, college and university professors were the major dispensers of information at an advanced level and their institutions were repositories of information. In this day, however, we are an "information-rich" society and access to information is easy. Technology has changed the job of college instructors to focus not so much on the giving out of information, but to ensure that our students know how to utilize scientific information appropriately. Some introductory courses now include accessing data bases through the Internet and using that information in course work. A part of this course component is to ensure that students learn how to evaluate the validity of information, how to make some sense of the vast amounts they can access, and perhaps most importantly, that students learn how to manage and apply that information.

Technology and the discoveries it has enabled have also affected what we can know and how we solve for answers. Most of the instruments used in research utilize computer technology in some way, extending the questions that we can investigate and what we can learn from them. Entire new areas in molecular biology, in nuclear science, in modeling natural physical systems, and in medical diagnoses and treatment have developed.

116

Some curriculum projects at the undergraduate level deal with incorporating some of this new material into courses to maintain connection with science at the cutting edge. In 1994 *The Society for College Science Teachers* published a monograph that showed how science at the frontier in the past few decades has influenced the content of

---

Table 2
Sample Projects Linking Teaching to Science Discoveries*

Teaching Creative Molecular Design
    Orville L. Chapman, University of California, Los Angeles

Ethics Discussions in Biology
    Judith Heady, University of Michigan, Dearborn

Chaos in the Undergraduate Physics Curriculum
    Eric Kincanon, Gonzaga University, Spokane

Ecology's Ikon from Space
    Ted Lopushinsky, Michigan State University

Optodes: Sensors for Chemical Systems
    Gordon Parker, University of Michigan, Dearborn

DNA and the Humanistic Study of Science
    Richard Rice, University of Montana, Missoula

Nuclear Magnetic Resonance Spectroscopy: A Tool of Modern Science
    Arlene A. Russell, University of California, Los Angeles

Cell Membranes
    Donald Schmidt, Fitchburg State College
    John Schmidt and Debra Wollner, Wichita State University

The Plates Can't Curl Down (Plate Tectonics)
    Dorothy Stout, Cypress College, California

*documented in Siebert and Estee (1994)

---

some college/university introductory science courses. (Siebert and Estee 1994). Some of the projects highlighted in Table 2 show how science at the cutting edge is being used in the context of learning fundamental science at the introductory level. For example, biologists are looking to *molecular biology* and at the molecular structure of biological systems to improve understanding of function and disease (Schmidt). *Molecular design* using computers (a technique that earned Donald Cram the 1987 Nobel Prize in Chemistry) is introduced at the introductory level of organic chemistry (Chapman). *Fiber optics* is used to gather data remotely (Parker), and advances in *analytical techniques* such as in nuclear magnetic resonance (NMR) are used to illustrate the principles of state-of-the-art instruments in the medical field (Russell). In physics, some aspects of *advanced theories* such as chaos theory are introduced in introductory courses to show the techniques of science at the frontier and wide-spread application in forecasting weather, population trends, chemical reaction rates and planetary orbits (Kincanon). In the Earth Sciences, the concept of *Plate Tectonics* developed in the 1960's has unified a host of natural phenomena (Stout).

There are also whole program developments at both the secondary and college/university levels which emphasize the interplay and interdependence of science, technology and society (STS). STS curriculum development and workshops are active areas of faculty development in many institutions of higher education (Piel 1997).

Reflective Thinking and an Ethical Dimension

In recent years the rapid changes in our lives driven by technical and scientific discoveries have added much complexity to decision-making. *Ethics*, the study of human actions carried out with knowledge and by choice, has become an important added dimension of many science and technology programs or courses. This has taken the form of the inclusion of ethics within existing courses as well as offering one or more separate ethics courses in specific academic programs. In 1985 the Accreditation Board for Engineering and Technology (ABET) required that engineering curricula contain engineering ethics and professionalism content, and the National Science Foundation has funded curriculum development projects in ethics. Examples of engineering programs where ethics is integrated into the technical curriculum may be found at The Illinois Institute of Technology and at Texas A&M University. A study of ethics often involves case studies which illustrate real world problems and analytical techniques to determine what is professionally correct and ethical. (Harris *et al.* 1995) These case studies direct students to reflect on decisions through an examination of ideals, motives for choice, and what is right and just for the common good.

Some science programs also emphasize the relationship of science to human endeavors through added course components which consider ethics and humanism. In Table 2, for example, you find that Judith Heady includes ethics discussions in her introductory biology courses about molecular technologies such as are associated with *in vitro* fertilization, the Genome Project and gene replacement therapy. Richard Rice brings a more humanistic study of science by embedding the wonderfully-human route to DNA discovery in a discussion of the scientific process and ethics (see also Watson 1968). A leader in teaching bioethical decision making, Jon Hendrix, at Ball State University, has a Web site with information on why college science teachers need to include ethics in science teaching today. (Hendrix 1997)

Impacting the Way We Teach

The impact of technology on education has been enormous, especially as technology has become more affordable and available to many classrooms and libraries. For one thing, technology has provided access to information through public data bases (*e.g.*, meteorological data, astronomical data, *etc.*) that is being used in many courses (Kincanon). Many instructors are using computers to present information in the classroom or in remote locations via teleconferencing. You will find discussions of the use of technology in teaching in many areas throughout this book, but an important challenge facing teachers is to use technology not just to spice-up class presentations or to access information, but to use that technology in a way to enhance learning. Can computers be used to expand students' thinking—to help them learn to ask better questions, to reason more logically, to read and write more critically? Robert Allen talks about using technology to enhance critical thinking (Chapter 3); Jungck, Soderberg, Stanley and Vaughan use it for interactive teaching (Chapter 16); and Kelly and Caprio (Chapter 6) emphasize how scientific literacy will soon become obsolete without information literacy. Computers used in the laboratory can allow students to better analyze and, thus, to better interpret data (Chapter 17); and computers can be used to simulate experiments that are beyond the means or facilities of the institution.

119

It is important that science teachers stay abreast of developments in technology, and it is imperative that we use technology wisely. Students who were bored by slides and overhead transparencies will soon be bored by computer presentations. Because teaching must be student centered, the use of technology for convenience or for the sake of innovation is not enough. You must make sure that your use of technology is appropriate and that it provides a way for learners to think differently about information and to use that information more productively (Chapter 16). Research on the effective use (and misuse) of computers in the science classroom is relatively new (Wilcox and Jensen 1997).

Impacting When We Teach Concepts

Finally, discoveries in the field of cognitive science have not only influenced *what* content is taught, but *when* it is taught, and *how* it is taught (Chapter 1). The advances in psychology and cognitive research in the 1950's forward has strongly influenced the order and rate at which science concepts are covered in the curriculum. Piagetian theory (Piaget and Inhelder, 1952) has convinced many instructors that it is not only important for the curriculum to start with what the student knows but with what the student has the intellectual capacity to learn. Much of our current science education theory and constructivism (Chapter 1) are outgrowths of Piaget's work. Piaget describes intellectual development in terms of four stages, the last two of which may be appropriate for college/university science teachers to know about. The first two stages, sensory-motor and pre-operational, are usually completed by the time a child is seven or eight years old. The last two states of development are stages of logical operation, and usually require a longer period of time to develop; an additional complication is that the time required to develop into a logical/abstract thinker varies greatly among individuals. Called concrete-operational and formal-operational, the first deals with learners who must have first-hand experience with objects in order to learn and the latter with those learners who can reason from logical and often abstract relationships. The notion of what is "developmentally appropriate" for students may guide not only your choice of content but also how that content is presented (Gipson 1989,1994). For example, concrete learners learn well when concepts are developed in laboratory/field settings, and Gipson argues that it may be futile to try to teach abstract concepts to many of the learners in introductory courses. The intellectual development of students in your classroom can be tested, and this may influence when and how you introduce more complex and increasingly abstract concepts at the college/university level. However, the interpretation of what content is appropriate to teach at the introductory level is subject to conflicting interpretations. In a critical review of genetics instruction (Smith and Sims 1992), the authors conclude that "effective instruction that takes into account the cognitive levels of students will clearly demand radical changes in teaching techniques, a drastic reduction of the number of formal concepts introduced, and a drastic increase in the amount of time students are allowed to make sense of these concepts." In other words, concrete learners can learn abstract concepts, but a new learning approach is essential. And so, introductory science courses continue to include reasonably abstract concepts such as genetics, atomic structure, and modern physics. In Chapter 1 of this manual, Leonard discusses learning theories and how this has been a result of research of classroom settings and of psychologists; you will find some guidance there on how best to present abstract concepts at the introductory level .

Keeping Up With the Times

Of course it is impossible to teach *all* that has happened or is happening, but it is possible to show how the truly life-changing discoveries of science arose from questions asked about the fundamental concepts of science. Wherever possible, these science discoveries should be related to the process of science—how we come to know—and to the overarching concepts of the fundamental science that we teach in our introductory courses.

There is a contagion factor in incorporating cutting-edge science in our course material. It allows instructors as scientists to stay abreast of recent developments and promotes the notion that we need to read scientific journals or public articles that deal with science to present a "good" introductory science course. I find that time spent in this way gives a sense of perspective to my work and a satisfaction of understanding some of the science at a more fundamental level than covered in my courses. It reinforces the concept of a scientist and scholar in teaching. For students, the incorporation of cutting-edge science into the material also provides perspective and hopefully will better prepare them to be fully-participating citizens in the decisions of their time.

References

Gibson, M.H., Abraham, M.R. and Renner, J.W. (1989) Relationships Between Formal-Operational Thought and Conceptual Difficulties in Genetics Problem Solving," *Journal of Research in Science Teaching*, **26**, 811-821.

Gipson, M.H. (1994), Jean Piaget's Influence on Science Education, *Science Discoveries and Science Teaching: The Link*, see Siebert, E. D. and Estee, Charles R.

Harris, C. E., Pritchard, M. S. and Rabins, M. J. (1995), *Engineering Ethics, Concepts and Cases,* Wadsworth Publishing Co.

Hendrix, Jon R. (1997) Address: http://www.bsu.edu/bio/faculty/hendrix.html.

Moore, John A. (1993) *Science as a Way of Knowing, the Foundations of Modern Biology,* Harvard University Press.

Moore, John A. (1994) Introduction, *Science Discoveries and Science Teaching: The Link*, see Siebert, E. D. and Estee, C.

Piaget, J. and Inhelder, B. (1952) *The growth of logical thinking from childhood to adolescence.* Paris: Basic Books, Inc.

Piel, Joseph E. (1997) Science/Technology/Society Curriculum Development, Teacher Workshops Secondary Schools and Colleges; can be reached at epiel98502@aol.com.

Siebert, E. D. and Estee, C., eds. (1994) *Science Discoveries and Science Teaching: The Link*, Society for College Science Teachers.

Smith, M.U. and Sims, O.S. (1992) "Cognitive Development, Genetics Problem Solving, and Genetics Instruction: A Critical Review," *Journal of Research in Science Teaching*, 29, 701-713.

Watson, J. D. (1968) *The Double Helix*, Atheneum, New York.

Wilcox, K. J. and Jensen, M.S., Computer Use in the Science Classroom: Proceed with Caution!, *Journal of College Science Teaching, 26* (4).

Leona Truchan
George Gurria
Georgine Loacker

Chapter 12

ASSESSMENT: CONNECTING TEACHING AND LEARNING

Assuming assessment is an essential part of learning—a part that tells the student and the instructor how each is doing—its essential conceptual connections to all the other aspects of learning are relatively clear. To make those connections operational is the challenge of each instructor individually and in collaboration.

The principles one espouses to inform practice determine the connections between assessment, teaching and learning. For example, one principle of learning many science educators are apt to hold is that *learning begins with the student.* Thus, it seems to make sense to begin with an individual student assessment and design program and institutional assessment based on it.

Both for assessment as a part of learning and for learning in general, explicit outcomes are essential, and the student should be aware of them. Outcomes focus the learning, teaching, and assessment: what *can* and *will* the student learn in this class? what will I teach? what will I assess? The *course outcomes* determine all of these. In whole or in part, they constitute *assessment* outcomes.

Writing Course Outcomes
How can we assure that science course outcomes are what they should be? The first step is to make sure that they express an aspect of what a scientist should know and be able to do. It clearly helps if a given

department has articulated, for their majors, student outcomes that present a picture of the effective scientist—even better if the institution has a set of agreed-upon outcomes for all graduates. Then students can see connections from their day-to-day learning to their understanding of what they can, and in fact *must*, accomplish in order to earn a degree.

One can evaluate the relevance and completeness of course outcomes by using a set of guidelines such as the following:

- Is the set of outcomes multidimensional (*i.e.* integrates knowledge, abilities, behaviors, values, dispositions)?
- Do the outcomes represent something students can use in their personal and/or professional lives?
- Are they appropriate to the mission/aims of your department and/or institution?
- Would they be applicable to varied contexts?
- Do they embody potential levels of development?
- Together do they give you an expected picture of someone who has completed your course? (Alverno College Faculty, 1994)

Because we believe that scientists in a given institutional context can best articulate the science outcomes, we also believe that those scientists can best critique those outcomes, though certainly external evaluation is an important supplement.

The following example of a selected outcome of an Organic Chemistry course illustrates how an outcome might describe aspects of a scientist's competence as well as direct students' learning and assessment.

Organic Chemistry:
To show understanding of and ability to use laboratory experimentation as a means of investigating organic substances and their reactions. This includes:
1. Ability to analyze data obtained through experimentation based on relationships between and among observations and inferences resulting from the experiments;
2. Ability to create a design for the solution of a problem by use of laboratory experimentation, using the scientific method of problem solving;
3. Ability to apply a complete problem solving strategy to the definition and solution of a complex laboratory problem individually and in a collaborative mode.

Course outcomes, like assessment, need to embody the principles of learning that the instructor (and ideally the department and the institution) hold. If one believes that *learning should be active,* course outcomes should suggest active learning and performance assessment. In other words, if a course outcome expects students to create a design for the solution of a problem by use of laboratory experimentation, using the scientific method of problem solving, then their learning needs to include their active engagement in problem solving. Their assessment needs to elicit from students more than a summary of their knowledge; it needs to enable them to show, in performance, that they can use laboratory experimentation to solve a problem by the scientific method.

If one believes that *learning should be interactive,* one's course should be meaningful and accessible to the student in terms of the criteria which determine how to judge the outcomes. For example, it should be made clear to students that in order to demonstrate that they can create a design for the solution of a problem by use of laboratory experimentation, using the scientific method of problem solving, they must meet the following criteria:

- The student defines the problem or poses a question that is answerable by scientific inquiry.
- The student selects or designs an appropriate chemical framework and approach to solve the problem.
- The student uses the vocabulary of organic chemistry and chemical frameworks appropriately.
- The student uses strategies appropriate to the laboratory science of organic chemistry.
- The student develops a scientific plan to achieve a solution that is consistent with the framework she selected.
- The student articulates her rationale for the strategies used.

Another significant implication of the belief that learning should be interactive is the importance of instructor feedback on the students' development of the abilities inherent in the course outcomes. In our practice and research on that practice at Alverno College, we have found that such feedback assists students in their learning when it is specific to the criteria. It needs to point out what aspects of a given outcome they have demonstrated with more or less thoroughness, where other aspects are lacking or perhaps faintly hinted at, and how they can build on what they have already shown they can do.

If one believes that *students should take responsibility for their learning,* then it is imperative to find ways to assist the student to develop the ability to self assess. They might not, at the beginning of a course, understand all that a given set of course outcomes entails. By the end of the course, however, their understanding should enable them to evaluate their own performance of the outcomes with a clear perception of their strengths and areas still in need of development.

Course outcomes, therefore, prove to be a core-connecting link between all aspects of assessment, learning, and teaching. They determine the nature and level of the educational experience.

Constructing Assessments

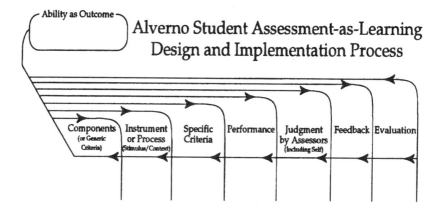

The above heuristic from *"Student Assessment-as-Learning at Alverno College"* illustrates the relationship among the several identifiable components of an assessment process as well as provides a framework for the design of assessment. Assessment design may begin once an outcome to be assessed is identified. The outcome may be just one of the set that describes what the successful student should be able to know and do as a result of a specific course. It may be a combination of these outcomes or a single portion or aspect of one of them. For example, in an assessment from an Organic Chemistry course (see Chapter Appendix), the outcome to be assessed may be a combination of the course outcome regarding "relationships" in chemistry; the analysis of structure and function outcome; and the information search and speaking aspects of the communications outcome. The specification of outcomes is one step in the process that ensures the connectedness of teaching, learning, and assessment.

Before leaping to the creation of an assessment instrument, it would be wise first to consider some *general criteria* for the demonstration of the outcomes. Criteria at this level help teachers as designers to paint a picture of what an outcome means and to consider the different ways in which an instrument might elicit that outcome. Taken together, the general criteria should give one a better picture of the outcome.

This *instrument* then is the device that gets students to perform and thus provide evidence of their capability. It is in part a *stimulus*: a question or incident or situation that students can respond to and through their response demonstrate the outcome one seeks. The instrument also sets a *context*: the discipline or content to be considered, the audience to be addressed, the purpose for the response. While many assessment instruments consist of a stimulus for students to read and require writing as the expected mode of response, designers should consider modes that may better connect to the outcome and to the level of the student, and may be more engaging to students and therefore draw out a more representative performance.

Once one has identified in the design the nature of the performance—a performance which will provide the evidence of student ability—there is a need to recast general criteria into specific criteria that fit this context. These *specific criteria* collectively should describe rather than prescribe a successful student performance. That is, students should be able to meet these criteria in more than one way despite the constraints of a specified stimulus and mode. Criteria should be written keeping the developmental level of student in mind: students at a beginning level (true in most introductory courses) often use criteria as a guide to planning their performance, as a set of directions. Later, students use sets of criteria to picture the outcome/ability and to infer a performance that shows that ability. Knowing that these criteria direct the judgment of the student's performance, one should ensure the they have a qualitative dimension to them so that judgments can accommodate a range of performance.

Whether it is in the form of writing or visual representation, speaking individually or as part of a group discussion, actions carried out, or some combination of these, the student's *performance* is the evidence that assessors judge and students *self-assess*. Judgment of this performance is based on the criteria specified. The communication of this judgment to the student is the process called *feedback*. The inclusion of strategies for assisting students to self-assess their work is critical in their development as life-long learners. As students develop in the ability to self-assess they can progress from a checklist approach to criteria to articulating ways in which they have demonstrated improvement and charting plans for future work based on present performance. Parallel to this, faculty approach to feedback ought to include prescriptive advice as well as analysis of the student's current level of performance.

Multiple Modes of Assessment

Student assessment-as-learning demands multiple approaches and strategies to assure that one taps into different styles of learning in the integration of science concepts and process skills. If inquiry skills are important outcomes for a science course in botany or introductory chemistry, then students should take assessments that require the integration of key concepts and inquiry skills. Identification or recall of factual content-based assessments alone rarely solicits this type of integration of concepts and skills in any science. An Internet resource on this topic is *Beyond Bio 101: The Transformation of Undergraduate Biology Education* developed by the Howard Hughes Medical Institute. It contains six chapters highlighting current trends and changes in undergraduate biology teaching. Three chapters of particular interest to this section on assessment are Chapter 2, "Changes in the Classroom"; Chapter 3, "The Laboratory Experience"; and Chapter 6, "Lessons Learned". Although no one chapter focuses totally on assessment, in Chapter 3 there is a section on "The Challenge of Assessment" (p. 40) which presents excellent questions that address assessment. The *National Science Education Standards* presents program evaluation as assessment. However, with the strong emphasis on outcomes and teaching, one can take the material on changes in teaching and extrapolate much of it to individual student assessment as well as to the development of consistency and coherence in a science curriculum.

Another reference is Gordon Uno's *Handbook on Teaching Undergraduate Science Courses* (Uno 1997). On pages 80-83, there is a graphic synthesis of a variety of assessment techniques and methods that summarize alternative assessment modes with brief descriptions and examples. These modes begin with the traditional multiple choice, two-tier multiple choice, free response, essay, to more current and diverse modes such as concept maps, clinical interviews, laboratory practicals, long term investigations, problem-based learning, and portfolios. Each of these modes needs to have a relationship to the outcomes of the course and needs to engage the students. Another approach to multiple modes of assessment appears in Appendix D of *Student Assessment-As-Learning at Alverno College* (pp. 117-118). These two pages describe a framework of assessment modes, stimuli, and student responses. The emphasis is on stimuli in assessments that solicit engagement of the student. The framework includes how students receive input: written work or record (reading something), aural (listening to something recorded), visual (viewing something), lived event (being in the lab, in the field or clinical setting), simulated event (being there in the pretended event or computer simulated event), following a set of directions or questions to create something such as a concept map, or any combination of the above. The student is actively involved in the performance response. The implication of both these references is not that there are multiple ways to assess, but that there is a need for a set of guidelines for an assessment design. The guidelines faculty at Alverno College have used for over twenty years appear in Part B of the document. (Alverno College Faculty, pp. 113-115, 1994) The questions regarding the outcome of the course, the choices of assessment modes, specific criteria, and structured feedback all assist in the assessment design.

In the *Journal of College Science Teaching,* Slater walks through his use of portfolios as a mode of assessing students in science and reflects on the strengths and student responses to using this approach. He states: "Whereas multiple-choice tests are designed to determine what the student *doesn't* know, portfolio assessments emphasize what the student *does* know." One of the components of the article is a quantitative comparison of students assessed by portfolio and students assessed traditionally. He concludes that "The results of these studies suggest that portfolio assessment procedures enhance conceptual understanding and attitudes toward learning and evaluation in the college science classroom....Portfolio assessment procedures allow instructors to view student achievement in a longitudinal and holistic perspective." (Slater, 1997)

Whether one selects performance assessments or portfolio assessments, the assessment design provides clear criteria by which one identifies whether students meet the intended outcomes.

Using Assessment to Improve Teaching and Student Learning

The fifth chapter of the *National Science Education Standards* addresses assessment, with a strong emphasis on classroom evaluation. One of the values of this chapter, although the intended audience is K-12 teachers of science, is the summary of changing emphases regarding assessment standards. These can act as a starting point to reflect on where teacher-designed assessments fail in science.

The national norms (National Research Council, 1996) say there is *less* emphasis on:
- assessing what is easily measured
- assessing discrete knowledge
- assessing scientific knowledge
- assessing to learn what students do not know
- assessing only achievement
- assessing only at the end of the term by teachers
- use of instruments developed by measurement experts for external assessment.

and *more* emphasis on:
- assessing what is most highly valued
- assessing rich, well-structured knowledge
- assessing scientific understanding and reasoning
- assessing to learn what students do understand
- assessing achievement and opportunity to learn
- assessing in an ongoing period of their work
- use of instruments developed by teacher for external assessment.

If one would use the above statements and add two questions to them, then an ongoing improvement in teaching and student learning would be very possible. They are:
- what are the specific outcomes you hope students will develop in your course?
- what criteria will you use to know that the students have developed them?

If it is correct that what one teaches and what one assesses are connected, how close are science syllabi outcomes connected to teaching and assessment? Reflecting on the quality and design of student assessment would be very conducive to substantive classroom research and could be the basis for judging how students do or do not achieve the outcomes of a given course. Using the data obtained from student assessment, faculty will be in a better position to improve science teaching and learning in an informed manner.

References

Alverno College Faculty (1994) *Student Assessment-as-Learning at Alverno College,* Alverno College Institute, Milwaukee, WI.

Beyond Bio 101: The Transformation of Undergraduate Biology Education (1997) ed. by Howard Hughes Medical Institute. Washington, DC. (Order through Internet: http://www.hhml.org/BeyondBio101).

National Research Council (1996) "Assessment in Science Education" ch. 5 in *National Science Education Standards,* pp. 75-102, National Academy Press, Washington.

Slater, Timothy F. (1997) "The Effectiveness of Portfolio Assessments in Science in March/April issue of *Journal of College Science Teaching.*

Uno, Gordon E. (1997) "The Task of Assessing Your Students" ch. 8 in *Handbook on Teaching Undergraduate Science Courses* (NSF funded), pp. 65-85, Oklahoma University Press.

Chapter Appendix: Examples of Assessments

Introductory Science

Course Outcome

The student demonstrates the ability to think critically and problem solve in a scientific context to observe, measure and analyze phenomena.

Summary Description of Stimulus

Pairs of students work together to construct, from paper and tape, a marble slide which will allow a marble to roll at least 7 meters. Students are guided by prompts from a problem solving protocol used in basic science: understanding the problem, exploring strategies, selecting strategies, evaluating strategies. Students are asked (individually) to describe themselves as problem solvers.

Criteria

Using appropriate problem solving vocabulary, the student describes herself as a problem solver, citing strengths and weaknesses and providing evidence of each.

Organic Chemistry

Course Outcome

You will be able to:

- demonstrate the relationships between structure and physical properties for organic compounds.
- analyze the structure and function of organic compounds using the frameworks of structure, energetics, and equilibrium.
- retrieve the published information that constitutes the knowledge base of organic chemistry, and to effectively communicate to an audience your understanding of that knowledge base.

Summary Description of Stimulus

Pairs of students are assigned "patent rights" to a technique, apparatus or material from Organic Chemistry (*e.g.*, gas chromatography, continuous liquid-solid extractor) and prepare to present and exhibit at the (fictitious) Annual Organic Trade Fair and Exposition. Students prepare a 15-minute presentation, with media and demonstrations, to illustrate the theory of, practical uses for, and limitations of their patent items.

Criteria

In your presentation:

- you accurately describe for your audience how to use your patented item
- you use appropriate concepts from organic chemistry to describe how your item does what it does
- you accurately relate these theoretical concepts to practical applications of your item and to address when not to use your item
- you use appropriate media and/or demonstrations in ways that assist your audience to understand the content of your presentation
- you and your partner demonstrate appropriate team behaviors
- you meet college-wide criteria for effective speaking

Botany

Course Outcome

Through the study of plants, you will gain a new awareness of the physiological complexity and adaptability of plants as organisms, a new area of knowledge that makes up the multifaceted areas of sciences, and further perception that science is a way of thinking and an approach to selected issues and problems.

Summary description of stimulus

Learning occurs over a five week period of an integrated lecture/laboratory sessions meeting four hours/week. The course is divided into three sections, each with a culminating assessment integrating structure and function and assisting students to see two- and three-dimensionally. In the assessment for the second section, the students are given a packet containing 9 questions (seven in graphic format). Students are asked to select and answer five questions.

Students are to write for an audience of their science peers. Students are encouraged to use examples, drawings, and maps to enhance and strengthen their explanations.

Criteria

- The student appropriately uses technical language regarding plant structure and function.
- The student makes relationships beyond a one-to-one level of complexity in her explanation of water transport or photosynthesis.
- The student accurately interprets models or graphics without significant omissions.
- The student consistently addresses designated audience in her answers.
- The student organizes answers rather than listing discrete pieces of information.
- The student synthesizes basic principles or patterns correctly.
- The student completes the assessment and self assessment in the given time.

Microbiology

Course Outcome

You will develop your ability to work with multiple pieces of data, weight them, and be able to organize these data into a meaningful framework or flowchart demonstrating a more complex view of the microbial organism.

Summary description of stimulus:

Conducted over an eight week laboratory period of four hours/week.

- Part A - Identify to the species level an unknown microorganism by going through multiple tests; using software and Bergey's taxonomic keys use your data and try to come up with a "best fit" relationship; synthesize your findings in a formal report analyzing why you made the taxonomic decisions that you made.
- Part B - Given your mastery of a specify bacterial system, your unknown; design and implement an investigation using your unknown, your partners, or both. You will present this investigation to your peers, drawing an appropriate conclusion from the data, and identifying how you would modify your design if you were to repeat it.

Criteria

For Part A: Your individual report includes:

- a clearly designed flowchart showing your experimental movement to reach a conclusion to the species level
- an analytic written explanation stating the basis of your key decisions
- an accurately completed official Descriptive Chart
- a timely selection of 2 or more references showing how your unknown is used in research

- an appropriate statement of how this process is generalizable and can be used in other science courses

For Part B: Your joint investigative project includes:
- an oral report meeting the college-wide criteria for communication
- a co-authored written report employing a standard science journal format
- a one-page written report with a reflective statement comparing the two problem solving approaches used and what you have learned - part A: identification; part B: hypothesis generated and implemented.

Physics

Course Outcomes
You will be able to:
- solve traditional physics problems: individually on paper, working collaboratively in a group, in a presentation mode at the blackboard or overhead, or using a computer.
- work more effectively in a group whose goals are to discover or use physical relationships in an experimental or theoretical setting.

Summary Description of Stimulus
Four students, two with calculus background and two with algebra/trigonometry background, work as a team on a problem. The problem assigned requires the use of course material from a later portion of the class calendar. This makes the problem more difficult and more realistic.

Criteria
You/the group:
- explicitly identify the problem or goal
- plan a process for achieving the goal and identify any constraints or assumptions
- establish criteria for the decision
- explore and encourage differences of opinion
- derive tentative solutions
- combine input to produce a decision
- compare the decision to the criteria established
- reach consensus and evaluate the group process and individual contributions

III

Introductory Courses and the Classroom

Introduction

INTRODUCTORY COURSES AND THE CLASSROOM

Unit I of this book focuses on the ways people learn, and Unit II on the art of teaching; now it is time to cover some of the details that will set the stage for creative and effective change to take place in your courses. In Unit III, the authors suggest ways to create good learning environments in your classroom and laboratory and offer concrete steps toward building these components into your course experience.

First it is important to know what kind of introductory science course you will be teaching: will it be one for non-majors, for majors, or for both? What do these courses have in common? How do they differ? Chapter 13 discusses each course from the perspective of students, according to their self-selection as "science majors" or "non-science majors". We can better meet the needs of our students if we first understand them, and we must be very well acquainted with the alternative forms of the introductory courses we have for them. They are as different as the students they were designed to serve.

A separate yet crucial consideration in teaching is the students' differing backgrounds and learning styles. Regardless of gender, ethnicity, and special needs—such as physical challenges, limited English proficiencies, and many learning disabilities—all students can learn science. And for the future of our society, all students must learn science. Chapter 14 offers compelling suggestions for implementing supportive learning environments for all students. We are all challenged to examine our own beliefs and assumptions and to develop an action plan that will ensure equity in our course.

While large classes are not an ideal teaching and learning setting, they are a reality at many institutions. In Chapter 15, the author asserts that large classes can be effective learning environments and provides suggestions for offering "small-class" learning techniques in the "large-class" setting. Concrete suggestions are given for presentations, active learning and assessment as well as for dealing with equipment, instructional staff, and problem behaviors. The chapter also considers the added coordination details necessary to ensure the success of the large class.

Chapter 16 is a chapter on using technology in education. But this is not just a chapter on accessing data bases or electronic communication; the authors here provide useful strategies for enhancing collaborative learning with technology. The theme of this chapter is an emphasis on the ways in which technology can be used to engage students in new types of active and collaborative experiences. Many of the key concepts developed in earlier units of this book are embodied in this chapter.

As scientists, we all know that laboratory/field experiences are integral to most science disciplines; but how should we provide these experiences for our students? How do we maximize their efficacy? How do we choose or craft the experiences for our students? How do we let students explore and inquire in a large laboratory where hazardous materials are involved in the exploration? Crucial to laboratory teaching are safety considerations and many important managerial details. Chapter 17 is the guide for designing, teaching—and especially for managing your laboratory course.

Nathan Dubowsky

Chapter 13

WHAT KINDS OF COURSES WILL I BE EXPECTED TO TEACH?

Congratulations! You have completed most or all your formal education in your chosen scientific discipline and are about to embark on a career teaching that discipline. How you perceive this new academic challenge depends on your personality and your prior academic experiences.

You may envision yourself standing in front of a large lecture hall delivering a brilliant dissertation on some esoteric topic to a fascinated audience of bright and eager students in much the same way as your favorite professor did. Or, you may be entirely in awe of your new responsibilities, not knowing how or where to begin, beginning to wonder whether you really want to begin at all. Ideally, you would like the classes you teach to be models of pedagogical excellence—nurturing environments where your students can enjoy learning science and can gain an appreciation of the potential of science in shaping the future in which they will spend the rest of their lives.

You have learned your subject well. But now, to meet your pedagogical responsibilities, you must begin a second less formal, but equally important component of your professional education. You must learn the art and skills of communicating what you know about your discipline to your students—you must become a science *teacher*! Did your past academic training really prepare you for the teaching career you will soon begin? Although there is the chance that you will begin it in the familiar environment of a research institution like the one that granted you your graduate degree(s), it is more likely that you will find yourself employed at a community college or at a small four year school (Johnson 1995). Here, you will probably teach students whose abilities, academic preparations, and career goals are very different from yours and the other students who were in your undergraduate classes. You may already have some limited experience, perhaps as a graduate teaching assistant, where you graded term papers and exams. You may even have been responsible for conducting a laboratory or discussion section filled with students who were high academic achievers carefully screened for admission to your highly competitive university. However, in that environment, it would have been unlikely for you to have ever developed a full-length lecture or constructed a major examination (Johnson 1995).

Your first full teaching assignment will probably be an "introductory science course" or a "science literacy course" specifically designed for "non-science majors." How do you:

1. create a course syllabus? (Chapter 19);
2. translate the course syllabus you create into the day to day activities that will make attendance in your class an academically rewarding experience for your students?
3. select an appropriate required text and supplementary enhancements to use for your course? (Chapter 18) ;
4. create the kinds of assessment instruments that will allow you to evaluate student performance fairly and accurately? (Chapter 12).

How will you effectively teach courses to students with such wide-ranging academic preparations, abilities, and goals as you are sure to encounter in your classes? These are the questions to which you must find answers. But these are the questions that your graduate studies left you least prepared to answer. As one pessimistic report summed it up,"...if the professional preparation of doctors was as minimal as that of college teachers, the United States would have more funeral directors than lawyers..." (Association of American Colleges, 1985).

Fortunately, much assistance is available to you long before you need to begin your first class. Unless you are beginning at a new academic institution, there will be experienced instructors to support you by sharing their expertise with you; bookshelves of standard texts to examine; files of "old" syllabi to review; and descriptions of the courses you will teach to read.

After studying all of the resources available, you should find that the seemingly bewildering array of introductory science courses offered by your institution are actually variations on a single theme. All emphasize, or should emphasize, the fundamental idea that science and the methods of science are actually powerful ways to observe the natural world and to develop the logical and rational explanations for observed natural phenomena. All introductory science courses should emphasize process, not encyclopedic collections of "facts." Woven into the fabric of all introductory science courses should be discussions and hands-on, minds-on activities that assist students to develop the skills needed to:

- *make careful observations of natural phenomena;*
- *develop rational explanations for their observations;*
- *formulate predictions based on their explanations;*
- *develop and implement objective tests of their predictions; and*
- *evaluate their explanations based on the outcomes of their tests.*

In fact, your own studies should lead you to the realization that all introductory science courses have many shared objectives modified only to reflect the specific needs and career objectives of the students taking them. These modifications typically result in three readily identifiable categories of introductory science courses:

science literacy courses designated for "non-science majors";

introductory courses designed for science "majors"; and

general studies hybrid courses to meet the needs of both groups.

Science Literacy or "Non-Science Major" Courses

Biol 101. Biological Science. An introductory, one-semester course in biology for students with limited backgrounds in the sciences. Covers such fundamental issues as the meanings and origins of life, the evolution of life, human reproduction, and heredity. Designed to fulfill the general science requirement for the non-science major. Class hrs. 3; Lab hrs. 2. (Westchester Community College, 1995)

For many years, it has been believed that, for a person to be considered well-educated, he or she must have a basic knowledge of the natural sciences along with a fundamental knowledge of literature and languages, the humanities, and the social sciences. To satisfy this need for a basic knowledge of science, many colleges offer and require students not

141

majoring in one of the sciences to successfully complete one or more *non-science major science survey* or *science literacy* courses. Unfortunately, these courses often proved to be—and in some cases continue to be—little more than "watered down", or "dummied up", versions of traditional introductory courses offered for science majors (Hartman and Dubowsky, 1995; Bunce 1995). These non-science major survey courses were often assigned to and taught by inexperienced junior faculty who viewed them in much the same way as a college freshman views pledging for a fraternity or a sorority—something that had to be endured until he or she is recognized for achievement and has earned the right to teach real science courses. The result was as expected. Students invariably reported non-science major survey courses to be filled with minutiae; they were boring, unpleasant, irrelevant, and did little to kindle interest in or understanding of the subject they were offered to foster (Hartman and Dubowsky, 1995; Kugler 1994).

Today, we widely recognize that our society, with its largely scientifically/technologically dependent economy, is rushing headlong into an ever more scientifically/technologically dependent 21st century and cannot afford to have citizens who possess only "...some basic knowledge of science...." Instead, if we are to function, to compete, and to survive in the world economy of a decade or two from now, our society we must have a universally scientifically literate citizenry (Ireton, Manduca and Mogk, 1997). There is also general agreement that the best way—arguably the only effective way—to ensure universal science literacy is through our educational system (Caprio, Dubowsky, Micikas, and Wu, 1997). For those of us teaching at the college level, the message and the warnings are quite clear. We must teach meaningful science literacy courses developed and taught with the same effort and diligence as that devoted to develop and teach courses designed for our future scientists, engineers, and technicians.

If you are given the responsibility for developing and teaching a science literacy course, the first logical step you must take is to create your own working definition of what science literacy is. Conceiving such a definition can be a formidable task since so much has been written on the subject (Hartman and Dubowsky, 1995). However, you will find that most definitions of science literacy include a common core of ideas, much as they are articulated in the introduction to *A Society for College Science Teachers Position Statement on Introductory College-Level Science Courses* (see Chapter 7).

For a person to be scientifically literate, he or she must have not only a basic knowledge of science content but must also have the intellectual skills needed to make rational, responsible, and ethical judgments concerning scientific/technological discoveries and the effects they will have on all of us.

In practical terms this means that, if the course you are to teach is truly a science literacy course, you must include more than traditional science content. You must also provide students with the skills they need to evaluate how science and technology impact on the world and how advances in science and technology will alter the world that lies in their futures.

The next logical step in the process of developing a science literacy course is to convert your working definition of science literacy into a specific course description and syllabus. You must teach content, but you must also include ways to enhance the skills your students will need to evaluate content. At the same time, your course must be designed to motivate, engage, and capture a broad range of students: students with diverse academic backgrounds; students who harbor negative preconceptions of what science is; students who fear science and lack confidence that they are "smart enough to learn science;" and students with what they consider to be non-scientific career goals who wonder why it is that the school requires them to take any science course at all. Fortunately, here again, there are many resources you can call upon. One of the best ways to begin your specific science literacy course syllabus development activities is by reading past issues of science educational journals like:

The Journal of College Science Teaching
The American Biology Teacher
The Journal of Chemical Education
The Journal of Geological Education
The Physics Teacher

In them you will find descriptions of how experienced science education professionals develop, restructure, and improve the science literacy courses they teach. Interestingly, you will find that, because there are no traditional syllabi for most science literacy courses and no pressure to "cover" a prescribed body of content, teachers of science literacy courses can have the freedom to explore:

Different overall course topics and ways to teach these topics. In fact you will find examples of :

- courses that appear to be little more than traditional discipline-limited survey courses but with dramatic "twists" and variations when they are constructed with the non-majors perspective in mind;
- courses that cross traditional discipline boundaries blending subject matter from several disciplines into a seamless interdisciplinary whole (*e.g. Life: Origin and Evolution*); and,
- single issue courses that are of special interest to the instructor (*Energy and the Future, The Biology of Human Sexuality,* and *Chemistry and the Consumer*).

Different kinds of supplementary materials that can be used to augment classroom learning experiences. These include:

- a wide range of conventional and less than conventional commercially prepared "texts" specifically written for science literacy courses;
- compendia of trade books blended together with current articles in popular magazines and newspapers, films, and television programs;
- custom texts written by course instructors for their own unique courses and printed either on campus or off campus by custom printing divisions of major textbook companies.

Different teaching strategies. So, in addition to the rigidly structured, traditional lecture-laboratory learning environment, instructors can experiment with and, if successful, continue to utilize:

- community service projects and independent research projects as alternatives to traditional laboratory activities;
- "learning by doing" and "hands-on activities";
- peer teaching ; and/or
- the whole range of activities associated with the constructivist approach to learning. (see Chapters 1,2, and 9 for examples)

Different assessment instruments to measure student success in meeting course objectives and goals. (see Chapter 12)

However, along with the challenges, the opportunities, and the intellectual stimulation that come with teaching a science literacy course comes a unique responsibility. You must always keep in mind that, for most of your students this is not an introductory science course. For most of the students in your college science literacy classes, this will likely be the *last* formal science learning experience they will ever have. Taking notes in your lecture class or peering through a microscope in your lab you will find the future lawyers and statesmen of our society. These individuals will someday authorize the funding for government sponsored research projects and draft the regulations that will determine how the results of these government sponsored research projects will be utilized. You will have in your classes the future men and women of business who will incorporate the ideas you taught them into decisions about which scientific ideas will be taken from the drawing board to the factories and which ideas will be rejected in their earliest conceptual stages. You will have the elementary school teachers who will provide generations of future scientists, engineers, technicians and, hopefully science literate citizens with their first formal science education experiences. Finally, virtually all students in your classes will become the very first science teachers to the next generation of our society when they become parents. What do you want your students to know about science? How do you want your students to feel about the processes of science and the scientific enterprises? What message do you want your students to convey to their students? The answers to these questions should determine the kind of science literacy course you need to create.

Introductory Courses or Courses for the "Major"

> *Biol 115, 116. General Biology I and Lab. A first course in a two-semester sequence designed to fulfill the science requirement for the college degree as well as for the science major. Covers basic chemistry, cell energetics, genetics and evolution. Class hrs. 3; Lab hrs. 2.* (Westchester Community College, 1995)

You were most likely an undergraduate science major, and you probably enrolled in, participated in, and successfully completed several different college level *introductory* science courses. You should be familiar with what an introductory course for "majors" is like—at least from a student perspective. Because of your experiences, you should find developing and teaching of an introductory course in your discipline a much easier assignment than the challenge of a non-majors program. As you well know, most traditional introductory courses for majors are actually two-semester sequences with each course divided into a lecture and a laboratory component. Introductory science courses provide students who are majors in the field, students who are majors in related scientific disciplines, and students in science-related pre-professional programs (*e.g.*, pre-med and pre-dent) with "a thorough grounding in the basics of that discipline" so that they are prepared for more advanced courses (Bunce 1995). There is almost always a standard curriculum or syllabus to follow and a number of standard books that can be adopted as the required text for the course. Laboratory manuals and laboratory activities are often described as "cookbook" in nature with little opportunity for faculty innovation or for the student to think critically or explore a specific issue in detail. Students enrolled in introductory science courses tend to be more motivated, interested, ambitious, competitive, and they are usually better prepared to study science.

However, introductory science courses are also undergoing review and, in many cases, dramatic revision. College science faculty have come to realize that "times are a changin'" and so are the needs, expectations, and aspirations of the students who take the introductory courses. And we are beginning to grasp the point that even science majors need to be science literate. Although introductory science courses are usually "crowded" with content, and becoming more so every year (Paldy, 1994; Dubowsky and Hartman 1994; Micikas,1995), innovative instructors are finding ways to:

- be more selective in the content they include in their courses and the methods they use to teach what they incorporate;
- include a range of different activities that stimulate students' critical thinking abilities;
- enhance student understanding and appreciation of the interdisciplinary nature of science and the consequences of scientific/technological advances on their own lives and on the lives of others with whom they share the planet.

Here, too, challenges to the "*status quo*" provide opportunities for creativity and innovation in the nature of the content to be included, in the ways that this content is offered to the student, and in the ways student achievement is measured. Here, too, you are not without resources. In fact, the very same resources and techniques recommended for the development and teaching of science literacy courses can be used as guides to the development and teaching of innovative introductory science courses.

Hybrid Science Literacy/ Introductory Science Courses: A Course for All Americans

At some colleges and universities, the first science course offered in each of the traditional scientific disciplines is a hybrid science literacy/introductory course designed to meet the needs of all of the students studying at that college or university. The philosophical basis for this approach is that it is both prudent and beneficial not to separate potential science majors from those who do not elect to pursue a career in a scientific discipline at the start of the collegiate experience. In fact, science educators at these colleges believe that much can be gained when future scientists interact with future humanists in a formal classroom environment where they can collectively study the fundamentals of a scientific discipline and then discuss and debate the "...vast... (ethical, moral,)...political, technical, and environmental implications..." of advances in it (Dubowsky and Hartman, 1994). These additional course objectives do add to the overall work load for the teacher as well as the student. However, judicious selection of content and creative and innovative teaching methods can result in science courses that make a significant contribution to the education of a sub-population of scientists within the total population of citizens of a society who :

> *...[are] aware that science, mathematics and technology are interdependent human enterprises with strengths and limitations; ...[understand]... key concepts and principles of science, ...[are]... familiar with the natural world and ...[recognize]...both its unit and diversity; and ...[use]... scientific knowledge and ways of thinking for individual purposes.* (Rutherford and Ahlgren, 1990).

Conclusion

In recent years, "Science literacy—which embraces science, mathematics, and technology—has emerged as a central goal of education." (American Association for the Advancement of Science, 1995). This means that the finest quality science education must be provided to all citizens of this nation not only to a "...select group of future scientists and engineers..." (Arambula-Greenfield, 1996; Ireton, Manduca and Mogk, 1997). For science educators, this means developing and teaching the kinds of courses that will provide every resident of our nation with the knowledge and skills needed to understand the basic principles of science, to be able to use scientific methods of problem solving in their daily lives, and to be able to evaluate the consequences of scientific/technological advancements on their lives.

At the collegiate level, the primary responsibility for enhancement of science literacy begins with three categories of courses:

- *Science literacy courses offered for those who do not intend to pursue a career in a traditional scientific discipline,*
- *Introductory Science courses for those who do intend to pursue a career in a traditional scientific discipline or for those who*

> are preparing for careers in such fields as medicine and dentistry, and
>
> • *"Hybrid" or "General Education" courses—courses designed for both science majors as well as students who do not seek a career in science.*

The activities associated with the development and teaching of any course that enhances science literacy can be most demanding, calling upon every bit of your knowledge of your discipline's content as well as your best creative and innovative teaching skills. However, this task is not insurmountable. First define, for yourself, what science literacy is. Then, designate it as a fundamental goal of that course (Hartman and Dubowsky, 1995). Finally, select the content, teaching methodologies, and instruments that will help you achieve this goal. And, most importantly, remember that you are not alone. There are many who have traveled this intellectual road before you. They have left maps to guide you on your way. Don't hesitate to use them!

References

American Association for the Advancement of Science. (1995) *Science for All Americans: Summary*, AAAS, Washington, D.C.

Association of American Colleges. (1985) *Integrity in the College Curriculum:A Report to the Academic Community*, Washington, D.C.

Arambula-Greenfield, Teresa. (1996) Implementing Problem-Based Learning in a College Science Class, *Journal of College Science Teaching*, 26 (1).

Bunce, Diane. (1995) The Quiet Revolution in Science Education-Teaching Science the Way Students Learn, *Journal of College Science Teaching*, 25 (3).

Caprio, M.W., Nathan Dubowsky, Lynda B. Micikas, and Yuan James Wu. (1997) It Happened in Phoenix: A Look at Opportunities and Obstacles in Achieving Science Education Reform. *Journal of College Science Teaching*, 26 (5).

Dubowsky, Nathan, and Elliott M. Hartman. (1994) Debating the Merits of "Science for Non-majors", *Journal of College Science Teaching*, 24 (3).

Hartman, Elliott M. and Nathan Dubowsky. (1995) The Nature and Process of Science: A Goal-Focused Approach to Teaching Science Literacy. *Journal of College Science Teaching*, 25 (2).

Ireton, Frank W., Cathryn A. Manduca, and David Mogk. (1997) Towards a Coherent Plan for Undergraduate Earth Science Education: A Systematic Approach, *Journal of College Science Teaching*, 26 (5).

Johnson, Margaret. (1995) Preparing Future Faculty for Unfamiliar Teaching Settings—A Process in Need of Revision, *Journal of College Science Teaching*, 25 (1).

Kugler, Charles, ed. (1994) *New Approaches to Teaching Biology.* Virginia Association for Biological Education, Radford, VA.

Micikas, Lynda, B. (1995) Teaching About the Nature and Processes of Science: Ask "Why?" Before Considering "How?", *Journal of College Science Teaching*, 25 (2).

Paldy, Lester. (1994) Science and Metascience, *Journal of College Science Teaching*, 24 (2).

Rutherford, James F. and Andrew Ahlgren. (1990) *Science for All Americans,* American Association for the Advancement of Science, Oxford University Press, New York.

Westchester Community College. (1995) *College Catalog.*

Gerald H. Krockover

Chapter 14

DIVERSITY AND EQUITY IN THE CLASSROOM

The face of society is rapidly changing in the United States and with it, the face of the college classroom. It is hoped that changes in the nation's demographics will be reflected in the mix of cultures, colors and gender in our college science courses. With diversity comes a richness of learning; and with diversity come special challenges for the college science teacher. When culturally-determined norms conflict with instructional methods, the learning of science can be inhibited. Unless our introductory science courses are more responsive to diversity and equity issues, we will as a society lose the talents of the majority of our population.

The demographics in the United States are rapidly changing—from the domain of primarily white males to a female majority. Ethnic minority groups have risen from 25% of the population in 1980 to approximately 35% in 1997, and it is predicted that this percentage will rise to 40% by the year 2015. These changes in demographics already show up in our college populations. With continued and rapid change in the demographics, it is very likely *and desirable* that our classrooms reflect those changes. Tomorrow's classroom should be rich in diversity; it is our job to ensure equity in the learning process to this diverse group of students. (George 1996)

This chapter requires active reading. Here I invite you to explore your deeply-held values, beliefs and assumptions, to become aware of possible bias in your teaching and course materials, and then to develop an action plan that will assure all students in your classroom (and beyond) excellent and equitable learning opportunities.

A Diversity and Equity Update

The National Science Foundation report, *Shaping the Future: New Expectations for Undergraduate Education in Science, Mathematics, Engineering, and Technology,* states that, "all students must have access to supportive, excellent undergraduate education in science" (NSF 1996, p.6). Furthermore, this report indicates that we must "believe and affirm that every student can learn science" (p.8). This report reinforces the goal that *every* student must have access to learning opportunities in science. Every student includes:

> women,
>
> minorities, and
>
> persons with special needs resulting from
>> physical challenges
>> learning disabilities
>> limited English proficiency

Diversity in the classroom requires that instructors be aware of and attend to issues of equity. Let's begin by reviewing the common definitions of each term:

diversity: *to give variety to; to variegate; to make diverse.*

equity: *state or quality of being equal or fair; fairness in dealing.*

Now let's consider what college science instructors need to do to provide excellent, equitable, and supportive learning opportunities in science.

The most common complaint I hear from students about teachers of introductory science courses is poor teaching. In fact, nine out of ten former science majors who switched to a non-science major and three out of four who persevered in science described the quality of teaching as poor overall (Seymour and Hewitt 1994). Students with whom I have worked at my university describe good teaching as characterized by the following ten values:

> openness
> respect for all students
> encouragement of discussion
> discovering science together
> warmth
> democratic values
> support
> student-teacher dialogue
> illustrations, applications, and implications
> non-competitive atmosphere

Notice that these are characteristics which define a classroom as a community of learners. Thus, good teaching is characterized by inclusivity—an inclusion of all students in the learning process.

> *Which of these ten characteristics for good teaching do you employ in your introductory science course? Make a list. Then, ask your students to make their own lists. How many of the characteristics that you listed made your students' lists? Why do you think that there were any differences?*

Diversity and Equity-based Values, Beliefs, and Assumptions

It is best to think of diversity and equity using a global perspective. If we could reduce the Earth's population to a village of 100 females and males, but maintain the existing human ratios, our village would be composed of [1]:

57 Asians, 21 Europeans, 14 North and South Americans, 8 Africans
70 non-whites, 30 white
70 non-Christian, 30 Christian
70 unable to read, 50 malnourished, 80 living in substandard housing
1 university graduate
50% of the entire world's wealth would be in the hands of six people, all citizens of the United States

With this global village in mind, what is the future of science and scientific research? Do you have any preconceived ideas of who can and should learn science, and who can and should contribute to the scientific enterprise?

> *Take a few minutes to list your diversity and equity values, beliefs, and assumptions.* Here are some of my beliefs and assumptions:
>   All individuals can learn science;
>   All cultures can contribute to the science knowledge base;
>   All individuals can have science career role models;
>   Persons with disabilities can contribute to understanding science.
> *As you compare your list with mine, think about why you may or may not have included these ideas in your list. What efforts might it take on your part to have these ideas added to your list and incorporated into your introductory science college classroom?*

---

[1] Association of Retired Citizens Newsletter, Vol. 16, No.5, June 1990, from United Nations demographic data.

Gerald H. Krockover

Diversity and Equity Bias in Student/Teacher Interactions and Instruction

Student/teacher interactions and instruction play a powerful role in embracing diversity and equity issues in introductory science courses. These issues, which affect college teachers regardless of their own gender or diverse background, are reflected in your classroom behavior. Consider these questions and the typical answers based on research studies:

Whom do you call upon in your class? College teachers tend to call on men more than women, white students more than minority students, US students more than international students, students proficient in English more than students with limited English proficiency, and non-special needs students more than special needs students.

How do you respond to students? College teachers also accept answers, wait longer, ask more interpretive questions, give more complex responses, and allow more talking time to the same groups previously indicated.

Do you have similar expectations for all students? College teachers tend to teach under-represented groups "learned helplessness". This means that if students act like they do not know the answer to a question or if they cannot operate a piece of laboratory equipment, the instructor answers or does the action for them. Thus, the term, "learned helplessness".

Do you tolerate stereotyping by others? Many college teachers fail to support underrepresented groups by not challenging stereotypical behaviors such as: women are not as good at science as men, visually impaired students cannot learn science, or science is not an acceptable field of study for Native American students.

Do you strive for an inclusive classroom? College teachers allow self-segregation by race, gender, limited English proficiency, country of origin, or special needs in their classroom seating arrangements, laboratory groupings, and course sections.

Do you provide equal learning opportunities for all students in your classroom? College teachers tend to provide under-represented groups with fewer experiences involving science instruments and equipment. They also assign different tasks on the basis of diversity and equity criteria.

Take time to review your own interactions and instruction with all of your students; for this purpose you may wish to either videotape several of your classes or have an observer in the classroom who keeps a record of your behavior as you interact with students. Some questions you will want to answer include the following thirteen items:

- *Whom do you call on?*
- *Do you wait an equal length of time (3-5 seconds) for responses to your questions by all of your students?*
- *Do you share answers to your questions between students rather than simply confirming the first response with a yes or no?*
- *Do you insist that everyone participate in non-lecture (discussion, recitation, laboratory) experiences?*
- *Do you use cooperative learning groups in order to respect and value each student's ability to contribute to learning?*
- *Do you use peer learning opportunities by having your students present to your class?*
- *Do you connect your instruction to real-world events, situations, and experiences related to more than one diverse culture, gender, or special need?*
- *Do you include science models from other cultures? Both genders? Special needs?*
- *Do you adapt your materials to meet the special needs of your students?*
- *Do you assign all tasks equally without regard to diversity, gender or special needs as your criteria?*
- *Do you provide criticism and praise equally to all students?*
- *Do you challenge stereotypical comments, jokes, and inappropriate behaviors?*
- *Do you adapt your instruction for special-needs students, including laboratory experiences?*

As you view a videotape of your teaching or interact with a colleague who has observed your teaching, you should discuss each of these previous questions and develop a plan of action to address the issues and concerns that have been identified. Then, practice addressing those issues and concerns over the next several weeks as you teach. You may wish to videotape your classroom again or have your colleague return to observe in order to find out if you have been addressing your issues and concerns that have been identified. You may also wish to encourage your students to provide you with anonymous feedback regarding the above questions two or three times during the length of the course. This allows you to continually identify and remedy your instruction.

Diversity and Equity Bias in Assessment

Assessment strategies should be carefully designed to prevent inequity. Perhaps the best approach to ensure there is no inadvertent or unintended bias is to use of a variety of tools to assess learning. Not all individuals learn science in the same way, thus a variety of assessment practices is most successful. In Chapter 12 of this manual, an array of assessment tools is discussed as well as the importance in using assessment in the learning process.

Do you provide for more than one type of assessment? Written examinations are used in most college science courses. Do your written examinations require different types of responses— i.e., multiple choice, short answer, or essay answers?

Group examinations, open-book examinations, and essays are other types of written assessments. Consider giving oral examinations or reports, laboratory assessments, computer simulations, and portfolios. These are all ways to support diversity and equity in your teaching.

Diversity and Equity in Instructional Materials

The instructional materials that you use will send a powerful message to your students. As a result, it is important to review all print and media materials for diversity and bias prior to using them. Chapter 18 provides a broad discussion on criteria that might be used in screening instructional products. Some questions you may wish to ask prior to using any materials in your introductory science course are:

What groups are featured in the print and video materials and what are they doing? Who is conducting the experiment? Who is watching the experiment? Who is featured as the researcher?

What careers are featured? What groups are promoted for those careers?

Is there a sufficient variety of problems that include diverse applications of content? When you assign problems for your students to solve they should be applicable for most or all of your students—and not to just a few of them. For example, problems that refer to the inner workings of a jet engine may not be applicable for all students. Thus a variety of topics related to the same problem is a useful teaching strategy.

Do your materials constantly use the generic "he" that excludes certain groups instead of the preferred "you" that includes all of your students?

Do you use materials that ensure that all groups are included when the history of science is presented?

Do you and your students bring in articles from journals and newspapers or instructional media that promote science for all? This can have a positive effect upon your students.

> *What other questions related to diversity and equity would you ask about your instructional materials? List them.*

Supporting Your Students

Students must be supported in their educational endeavors. Within their course experience all students are encouraged through bias-free instruction, interactions and resource materials. However, your support of students outside of the course experience is also important. This is an *especially* crucial issue with respect to women, minorities, and students with special needs, including international students. Outside of class there are several ways that I support my undergraduate students throughout their college years and into their careers. They include:

- formal mentoring that includes regular individual or small group meetings and social events;
- dining weekly with students at their residence halls, fraternities, sororities, and cooperative housing units;
- maintaining electronic mail communication with all class members and former students to provide opportunities for class assignments, questions about the course, updates, and notices of professional opportunities;
- sponsoring and supporting student organizations;
- visiting my students in other classes that they are taking during the same semester;
- visiting my students at their job locations to understand the types of experiences that they are having; and
- encouraging my students to bring their children, spouses, friends, and relatives to visit class

> *What support opportunities will you provide for your students? List them.*

157

Developing An Action Plan

Research shows that caring, supportive teachers who recognize that *all* students can learn science make a big difference in the future of each of their students. It is now time to develop a plan of action that will actively address issues of diversity and equity in the course experiences you provide. Some suggested assignments for your students that will demonstrate the value of diversity might include:

- Researching scientists from a global, equitable perspective.
- Instituting a global, equitable science web site at your institution.
- Interviewing a scientist from a diversity/equity perspective.
- Shadowing a scientist at your college.
- Analyzing science print and media publications.
- Selecting media that portray the global/diversity/equity science perspective.
- Develop a course mentoring plan that includes all of your students.
- Develop a course portfolio that celebrates your students' contributions to your course.
- Develop a program to counteract bias in introductory science courses and present it to your students and faculty for action.
- Investigate the role of diversity and equity in your class materials with your students and colleagues.
- Conduct an inventory with your class to determine the interests of your students related to science.
- Have students monitor your teaching to provide you with feedback regarding any diversity/gender bias that they perceive.
- Observe the walls in your campus buildings. Do the wall hangings foster diversity and equity? Implement a plan to ensure that this will occur.

Now you can add your own action plan items!

Conclusion

There is a genuine and immediate need to recognize that diversity and equity issues are a function of context. The total college introductory science course experience—including teaching, classroom environment, resource materials used, assessment and personal support—must value diversity and minimize inequities. As college science instructors, we must employ techniques and attitudes that will ensure:

- equal educational opportunities in science;
- equal educational treatment and experiences in science;
- equal educational outcomes for science achievement; and
- positive attitudes toward science

FOR ALL PERSONS!

Beginning college students in introductory science courses are looking for positive role models—models that are supportive of science learning for all students. When those students arrive for the first day of your class with high learning expectations, will you be that role model?

References

Abdi, S. W. (1997) Multicultural Teaching Tips. *The Science Teacher* 64(2), 34-37.

Brooks, W. E., Chair (1993) *An American Imperative: Higher Expectations For Higher Education.* Racine, WI: The Johnson Foundation Wingspread Group on Higher Education.

Brush, S. G. (1991) Women in Science and Engineering. *American Scientist,* 79(1), 404-419.

Campbell, P. and Storo, J. N. (1994) *Girls are ... Boys are...: Myths, Stereotypes & Gender.* Washington, DC: Office of Educational Research And Improvement, U.S. Department of Education.

Committee on Undergraduate Science Education (1997) *Science Teacher Preparation in an Era of Standards Based Reform*, Washington DC: National Academy Press.

George, M. D., Chair (1996) *Shaping the Future: New Expectations for Undergraduate Education in Science, Mathematics, Engineering, and Technology.* Arlington VA: National Science Foundation.

National Science Foundation (1996). *Shaping the Future: New Expectations for Undergraduate Education in Science, Mathematics, Engineering, and Technology.* (NSF 96-139)

Rosser, Sue V., ed. (1995) *Teaching the Majority: Breaking the Gender Barrier in Science, Mathematics and Engineering*, Teachers College Press, Columbia University, NY.

Gerald H. Krockover

Sanders, J., Koch, J., and Urso, J. (1997) *Gender Equity Right From the Start: Teacher Education in Mathematics, Science, and Technology.* Mahwah, NJ: Lawrence Erlbaum Associates.

Seymour, E. and Hewitt, N. (1994) *Talking About Leaving: Factors Contributing to High Attrition Rates Among Science, Mathematics, and Engineering Undergraduate Majors.* Boulder, CO: Bureau of Sociological Research, University of Colorado.

Tobias, S. (1992) *Revitalizing Undergraduate Science: Why Some Thing's Work and Most Don't.* Tucson, AZ: Research Corporation.

Vetter, B. (1994) *Stereotypes: Manpower Comments.* Washington, DC: Commission on Professionals in Science and Technology.

Ann S. Lumsden

Chapter 15

THE LARGE CLASS

Teaching the large class is an important responsibility for which there is great satisfaction and reward. If you are successful you will have influenced the lives and thoughts of a great number of people, and you will have made it possible for your department to offer a wider selection of courses to more students. (Aronson 1987) The special challenges in teaching the large class include coordinating the course components so that all students receive excellent and equitable learning opportunities, and bridging the gap between instructor and students, who are mostly anonymous.

More and more colleges and universities are encouraging larger classes for a variety of reasons, mainly budgetary. Other reasons for large classes might be lack of classroom space and also lack of faculty. The large class means different things to different colleges, universities and their faculty. Some colleges have 75 in a large class, some universities have 100-300 in large lecture halls, and others have 1000-1500 students in auditoriums. Each class must be run smoothly and professionally to attract students to these science courses. Maryellen Weimer (1994) suggests there are seven major challenges for instructors of the "Big Class" (see Table).

Major Challenges for Large-Class Instruction

1. Make learning active
2. Personalize the class
3. Work with diverse learning needs and preparation levels
4. Manage disruptive behavior
5. Assess learning
6. Adapt teaching style to the "stage"
7. Enjoy teaching large classes on a long-term basis

The large class—with an enrollment of 100 or 1000—can be effective! When students were surveyed about their learning in large classes, they felt that their best large classes were as good or better than their best small classes. They felt that effective teaching rather than class size reinforced their learning. The most frequently mentioned aspect about a good class was that the professor assisted them in learning; the second most frequently mentioned factor that enabled student learning was the interaction with other students (Wulf, Nyquist, and Abbott, 1987).

Large classes have been part of the educational scene for many years, and they will continue to be an educational experience for many students in the future. Weimer (1987) adds, "to those students who will attend large classes, we have an obligation to do something more than debate the propriety of various class sizes." To the faculty teaching large classes, learning to teach them well is a fundamental professional obligation.

Teaching a large class is challenging to all instructors, and this chapter will offer suggestions and ideas that can make large classes easier to manage. This chapter considers: in-class presentation options, instructional staff, support staff and course coordination, learning resource materials, assessment, facilities and equipment, and the first day in class.

Presentation Options

The most common mode of content presentation in large classes is through the lecture format, and the large-class lecture can be effective when computer presentation programs are utilized. The use of computer presentation programs (such as Power Point) which organize and display outlines, slides, action clips, charts, diagrams, and many other forms of media work well. Media in a large class should be professional and timely. The overhead projector with well-made transparencies, slides, movies, and film or video clips is also useful in large classes, and the blackboard is still used by some instructors. A point to remember with any media presentation is that the students must be able to read the written word, and hear the spoken word.

Research has shown and this book has been about active learning as the most effective learning mode (Chapters 1,2, 9, among others), but we don't ordinarily associate active learning with large classes. However, Frederick (1986) suggests that active learning is one of the answers to large classroom settings, and he describes five areas where active learning can occur in them:

1. *Interactive lectures* where students add comments and information to the class as the lecturer moves through the lesson.
2. *Questions* which shift the energy back and forth between the students and the teacher. Both student questions and instructor questions are important.
3. *Small groups discussion* within the large class can be used with each group reporting to the entire class.
4. *Problem solving with the class* will reinforce critical thinking skills. Moreover, the process of participating together in the analysis of a common context is interactive, investigatory and intimate.
5. *Whole class debates, simulations, and role playing* are very effective at engaging students in large classes.

Teachers will need to decide where active learning strategies fit into their own teaching styles. If you decide to use active learning to make your teaching more effective, choose approaches that meet the learning goals for your students, that fit your personal level of comfort, and those which furnish sufficient learning support for students (Bonwell and Sutherland, 1996).

Instructional Staff

An important, and perhaps the most important, decision about any large course is who will be assigned to teach it. The instructor should be comfortable in front of a large class, positive about teaching undergraduate students, and have organizational skills to deal with the logistical challenges of the large section. Some colleges and universities use one instructor; some use multiple instructors each teaching their own unit of interest; and others assign one instructor and several teaching assistants that meet once per week in smaller recitation sections.

What are the ideal attributes of an instructor for a large class? The instructor must be responsive to the enthusiasm and excitement of the students. When students were asked what motivates them, they responded, *"I get motivated by an instructor who enjoys what he or she is teaching." "The enthusiasm presented by the instructor is the best motivator,"* another student said. And another said, *"Energetic professors—who not only have a great deal of knowledge, but truly want to share their knowledge and will go out of their way to enable us to learn from them are what motivates me the most."* (Weaver and Cotrell, 1987) Instructors need to be warm, considerate, cheerful, and friendly; several sensible suggestions offered by Weaver and Cotrell are:

1. Adapt your lecture to your students;
2. Do not try to pack your whole education—all that you have learned—into the lecture or course; cover in depth fewer points or topics;
3. Use a wide variety of examples, stories, jokes, and illustrations, to maintain student interest;
4. Use humor where appropriate;
5. Demonstrate an active commitment to the topic;
6. Demonstrate an emotional interest in the topic; and
7. Be intellectually and physically convincing.

A large class usually requires more than a single instructor. Depending on the size, additional instructors, teaching assistants and a faculty coordinator may be involved. One successful science program which has large introductory classes assigns four instructors who are selected from the full professors in the department. The professors each present a unit of specialty from their research area. Each professor writes a booklet for his or her unit, presents in class, and each develops student evaluations for the unit. There are three tutors in this program who offer one-on-one help to students outside of class for 12 hours per week. There is also a faculty coordinator who is permanently assigned to work with this program. The coordinator attends every class and handles the logistics of the class. The faculty coordinator works with teaching assistants assigned to the class, oversees the tutor program, handles the facilities and equipment, checks all evaluations and assessments and handles student grades.

Course Coordination

It is imperative to have the large class well organized. Either a faculty coordinator or, in some cases, the instructor must assume responsibility for the coordination of the course. Added responsibilities for the large class might include creating the course syllabus, scheduling the course activities, working with Teaching Assistants, hiring tutors, and coaching graders. When multiple course sections and/or multiple instructors are involved, additional responsibilities might also include coordinating communication among instructors, organizing the smaller recitation meetings, and making the overall course decisions.

Dr. Robert Brooks of Pennsylvania State University teaches a lecture course with laboratory that involves guest lecturers, a variety of audiovisual media, and buses to be scheduled for field trips. He suggests that in setting up a large class you must organize and plan all of the logistics well in advance. "At least two months in advance I confirm dates for speakers, order films, and projectionists, visit potential sites for field trips and make sure buses are available at the right place for the correct amount of time." (Brooks 1987)

The coordinator or instructor in charge often must put together the syllabus of the course. (See chapter 19 for a full discussion of syllabus preparation.) For the large class, the syllabus must include complete and correct information about:

- *Course Information*: Telephone numbers, office hours and location, tutor hours, e-mail addresses, course homepage, and instructor's homepage (if any) must all appear on the syllabus.
- *Course schedule*: If there are multiple teachers, then the dates of each unit, titles of the units and faculty member in charge of that unit must be on the syllabus. All holidays must be printed and test dates must be set.
- *Assignments*: All assignments for the semester, as well as any deadlines or due dates must be provided.
- *Grading Policies*: The grading scale for each test and for the overall class must be printed, including whether the class uses plus and minus scoring. Students need to know whether make-up exams are allowed, whether tests are cumulative, and whether surprise quizzes are a possibility. How and where tests will be administered and adherence to assignment due dates is another consideration. (Brooks 1987)
- *Course policies*: Attendance, homework and assignment policies, and make-up procedures (if any) must be communicated in writing.

In a large class you cannot just teach and announce as you go; every date must be set before the class begins and printed in the syllabus.

Finally, the faculty coordinator is generally responsible for selecting the text and ancillary materials to be used in the large course. There are many interesting and well-written texts on the market today from which science faculty can choose, and selection criteria for this important decision can be found in Chapter 18. Also there are many supplements such as CDs, newspapers, and Internet access offered which encourage outside reading and computer interaction among the students.

Large classes with multiple instructors can benefit by having each instructor assigned to teach in the large lecture class develop and write their own unit outlines and class notes. The course coordinator oversees the assembly of these notes into booklets which are copied and made available for purchase by the students. These booklets enable faculty instructors to update their material each semester and gives them more class time to spend on in-depth explanations and on exploring the excitement of the discipline.

Additional Staff

In addition to course instructors and a faculty coordinator, teaching assistants, tutors and audiovisual helpers may be needed to assist with large classes. Both graduate students and seniors in the department can be hired; they have the advantage that they know the science content. Seniors are excited to be working in the department of their major, and they are knowledgeable about your department and the university policies and procedures. Senior undergraduates tend to be excellent in working with students, and they often want the experience. Additionally some colleges do not have a graduate student population from which to draw, so seniors could fill this need.

When class is held in a very large lecture hall or auditorium, a good investment is a graduate student or talented senior who will handle the sound equipment, lights, overhead projector, slide projector, and/or the computer set up, video disk player, video player and projector. You will need someone to run this expensive equipment during class, to maintain it in working order, and to set up before and put away following your class—since other classes will likely use the room prior to and following you.

Facility and Equipment for the Large Class

Most universities and colleges have large lecture halls that are used for large classes. Some of these lecture halls hold 150-300 students and others 300-600 students, or perhaps even an auditorium is used for the class. For any size classroom there are certain considerations that are essential. Safety is a primary concern and a fire exit plan must be well understood. In addition, lighting, seating, acoustics, and visibility are all essential. If the students cannot see what is going on or hear what is being taught, there can be no learning. *Never* use an overhead to put up a transparency and say "I know you can't read this, but I will read it to you"! You must have equipment that is effective in the large classroom; this equipment is made specifically for large rooms, so don't use equipment from a small classroom in the auditorium.

Large lecture halls need a powerful computer (*e.g.,* a Power Mac computer), a video camera, video player, and a projector. The screen should be visible for all of the students where slides, movies, motion clips, demonstrations, and writing can be easily read. Purdue University uses several TV monitors attached to the side walls in one of their large lecture halls; each student can easily see any information that is presented. An adequate sound system needs to be set up to ensure that each student hears the instructor and any questions that other students might ask. Student questions are either repeated by the instructor or asked over a student microphone monitored by the Teaching Assistant in class. A cordless microphone can be used to enable the instructor to move from the podium. (Lumsden 1993)

Assessment in the Large Class

Assessment and evaluation are two of the most challenging aspects of teaching, and this is equally true in the large class. Assessment should be consistent with the type of students (*e.g.*, majors *v.* non-majors) and the course objectives (see Chapter 12).

In courses with large enrollments, organization and care must be used in teaching and assessment as well as in providing feedback from instructors. It is recognized that a variety of assessment instruments is generally superior to any single method of evaluation (Lowman 1987; Chapter 12). While the range of assessment options for large classes is limited—primarily by the time required for a thorough evaluation of student work—the following types of assessments have been used in large classes.

> *Written examinations in class*: In classes with 400 or more students there is little choice as to the kinds of examinations given. These students will take written tests with short-answer questions in a single class period (usually about one hour). Teaching assistants and tutors hand out and collect tests in a large class; also they monitor and answer questions during the tests. Graduate students, and seniors in some situations, are used as graders.
>
> *Testing center*: At one large university a testing center is used for large lecture classes. Each student is allowed to take the non-major biology test two times, and the higher score is recorded. The tests consist of 25 multiple choice questions. There are 4-6 versions of each instructor's test. The tests are graded immediately and the students given feedback before they leave the test center. On the feedback sheet is the grade for that unit, the cumulative grade in the class, and from which teaching objective or chapter the student missed questions. The grades are then sent to the faculty coordinator to be recorded.

Electronic assessments: The Internet is being used to develop additional modes of assessment; *e.g.*, papers and special readings can be assigned and submitted for grading over the Internet.

One-minute papers: This assessment tool is used in chemistry and biology departments at my institution. At the end of a lecture the instructor gives a question that was covered in the day's lecture or asks the student to write a one or two sentence summary of the day's lecture. The student is given 3-4 minutes to answer the question on paper. These are collected and read by the instructor to see where information given in the lecture may have not been clear. (Lumsden 1993)

Problem Behaviors

Cheating in the large class can be a problem; the best way to handle it is by prevention. Design the examination so that cheating is difficult.

- *Use several versions of the test.* In a classroom where students sit side by side, have three or four versions of the test. When we have different versions, we tell the students and color code the versions. Different versions may have the same questions with different answers and certainly in a different order.
- *Be vigilant.* Having more than one test proctor in the classroom is advisable; we find that one proctor for every 50 students is a good guideline. Also the instructor should not work on anything during a test; watch the students and move around the room during the entire time. Never leave the room.
- *Prevent talking among the students.* Answer questions and put any announcements and corrections about the test on the board; make it clear that students should not talk to each other during the test.
- *Enforce academic honesty policy or honor code.* Reminding students of these policies, why they are important, and consequences for violation may help.
- *Be aware of ways that students cheat.* For example, calculator covers can contain notes, and baseball caps are so popular that most instructors now have students turn the bill to the back during a test! Talk to students to keep up on the latest!
- *Be on the lookout for "ringers" or surrogate test takers.* If your enrollment numbers are approximately 100 to 150, each student's ID may be checked. With very large classes (enrollments of 500-1500), utilize a testing center which will check in students and verify their ID.

Disruptive student behavior during class keeps some talented scientists from teaching large introductory courses. The management of student behaviors in the classroom is difficult, and especially in classes with 100-1500 students. These suggestions have helped me.

- *Have an additional helper in the room.* Any instructor with 200 or more students, for safety reasons and for management reasons, needs another person in the classroom. This person might be the faculty coordinator, a graduate student or senior (hand picked for management), or other colleagues. A confrontation between an instructor and a student during class often causes more harm than good. The instructor is at an extreme disadvantage with disruptive behavior and needs another person to handle management while he or she teaches.
- *Circulate.* In the class that I coordinate, I move throughout the auditorium during the entire class when I am not teaching. If there is talking (loud enough for me to hear) I ask the students to write their comments to each other or move to the foyer for important discussions with friends.
- *Be prepared for class.* The instructor should be prepared for class, punctual, and demonstrate confidence (Brooks 1987). Know the information that is important to communicate, engage students, and organize the activities effectively.
- *Be aware of student reaction while teaching.* Watch for the decline of student interest and respond immediately. Move around in the lecture hall, change the class routine, open windows, or ask a question.
- *Personal interactions.* Treat all students with respect, recognizing their personal value; require that they treat you the same. For example, learning the students' names tells them that you value their person and is another way to control the class behavior. One of the authors of this book learns 110 students' names in three weeks by studying the roster outside of class, talking with students before and after class and inviting students to stop by the office. Using the student's name in class is important to help control disruptive behavior, to encourage a shy student, and to reward good behavior.
- *Class attendance.* If you want to monitor class attendance, roll can be taken in the large lecture class by passing several sheets of paper around and asking for printed name, signature and social security number. The teaching assistants can help to pass these during the class. This would be unwieldy every day, but to take attendance occasionally during a semester is not prohibitive. Some universities use an ID and a check in point for attendance. This is

still time consuming and probably not necessary every day. Having assigned seating that does not change during the semester can be used to take attendance. (Be sure with assigned seating that you are mindful of students with special needs, such as hearing, sight, and wheelchair.)

- *Invite student input.* A question box is helpful in very large classes. Each day at the end of class questions are collected from the three or four boxes around the entrances and exits of the lecture hall or auditorium. At the beginning of class each day, the professor goes over the questions from the class before. This encourages questions from shy students or students who will not ask questions in front of their peers.

The First Day in Class

Setting the tone on the first day for a well organized and exciting class helps to minimize student problems.

- Be familiar with the facilities. Visit the classroom before your first class; stand at the podium, try out the microphone; write on the overhead and see if you can read it from the back of the room or the balcony; write on the board and determine whether the letters and writing are large enough for students in all seats in the classroom to see. Brooks suggests trying your transparencies, and I like to try the Power Point presentations running through at least 10 of the slides.
- Be on time every day, and *especially* the first day.
- Introduce yourself and any Teaching Assistants or other faculty helping in the class.
- Go over the syllabus and the semester schedule.
- Begin with the first lecture on the first day so that students realize you are serious about this class and their time.
- Be prepared with what you will say. Aronson (1987) suggests that the first lecture be practiced aloud before the first day of class. If you have video equipment, taping your first lecture and watching it will be a great way for you to practice before you teach to the 500 students in class. Even just presenting your lecture in your office aloud helps to go through the wording and explanations of certain concepts. Being prepared *and knowing you are prepared* is important.

Conclusion

Large classes can be as effective as smaller classes, but extensive preparation and organization before the class begins is necessary. Adequate personnel and equipment to support it are essential. Large classes should never again be boring because there are no limits to the creativity of presentations in classes; multimedia, computer simulations and even the access to the World Wide Web during class opens many doors to science class presentations. Departments must assign their best faculty to teach large classes—faculty who want to teach and present the science program to a large number of students. Large classes present challenges, but they can be effective ways to teach science to large numbers of students. By considering the recommendations here, you can be on your way toward a successful and rewarding experience! I know how rewarding it can be.

References

Angelos, T.A., Cross, K.P. (1993) *Classroom Assessment Techniques.* 2nd Edition. San Francisco: Jossey-Bass, pp 3-11.

Aronson, J.R. (1987) "Six Keys to Effective Instruction in Large Classes: Advice from a Practitioner," *Teaching Large Classes Well*, In New Directions of Teaching and Learning 32:31-38. San Francisco: Jossey-Bass.

Bonwell, C.C.(1996) "Enhancing the Lecture: Revitalizing a Traditional Format," *Using Active Learning in College Classes: A Range of Options for Faculty,* in New Directions of Teaching and Learning, 67:31-44. San Francisco: Jossey-Bass.

Bonwell, C.C., Sutherland, T.E. (1996) "The Active Learning Continuum: Choosing Activities to Engage Students in the Classroom, *"Using Active Learning in College Classes: A Range of Options for Faculty*, In New Directions of Teaching and Learning 67:3-16. San Francisco: Jossey-Bass.

Braskamp, L.A., Ory, J.C. (1994) *Assessing Faculty Work: Enhancing Individual and Institutional Performance.* San Francisco: Jossey-Bass.

Brooks, Robert P. (1987) "Dealing with Details in a Large Class," *Teaching Large Classes Well*, In New Directions of Teaching and Learning, 32:39-44. San Francisco: Jossey-Bass.

Frederick, Peter J. (1987) "Student Involvement: Active Learning in Large Classes," *Teaching Large Classes Well,* In New Directions of Teaching and Learning, 32:45-56. San Francisco: Jossey-Bass.

Lowman, J. (1987) "Giving Students Feedback," *Teaching Large Classes Well,* in New Directions of Teaching and Learning, 32:71-83. San Francisco: Jossey-Bass.

Lumsden, A.S. (1993) "The Rewards of Institutional Commitment." *Journal of College Science Teaching*, pp 192-194.

Lumsden, A.S. (1996) Instructor's Manual and Test Bank to Biology, *Understanding Life.* St. Louis, Missouri: Mosby.

Rushin, J., Lumsden, A.S., *et al.* (1997) "Graduate Teaching Assistant Training." *The American Biology Teacher*, February, pp 86-90.

Weaver, Richard L., Cotrell, Howard W. (1987) "Lecturing: Essential Communication Strategies," *Teaching Large Classes Well*, In New Directions of Teaching and Learning, 32:57-70. San Francisco: Jossey-Bass.

Weimer, Maryellen (1987) *Teaching Large Classes Well.* New Directions for Teaching and Learning, 32. San Francisco: Jossey-Bass.

Weimer, Maryellen (1994) "Facing the Challenges of the Big Class," *The Teaching Professor*, February, p 1.

Wulff, D. H., Nyquist, J. D., Abbott, R. D. (1987) "Students' Perceptions of Large Classes", *Teaching Large Classes Well*, In New Directions of Teaching and Learning, 32:17-30. San Francisco: Jossey-Bass.

John R. Jungck
Patti Soderberg
Ethel Stanley
Virginia Vaughan

Chapter 16

COMPUTER-ENHANCED COLLABORATIVE LEARNING

This chapter focuses on educational technology, but in ways that it can be used to enhance collaborative learning. When used in this way, we have found that it promotes curricular and conceptual change.

BioQUEST Curriculum Consortium

"Don't expect a fish to discover water" is a phrase often used by cultural anthropologists. It sometimes takes an outsider's eyes to offer a fresh and insightful look at the tacit knowledge and actions of a particular community. If we are to incorporate a substantially different perspective on the role of technology in science education, it may be profitable to look beyond our own discussions to what others have been doing. In particular, we have looked at the teaching of creative writing because there is often a different set of assumptions from the beginning in writing education. If the content of writing, namely the material for poetry, plays, novels, short stories, and essays, comes from the students' experiences, commitments, and interests and, if the students anticipate that their teachers' role will be to help them express *their* ideas, then the expectations of students' and teachers' roles are, from the beginning, quite different from the expectations in the usual science course. How often do we begin with asking students what hypotheses they have been dying to test or that they bring in their portfolio? Hence, it is not surprising that we appreciate the insights of an English professor who has suggestions for us on collaborative learning in science education. Kenneth A. Bruffee's

John R. Jungck et al.

Collaborative Learning: Higher Education, Interdependence, and the Authority of Knowledge (1993) has two chapters entitled "Science in the Postmodern World" and "Mime and Supermime: Collaborative Learning and Instructional Technology" that are particularly relevant to college science professors as we are constantly challenged to define what we mean by "open-ended" problem solving. Bruffee states:

> Yet simply adding "small groups" to science classes, without integrating collaboration systematically into the course by changing the nature of the tasks that students undertake together, will not achieve the fluency in the language of the relevant scientific community that an interpretive approach to science can achieve. The problems that this chemistry student and her fellow students were solving together were closed-ended, result-focused jigsaw-puzzle tasks..., the kind of tasks usually found in problem sets. In the context of an interpretive course, in which the goal is to confront the uncertainties of science as well as its certainties, problems of an open-ended, interpretive, tool-making kind, ... would make peer-group work more rewarding still.
>
> Under these conditions, that is, collaborative learning, student conversation would go beyond helpful cooperation and teamwork to active construction of knowledge, although of course of limited scale and authority. (Bruffee, p. 153)

Within the BioQUEST Curriculum Consortium, we have always strived to develop approaches that try to strengthen students' abilities to construct long-term strategies of research in their problem solving investigations as well as their abilities to convince their peers of the quality of their experimental protocols, theoretical foundations, data collected, analyses performed, and conclusions inferred. Bruffee's claim that collaborative learning is crucial, not simply as a motivational device, but because all learning is ultimately social, will serve as the focus for this article as we collectively explore how to instantiate research approaches to learning with our college science students.

Of particular concern in the use of technology in education is the intelligent design and use of computer software. If we assume that one important purpose of the software that we design and employ is to enhance collaborative exploration, then:

> To devise programs that help people at the computer keyboard...to make contact not just with the authority that the program represents but with one another, producers and programmers will have

174

to strive to "lose their audience" constructively. Software writers...will have to find ways to weaken the bond that glues people to the tube and to intensify instead the excitement, interest, and understanding that people derive from conversation about what they are seeing or have seen on the tube..... programmers can get to work on at least three fronts: (1) designing learning tasks to be undertaken collaboratively and directed toward achieving consensus, (2) designing programs that help students learn the social conventions of working successfully in small, semiautonomous groups, and (3) designing programs that supply the information, assumptions, tasks, and evaluative criteria that guide collaborative work constructively and help people learn from each other. (Bruffee, p. 106)

For the past eleven years we have developed modules for *The BioQUEST Library* with many of these challenges in mind. Bruffee eloquently provides us with some explicit guidelines that neatly summarize what Consortium members have found difficult to articulate. We have stressed collaborative learning from practical experience: our students took on greater challenges, engaged heartily in discussions about their problem solving activities and the hypotheses that they generated, and convinced their peers of their inferences. In this chapter we explicitly address the challenges of using newer technologies in a theoretically informed fashion which will allow us to design better strategies for engaging students in problem posing, problem solving, and persuading peers.

Changing Computer Technology:
From Individualized to Collaborative Learning

In order for teachers to substantially rethink their curricular commitments they need to have an opportunity to intensively interact with peers who are actively engaged in curricular reform on their own campuses and to have the time for reflection, critique, and construction of curricular materials. In other words, if teachers are having students involved in collaborative learning, they are probably only authentic participants if they practice this collaboration with their peers within and outside their own institutional and professional contexts. Within the BioQUEST Curriculum Consortium, we have explicitly tried to provide a forum for this collaboration in the form of workshops, newsletters, web-pages, and a collection of peer-reviewed software for biology education. Teachers explore the use of new technology-based tools with four specific agendas: (1) to promote collaborative learning in biology, (2) to enhance peer review of scientific problem solving, (3) to examine the new opportunities for visualization in biology, and (4) to develop their students' skills of scientific persuasion. In addition, we have asked participants to consider possibilities regarding communication and uses of communication means (traditional and electronic) between students, between students and faculty, between students on other campuses, between campuses and research labs and/or science-based businesses.

Twenty-two years ago, some us began promoting the general use of computing in undergraduate science education. We were aware of the previous educational failures of assembly language encoding of switch driven mainframes, massive stacks of Hollerith key punch cards and batch processing which resulted in the response: "job control error" two days later, and even the highly interactive, paper-tape driven teletype minicomputers. Early visionaries recognized both the potential and the problems of the new technologies. Arthur Luehrmann's (1972, reprinted 1980) eminently readable parable on the invention of writing (and hence reading) is still a classic. In *Run, Computer, Run: The Mythology of Education* Anthony G. Oettinger (1969) wrote that he was critical of the use of technology in education,

> ...not as a Luddite fearful of the Machine nor as a shrinking humanist living in the past, but as a scientist and engineer convinced that educational technology holds great promise. My aim in analyzing the myths, the institutional failures, the brazen exploitations, the oppressive self-delusions that make a mockery of technological change in education is not to deny the promise, but to rescue it from unmerited disillusionment. I say there are no easy victories, no quick answers, no panaceas. If we are to realize the promise, we must not allow our human and material resources to be diverted into showy changes in form that continue to block change in substance. (Oettinger 1969)

Dwyer (1974) realized that there were enormous revolutions in computing beyond "the safe but shallow waters of drill and practice" educational computing:

> Recent advances in technology, especially those related to the ideas of computer science and human problem solving, offer fascinating potential as agents for implementing a rich and quite deep view of education. Yet many educational programs involved with computer technology studiously avoid entanglement in such issues, preferring instead to accept the safe but shallow waters of drill and

> practice, frame-oriented tutoring, computer-aided testing, and other traditional management-of-student applications. [Thus] There has undoubtedly been a tendency to associate technology with some of the more mechanistic aspects of instruction. ..."deep technology is of little value without a deep view of education." (Dwyer 1974)

However, in reality very few college science educators had access to computers that they could comfortably use with students in their own classrooms, laboratories, or in the field.

In 1975, we packed our twenty thousand dollar microcomputer in the VW bus and went on the road with the message that microcomputers allowed us to build "strategic simulations" or computer exploratoria (after the Exploratorium in San Francisco) which allowed students to learn long-term strategies of research in such areas as Mendelian Genetics and protein biochemistry. However, we too joined the list of failed ventures in educational computing because we did not understand how to deal with costs, resistance, and the lack of breadth of materials for others to join in curricular change. Even the existence of convenient, inexpensive microcomputers in the early 1980's (Apple IIe's, Commodore PET's, and Radio Shack TRS 80's) and a substantial and growing body of literature, such as Seymour Papert's *Mindstorms* (1980), did not wholly make the difference.

However, by the time that we started the BioQUEST Curriculum Consortium in 1986, five critical factors had changed which made it much easier to collaborate with individuals at different institutions: (1) the development of strategic simulation and "construction kit" software in many different subdisciplines, (2) the widespread use of "wordware" (word processing, spreadsheets, statistical packages, and, graphing and graphics packages), (3) the availability of graphical user interfaces (WYSIWYG - what you see is what get) driven by WIMP (window-icon-mouse-pointer) systems that were easy to use "for the rest of us" (Apple Computer advertising slogan), (4) access to electronic mail, which had moved beyond the military's ARPA system to a small number of academic and industrial vendors, and (5) support from science education research, which was now focusing on deep senses of problem solving, constructivist and collaborative learning, and the social context of classroom education. All five of these historical components are worth considering when you currently "ask a fish to discover water" because they have become tacit knowledge in the contemporary context even though there are still adversarial aspects to each.

What has change in computer technology meant in terms of critical pedagogy? First, the ideology of one computer–one student was reinforcing to an objectivist conception rather than a constructivist view of learning (see Figure 1).

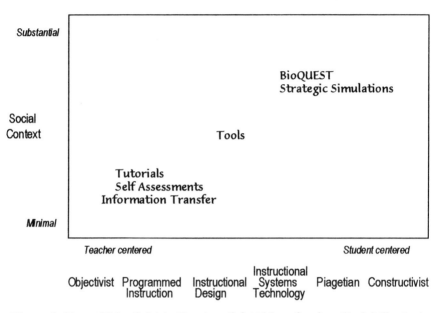

Figure 1: From Objectivist to Constructivist Education in a Social Context

The X-axis is from David H. Jonassen (1992) and the Y-axis is from Susan Jungck. (1990). The intent here is to suggest a spatial sense of the distribution of various computer approaches to education within both philosophical and social learning contexts.

When the computer is associated with a model of individualized learning that is oriented towards the computer as the disseminator as well as the evaluator of knowledge, with no attempt to differentiate between knowledge and information or to consider the social construction of knowledge, then it is easy to see why early inventions in educational technology were associated with turn-the-page tutorials, drill and practice, and assessment with behaviorist reinforcement (remember those sad faces and blah sounds for negative reinforcement?) However, when the computer is primarily conceived as an instrument associated with communication in many guises (see Figure 2), then it is much easier to focus on the development of constructivist education which encourages students to collectively raise questions, pursue them together, negotiate interpretations of data and directions to go in, and to communicate why they believe that their hypotheses are both warranted and significant.

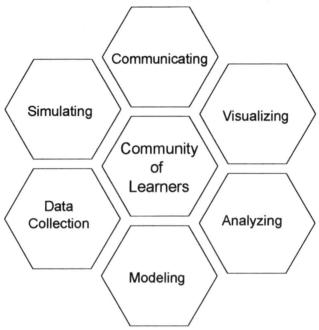

Figure 2: Technology as an enabler of communication amongst learners

Computer Software for Open-Ended Problem Solving

But what are the characteristics of software that enables this transition to more collaborative pedagogies? Within the BioQUEST Curriculum Consortium, we have identified three components of scientific practice that are reflected in supporting computer technologies: problem posing, problem solving, and persuading peers (Peterson and Jungck, 1988; Jungck and Calley, 1985). In Figure 3, we list ten criteria for the design of "strategic simulations" that should enable students to collectively explore all three components.

Strategic Simulations
1. Novelty of problems each time a program is run
2. Realistic outcome of each experiment performed
3. Infinite opportunities to perform experiments
4. Computational power
5. Speed in obtaining results
6. Large, complex data sets
7. Facilitates successive hypothesizing and logical and numeric testing
8. Sequentially developed problem difficulty involving an increased quantity of natural phenomena
9. Solutions as hypotheses
10. Peer review

Figure 3: Ten criteria for the design of "strategic simulations" for enhancing problem posing, problem solving, and persuading peers.

A second aspect of these software tools was the use of "construction kits" that allowed the development of different problem spaces in a variety of different areas. "Genetics Construction Kit" (Calley and Jungck, 1996), "Cardio-Vascular Construction Kit" (Douglas, Udovic, and Peterson, 1996), and "Environmental Decision Making" (Odum, Odum, and Peterson, 1996 - see Figure 4) are examples of software that make use of "construction kits".

In Perkins' (1992) description of "construction kits," he notes that: "Now learners can assemble not just *things* [emphasis his], such as TinkerToys, but more abstract entities such as commands in a programming language, creatures in a simulated ecology, or equations in an environment supporting mathematical manipulations" (p.47). "Construction kits" offer the nonprogrammer teacher or student most of the power of a programmer in deciding critical aspects of the problem solving environment that they will work in. So, not only is it important

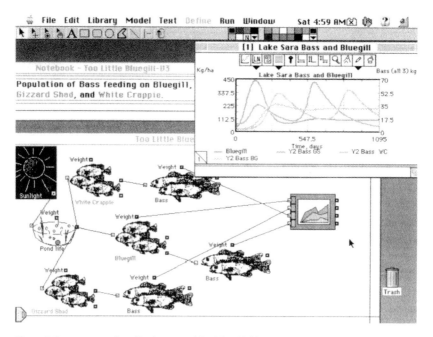

Figure 4: Screen output from Environmental Decision Making

Figure 4: Screen output from a student model constructed to mimic results in a pond where they found more predators (bass) than prey (bluegill sunfish). They were able to choose which type of fish, the solar source of energy, and the pond life as a food source for their prey from a library of entities, and they were able to choose the initial constraints on each parameter before running a plot of their results. "Environmental Decision Making" (Odum, Odum, and Peterson, 1996) uses the commercial programming environment entitled Extend by Imagine That!

that the computer enable education that could not take place otherwise such as in learning long-term strategies of research through a "strategic simulation", critical pedagogy demands that the potential power of the technological environment facilitate the participant's sense of posing as well as solving problems.

However, there is another critical component, the social component, that is necessary for these tools to be successful in a constructivist context. Three social aspects have to be considered in order to understand how computers can better serve the community of collaborative learners.

First, it is critical that the group context be established so that the peers understand both the philosophical underpinnings of and respect required for effective collaborative learning. In another article of by Bruffee (1995), he differentiates between "cooperative" and "collaborative" learning. While, unfortunately, these two phrases are often used as synonyms, Bruffee draws our attention to some major differences between the two concepts. In a "cooperative" situation group work may: (1) divide tasks to more quickly get a body of work finished, (2) be oriented in an objectivist context to learn the singular answers expected on an assessment device (particularly multiple choice, machine-graded exams), and (3) reinforce labor hierarchies such that differential status is conferred on each of the participants (*e.g.*, director, quality control manager, analyst, technician, wordsmith). On the other hand, a "collaborative" group may: (1) depend upon a constructivist notion that knowledge emerges from the social process of collaboration, (2) draw upon and respect the different talents that each member brings to the group, and (3) start from the assumptions that there are no singular, correct answers but that the solutions to problems will be hypotheses that other groups may want to consider as being worthy of their attention when they interpret their data. When you move from the positivist and nonhumanistic euphemisms: "data suggest," "research tells us," "results show," and "experiments indicate" to the language of constructivist science education, then students quickly learn they cannot settle for or hide behind such interpretations, but instead they must address and/or assume responsibility for the cultural connotations of their research agendas and the interpretations of the data that they have generated in that agenda.

Secondly, the social arrangement of classrooms has to deal with aspects of control and egalitarianism. In Figure 5, we illustrate two groups collaborating in the presence of computers. It is not only necessary that everyone can see the screen, grab hold of the mouse or keyboard, and have writing space for themselves, it is most important that the arrangement enables them to talk to one another without the computer totally dominating their interactions. To reiterate Bruffee (1993):

182

Software writers ... will have to find ways to weaken the bond that glues people to the tube and to intensify instead the excitement, interest, and understanding that people derive from conversation about what they are seeing or have seen on the tube (p. 106)

Figure 5: Two groups of college professors from the U.S. and Mexico who were participants at an annual BioQUEST Curriculum Consortium summer curriculum development workshop.

Finally, technological advances have changed the way that groups acquire and communicate information. With access to the world wide web, group members can find material germane to their interest which will help them understand the problem at hand, collect additional relevant data, explore opinions of others, and possibly have access to on-line tools which can perform technically difficult analyses for them. In this sense, e-mail and the world wide web have changed some specific constraints upon our community. In much of the past, one could have argued that telephones (as well as mail) could have been used to facilitate our communication;

however, we believe that it is qualitatively different to be able to share written, editable material including graphics and computer source and object code instantaneously and asynchronously via electronic communication. Furthermore, all of us (authors) have personally experienced departments where, even if we supposedly had access to telephones, in actual practice, budgetary constraints inhibited frequent and open communication with peers. While cut-and-paste word processing and desk-top publishing, FAXes, overnight delivery services, e-mail, and web-based publishing have accelerated the demands on our lives (making us into self-sufficient knowledge workers in one wag's vernacular), these communication avenues have also enabled a social connection that makes collaborative work much easier to accomplish across considerable geographic distances in several time zones and different personal work schedules.

Making the Field Experience Open-Ended

The design of technology to address problematic field experiences for undergraduates is also a concern. A major limitation to collaborative exploration of field problems continues to be the awkwardness of data collection during the laboratory field trip. Both students and teachers have come to regard these "situated experiences" in the field less as opportunities for open-ended investigation than marathons with specific obstacles to be run. Restricted in their choices of what they can reasonably investigate due to the time constraints, physical access barriers, and a limited "toolkit" for probing the field, learners are often handicapped by over-structured field assignments as well. Like "cookbook" laboratories, field exercises may be narrowly teacher-driven in order to insure that students going on a field trip "get something out of it." Often what students learn from field experiences is to cooperate with minimal interactive investigation in order to "get the job done." They do not learn about what it means to be a scientist within the scientific community or to value peer review, in any phase of research, as an advantage. Instead, they learn to wait to be handed the neatly packaged problems and the specific tools to probe them. Measuring "something" replaces making their own observations from which questions can be framed. They learn to ignore the complexity of real problems and to replace it with the minimalist "solutions" of field exercises completed under severe data acquisition constraints.

There are supportive technologies available today that may convince both students and teachers to re-examine their ideas about collaborative field investigations. However, both teachers and students must be persuaded to accept a broader view of data acquisition to include:

- Data collection need not be so laborious.
- Data collection need not be so divisive.
- Data collection need not be so limiting.
- Data collection need not be so intentional (teleological).
- Data collection need not be quantitative.

A handheld data acquisition device like the Newton combined with an interface and multiple probes could not only automate the collection of data such as temperature, pH, carbon dioxide level, or turbidity at specified intervals, but also store this data in files that could be transferred from the PDA to the lab computer for analysis after a field trip. Instead of each group of students partitioning field tasks and remaining focused on their task, students could be interacting with each other and the environment. Current communications technology would allow remote conversations between all participants in a field trip. Different kinds of data can be collected. For example, digital cameras provide a method for students to collect images which are instantly accessible. This rich visual data can be explored with programs like "NIH Image" to generate extended visual analyses either quantitatively or qualitatively. What to investigate and which tools to use become part of the collaborative research experience in the field. Inconclusive data need not carry the stigma of a failed field experience, especially if instructors modify assessment to include these evidences of both problem prototyping as well as methodology for problem resolution.

The design of technological tools that focus only on what to measure, how to measure it, and simple "teleological" data gathering de-skills these "scientists-in-training" by restricting social practices which are found routinely in professional field experiences. Students should be learning to negotiate realistic approaches to problem solving in the field by participatory experiential design, not just collecting data. Students who collaborate in the field are likely to value the role of social construction in science. As the design of field experiences expands from procedural (know how to do) data acquisition to include propositional (know what to do) use of the technology and treats the user as a collaborator rather than an isolated individual, our students and colleagues may see the field as a place for investigation rather than "cookbook" field experiences. If we value science as a way of knowing the world and envision problem posing, problem probing, and persuasion as an important part of our students' lifelong learning, we should invest in the supportive technology that enables collaborative explorations and open-ended experiences in the field.

Differences between Learning and Teaching

One of the major differences in using computer-enhanced collaborative learning with a problem posing, problem solving, and peer persuasion approach is that students have fewer requests to know what you (meaning "the" teacher) want, what will be on the quiz, and when are they done because the problems are theirs, the curiosity to forge on is their decision, and it is their peers (not just you) that they are trying to convince. Posner, Strike, Hewson, and Gertzog (1982) have likened the process of conceptual change that students go through to be very similar to Kuhnian versions of scientific change. If students value exceptions, modify hypotheses, and make revolutions in their paradigms, they indeed are reflecting major scientific changes within their own microcosms. There are many factors that may lead to resistance to changing models even in the face of contradictory evidence. Thus, Pintrich, Marx, and Boyle (1993) have focused on "The role of motivational beliefs and classroom contextual factors in the process of conceptual change." We as teachers need to be cognizant that when we change from the sage-on-the-stage or guide-on-the-side modes to becoming genuine collaborators in our student groups' research-like problem solving, that major changes in student behavior and expectations accompany these transformations.

Conclusion

Computer-enhanced collaborative learning mediates curricular, conceptual, and personal change in our learning practices and styles, our self perceptions as well as our social relations, our awareness of "hidden" curriculum lived through the lives of our students rather than mere requirements in a college catalog, and, importantly, our scientific world views. Students who are engaged in the production of scientific meaning rather than the assimilation of someone else's prescriptive information should have a better idea of the role of peer review in professional research, negotiations for acknowledgment in multiauthored papers, and some idea of the role of priority in scientific history. We are not asserting that every student will or should become a scientist in these approaches, but we do believe that they will have a better basis as citizens to weigh contradictory claims about scientific evidence in public forums if they have had multiple opportunities to perform their own deep investigations of a variety of problems.

References

Bruffee, Kenneth A. (1993) *Collaborative Learning—Higher Education, Interdependence, and the Authority of Knowledge*, The Johns Hopkins University Press, Baltimore, Maryland.

Bruffee, Kenneth A. (1995) "Sharing Our Toys: Cooperative Learning versus Collaborative Learning." *Change,* pp 12-18 (January/February)

Calley, John N. and John R. Jungck. (1996). "Genetics Construction Kit" In John R. Jungck, Virginia Vaughan, Ethel Stanley, John N. Calley, Nils S. Peterson, Patti Soderberg, and Jim Stewart, editors, *The BioQUEST Library,* The ePress Project, University of Maryland: College Park, Maryland.

Douglas, Sarah, Daniel Udovic, and Nils S. Peterson. (1996) "Cardio-Vascular Construction Kit" In John R. Jungck, Virginia Vaughan, Ethel Stanley, John N. Calley, Nils S. Peterson, Patti Soderberg, and Jim Stewart, eds, *The BioQUEST Library*, The ePress Project, University of Maryland: College Park, Maryland.

Dwyer, Thomas. (1974) "Heuristic strategies for using computers to enrich education." *International Journal of Man-Machine Studies* 6: 137-154.

Jonassen, David H. (1992) "Evaluating Constructivist Learning." In Thomas M. Duffy and David H. Jonassen, editors, *Constructivism and the Technology of Instruction: A Conversation.* Lawrence Earlbaum Associates: Hillsdale, New Jersey, pp 137-148.

Jungck, J.R., and Calley, J. (1985) Strategic simulations and post-Socratic pedagogy: Constructing computer software to develop long-term inference through experimental inquiry. *American Biology Teacher 47*(1): 11-15.

187

Jungck, Susan. (1990) "Viewing computer literacy through a critical, ethnographic lens." *Theory into Practice* XXIX(4): 283-289.

Luehrmann, Arthur. (1980) "Should the computer teach the student, or vice versa?" In R. P. Taylor, ed., *The Computer in the School: Tutor, Tool, Tutee.* Teachers College Press: New York, pp 127-135. (Reprint of 1972 article).

Odum, H. T., E. C. Odum, and Nils S. Peterson. (1996) "Environmental Decision Making." In John R. Jungck, Virginia Vaughan, Ethel Stanley, John N. Calley, Nils S. Peterson, Patti Soderberg, and Jim Stewart, editors, *The BioQUEST Library*, The ePress Project, University of Maryland: College Park, Maryland.

Oettinger, Anthony G. (1969) *Run, Computer, Run: The Mythology of Education.* Harvard University Press: Cambridge, Massachusetts.

Papert, Seymour. (1980) *Mindstorms: Children, Computers, and Powerful Ideas.* Basic Books: New York.

Perkins, David N. (1992) "Technology Meets Constructivism: Do They Make a Marriage?" In Thomas M. Duffy and David H. Jonassen, editors, *Constructivism and the Technology of Instruction: A Conversation.* Lawrence Earlbaum Associates: Hillsdale, New Jersey, pp 45-55.

Peterson, Nils, and John R. Jungck (1988) "The Three P's of biology education: Problem-posing, problem-solving and persuasion." *Academic Computing* 2(6): pp 14-17, 48-50, and 64 (March/April).

Pintrich, Paul R., Ronald W. Marx, and Robert A. Boyle. (1993) "Beyond cold conceptual change: The role of motivational beliefs and classroom contextual factors in the process of conceptual change." *Review of Educational Research* 63(2): 167-199.

Posner, G. J., K. A., Strike, P. W. Hewson, and W. A. Gertzog, (1982) "Accommodation of a scientific conception: toward a theory of conceptual change." *Science Education* 66: 211-227.

Sandra I. Lamb

Chapter 17

THE LABORATORY

The laboratory setting is unique and provides a powerful opportunity for learning science. It allows us to teach keen observational skills which are almost impossible in any other setting. Field study is one exception, but it is really an outside laboratory. The lecture, discourse, and seminar formats can adequately consider theoretical matters, but only the laboratory allows the transmission of how a science is really practiced. Learning in a laboratory prepares the novice to observe the world and to begin to draw conclusions about the amazing workings of nature.

Along with the unique learning and teaching opportunities offered in the laboratory setting come unique and important responsibilities of the instructor. For example, safety in the laboratory is a primary concern and a legal responsibility. Ultimately, too, the instructor is responsible for the materials and equipment to be used in laboratory work. This chapter outlines teaching and learning opportunities along with some of the administrative details associated with laboratory programs.

The Laboratory as a Learning Environment

The laboratory or field experience provides an opportunity for students to learn how to do science; in Chapter 1, it is described as the best instructional setting to learn scientific thinking skills and about the nature of science. Every science is built upon observation; and when observations are made to test a principle or effect, we define that as experimentation. The scientist is a person who finds out about the real world by making observations and designing experiments to confirm or disprove some known principle or to discover some unknown principle.

189

Making observations, taking and recording data, drawing conclusions and communicating these conclusions to other scientists are essential components of the scientific process. Science should be taught in a way for students to understand and develop through practice these essential skills.

Every student scientist in your course needs to be taught how to propose hypotheses, how to set up experiments that will prove or disprove the hypothesis, how to take data, how to draw conclusions, and finally how to communicate results. At the heart of all science is the ability to observe conditions and any changes in those conditions. Learning how to observe the world around us carefully is the crux of scientific exploration.

Technological advancements in recent years have improved the way data is taken, analyzed and even communicated. Precision instruments are able to measure minute amounts of materials and integral to most of these instruments are fast, reliable computers. Computers now control instruments, take data and plot changes, and the scientist needs to know how to use computers to simplify and enhance experimental methods. So as we delve into the use of the laboratory as a learning environment, we will include some of the computer applications that contribute to the instructional laboratory setting (see also Chapter 16).

Laboratory techniques and equipment differ among the science disciplines, but they share some commonalties such as the use of controls and precision measurements. While the chemist works with reagents and reactions involving specialized glassware and equipment, the biologist works with living systems, usually in aqueous media, at carefully controlled temperature and pH. In general, each science discipline has some established standardized techniques that are usually described in basic laboratory manuals or textbooks. In professional analytical and synthetic laboratories, care must be taken when following a standardized laboratory technique. Every effort must be made to obtain similar equipment, follow the procedure carefully and maintain the environment (heat, light, pH, *etc.*) as the procedure prescribes. When standardized techniques are used in instructional laboratories, students will need to be taught the importance of the details of conditions.

Planning the Program

Generally speaking, it will take much more time to plan a good laboratory program than to plan the lecture or discussion course. At some institutions the laboratory program is well established, and laboratory texts are available. If you are responsible for planning the program, a good place to start devising experiments is to review those described in laboratory manuals and journals, and then to modify those experiments to reflect your interest in a specific hypothesis or to match your resources. Most fields of science have laboratory texts that are good starting places to find different experiments. Journals, such as *The Journal of Chemical Education, The American Biology Teacher, The Journal of Geoscience Education, The Journal of College Science Teaching,* and *The Journal of Physics Education,* often include new and different experiments. While new experiments for instructional laboratories can be derived from the research literature, creating your own experiment is difficult. You will need to consider: Will the experiment enlighten or confuse students? Will the experiment work when performed by students? Does my program have the time necessary for the experiment to be carried to conclusion? Are the required equipment and instruments available in sufficient supply for the number of students to be served? What are the hazards of the experiment? How much waste will be produced and how can it be disposed?

Whether you devise your own experiment, or use one from a laboratory textbook, the experiment should always be given a trial run by you or an assistant under your direction to ensure that the experiment will be safe and produce valid results in the hands of students. Also, running the experiment yourself allows you to see the places where errors might occur.

It is also important to consider varying the experiments from year to year in order to keep the experiments current and meaningful. Too often the same laboratory experiments are done for years on end and they become out of date and meaningless for the student, and tedious and boring for the instructor!

An excellent way to keep up with new methods in your science discipline and to learn about new experiments is to attend workshops and meetings in your field. Teachers attend professional meetings to share their work, new experiments and results with others. Examples of professional organizations for science teachers and ways to communicate with colleagues are described in Appendices B and C of this manual.

Open-ended Experiments

The laboratory classroom or field setting is an obvious place to achieve a constructivist learning environment. Laboratory activities support the concepts of active learning (Chapter 1), collaboration (Chapter 2) and critical thinking (Chapter 3). Laboratory experiences also support criteria outlined in the *National Science Education Standards*

(Chapter 5) such as inquiry and constructivism and offer the opportunity for students to investigate phenomena as scientists do. Many teachers are devising new methods to move the laboratory experience from a cook-book directional mode to a more realistic scientific experimental mode. This type of experiment entails much more planning by the instructor, and it might require that students be motivated to find out how to perform a new technique by going to the library or accessing other resources. Such processes are usually set in a group environment, which is more akin to industrial and academic research. Each person in the group is made responsible for some aspect of the experiment, or recording data or writing a report. Generally groups of three or four are sufficient to see that everyone has a chance to work on the experiment. Cooperative laboratories are now being promulgated as the best way to motivate students to become interested in the sciences. (Nurrenbern 1995; Cooper 1996; Caprio 1993). Chapters 1, 2, 9 and 16 of this manual (among others) have more information about collaborative learning and laboratory activities.

Teaching in the Laboratory

The laboratory is where students learn how to "do" science, and so the laboratory environment lends itself to letting students explore and make discoveries. When specific techniques need to be taught, often the best way to teach is by example. That is, although you may want to talk about or discuss background theoretical material for the experiment, the best way to teach technique is usually to demonstrate the technique yourself. Any procedure which requires eye-hand coordination may be difficult for many of your students, so they may have to practice the technique as you offer suggestions and encouragement.

Effective laboratory instructors are almost always on the move among students—observing and asking questions. Don't sit in one place while the experiment is being performed and expect students to come to you with questions. Some students are shy about asking questions, don't know what to ask, are afraid to ask, or are not able to leave their work station while the experiment is in progress. To ensure that the experiment is being performed safely, to keep students thinking about what they are doing, to block errors before they occur, and to guide and share in their discovery process, circulate throughout the laboratory while work is being carried out. A good strategy is to have several simple questions to ask the students which will help you determine whether they understand the principles of the experiment and whether they are making connections that will reveal the overall purpose of the investigation.

A chapter could be written on how to formulate questions. In some cases you only want to know whether the student is prepared for lab or knows what she or he is doing; in other cases you want to ask probing questions that require analytic thought, synthesis and evaluation of the activity in developing an answer. Remember that the question you ask and the way in which you ask it will determine its effectiveness. Some of your questions should help students enhance their observational skills. Ask, for instance: "has there been a color change?", "have the temperature and pressure changed?", "have any other characteristics of the system changed?" Students make these observations when urged to notice details, and the small details in an experiment are often those that are the most important. Teaching students to observe details is the crux of teaching in the laboratory and the source of much added pleasure in life.

A chapter could also be written on how to answer questions from students. In general, avoid simple "yes" or "no" answers and answers that are ambiguous. Often the best answer to a question is yet another question which will guide the student to construct his or her own answers. For example if a student asks, "Is this red?"; you might ask, "What do you think?", "Should it be?", or "What have you just done?"

In summary, for our students to understand science we need to teach them skills of observation and inquiry coupled with skills of formulating hypotheses and conclusions. On the practical side, eye-hand coordination, recording observations, organization of data, and instrument use often must also be taught. Whether your student becomes a technician or a teacher, a research scientist or a politician, a farmer or banker, laboratory participation gives an understanding and, hopefully, an appreciation of what scientists do.

The Laboratory Record

Students should maintain a record of observations and laboratory measurements; this practice helps them to understand the importance of observations and provides them (and you) with a record of their experiences. (Kanare 1985) Some introductory course instructors use laboratory manuals that have blanks to fill. Students record their data in the blanks and remove the pages from the manual, which they then submit. This procedure is used for efficiency and ease of grading, but it does *not* reflect how science is performed. A laboratory notebook or journal is more reflective of real scientific inquiry; it is the ultimate record of scientific exploration. In the "real" world, the laboratory notebook can determine whether a patent is issued to one scientist or another. If you decide to use laboratory notebooks in your courses, students will need clear and detailed directions for organizing them. Further, they will need continued coaching, explanations, and feedback in order to learn to use their notebooks correctly. Teaching students how to keep a good laboratory notebook is important; it is particularly important for those students continuing in the sciences. The laboratory report, which is based on recorded observations and data from the notebook, can be included in the notebook or written as a separate document. At a minimum, the report should communicate the experimental observations and methods used as well as a summary of what was learned by the student from the experiment.

In addition to the more common laboratory manual and notebook, there are now computerized systems available that allow the experimentalist to type in the notes for the experiment in a computerized notebook. This procedure is appealing to people who prefer using computers and is the procedure now commonly followed in industrial research laboratories. (Lysakowski 1997) One of its advantages is that searching for specific results is easily accomplished and the computerized notebook usually includes a database for chemical properties. Advanced software, called LIMS (Laboratory Information Management Systems), can be shared by groups and is used to manage large data bases. Several companies produce such software (Axiom 1996; LabWare 1996; QSI 1996). There are also laboratory databases associated with two popular chemistry software packages (ChemFinder 1997; Isis 1997).

Assessment of Learning

Determining how much a student has learned in the laboratory is a difficult problem. Preparation for laboratory may be assessed though weekly *quizzes* and the *notebook* may be graded to assess laboratory procedures and observations.

Oral presentations are useful in evaluating a student's understanding of an experiment. The experience is also beneficial in that it helps students develop understanding, communication skills and self-confidence. The oral report helps students learn how to present results and, in this case, to a sympathetic audience. It teaches them how to think on their feet, a skill that will prove useful in all of life. Some students may be shy about talking in front of their peers, but this may be partially overcome in group presentations, with each person reporting on a separate aspect of the work. Or the student may use a poster to present the details of the report. The oral report may be graded by the instructor as well as by the peer group; peer feedback helps students learn how to evaluate each other and often provide insights that the instructor may have missed.

Another way to assess learning in the laboratory course is to give one or more different types of examination:

The practicum, or hands-on laboratory test, requires that students come into the laboratory and perform a series of techniques, which are then graded by the laboratory instructor. This is difficult to do in large classes, but it shows the instructor whether or not the student has learned the laboratory technique or experimental methods.

The written examination, with questions about the laboratory techniques and data analysis, is often more difficult to write than a classroom examination. In general the written examination focuses on the material learned in the laboratory and not the theory behind an experiment which may have been covered in another course.

The oral examination, such as a report on some experiment students have performed or research they have carried out, is also a possibility in smaller courses (*e.g.,* see above).

A group examination might be appropriate when assessing collaborative projects (*e.g.,* see above).

A grade for the laboratory course is usually determined from a combination of grades from quizzes, notebooks, laboratory reports, examinations, along with an evaluation of mastery of techniques and/or good citizenship. Chapter 12 has more information on assessment strategies for the laboratory.

Safety in the Laboratory

Both cleanliness and safety are of prime importance in the laboratory. Cleanliness is important to safety as well as to the quality of the experiment. This means that the laboratory work area must be clean and devoid of scraps of paper, extra samples, last week's biologicals, broken glassware and other items not being used in the experiment at hand. Safety is important *and* we laboratory instructors are responsible for the students in our care. Instructors are required to teach safe techniques in the laboratory and to make students aware of hazards and of procedures to handle waste.

Although the laboratory is a controlled environment in which to experiment, the instructor must be aware of safety in all areas. The law is quite clear: students must be informed about safety regulations, the safe handling of toxic materials and dangerous equipment, and the need to work carefully at all times. Anyone associated with a laboratory, including the custodians, must be informed on how to handle dangerous materials and how to dispose of toxic materials safely. Legislation requires those working in and around laboratories to be informed on a need-to-know basis about the chemicals and equipment with which they may have to deal. (Young 1987) Some special points about laboratory safety follow, but you should consult a safety handbook for more complete guidelines (American Chemical Society (ACS), 1993; 1994; Kaufman 1994; National Research Council, 1995):

Eye Protection In general, safety glasses or goggles are required in laboratory work. The goggles or glasses should meet ANSI Z87.1-1989 standards which means that the glasses or goggles are shatterproof. Goggles which protect the eyes from all sides are imperative when caustic hazardous substances are being used. It is important to remember that goggles will not protect the eyes from volatile solvents. This means that people with contact lenses are not protecting their eyes with goggles if they are working with volatile solvents. Contact lenses are extremely dangerous when organic solvents are being used because the volatile solvents can get behind the lenses and damage the eyes. Therefore, most organic chemistry laboratory instructors ask students to remove contacts and use safety glasses. On the other hand, if aqueous solutions are used, then contacts can help to protect the eyes. In most introductory laboratory courses, safety glasses with side shields offer sufficient eye protection.

Since goggles fit tightly around the eyes, most students prefer the safety glasses. It is much better to have students wearing safety glasses than uncomfortable goggles which they wear on top of their head. Remember: the instructor or teaching assistant should set a good example by wearing safety glasses at all times. (Emerson *et al.*, 1996)

Chemical Spills Most chemistry, physics and biology laboratories have safety showers and eyewashes. The safety showers are generally for use in case of fire or caustic or other dangerous materials that are spilled on a person. Modesty in time of danger can be harmful; if clothing has to be removed, it should be removed immediately to protect the skin. Any kind of acid or caustic burn can be treated by washing with excess water to remove the acid or base as quickly as possible from the skin. It is a good idea to pour corrosive chemicals into smaller containers for use by students. If the smaller containers are spilled or broken, there is less to clean up. It is a wise idea to have a tray of sodium bicarbonate available to clean up spills and drips from strongly acidic chemicals.

Even small chemical spills can cause problems when a student inadvertently puts a book or an elbow in a small puddle of caustic liquid; remind students to clean up all spills immediately and to keep work areas clean!

Fires Virtually all laboratories are reqiured to have fire extinguishers, and fire blankets are sometimes available. The location and type of each extinguisher should be noted by you and pointed out to your students. The usual carbon dioxide extinguisher works by smothering the fire, keeping oxygen away. Know how to use the fire extinguisher—especially in a panic. Always remember to pull the pin before using the extinguisher, and after the fire is over, see that the extinguisher is recharged and available for use again as soon as possible. There are several other types of fire extinguishers; be sure that you have the proper type for the flammable materials you will use. For example, the dry type is necessary for metal fires. If you will be working with flammable metals, be sure to have one of these extinguishers available. The important thing to remember about fires is that the best way to fight them is to remove the access to oxygen; smothering the fire or covering it is often more effective than spraying with water.

Safety Information New legislation requires that when working with hazardous chemicals, the Material Safety Data Sheets (MSDS) should be either on file in the laboratory or easily accessible. These MSDS forms are shipped with the chemicals when they are delivered or they may be obtained from the manufacturer. Several world wide web sites maintain files of MSDS forms and have the advantage of often being the most up-to-date. (WWW-MSDS, 1997) The forms should be available so that anyone working with these materials can look up their toxicity and danger. The MSDS forms should be available to anyone entering the laboratory, including custodians. They should be easily accessible and should include information about any chemicals being used in the laboratory. If they are only available by computer, a list of clear directions on how to access the information must be posted next to the computer. Many world wide web sites also have safety information. (WWW-Safety, 1997)

Safety Training Students should be made aware of all safety concerns. It is the instructor's responsibility to show the students the location and operation of both exits, fire extinguishers, blankets, safety showers, eyewashes and safety equipment. Give students an opportunity to inspect safety equipment and, if possible, let them test it. This experience may help them remember the location and procedures during an emergency. Students should know who to contact in case of an emergency, what to do in the event of an earthquake or fire and how to handle spills of acids, bases, mercury and other hazardous materials. The institution and department should have a safety plan on file that may be referred to by the instructor.

Guidelines or Lab Rules To ensure that safe and productive work can be accomplished in the laboratory, you may need to establish some rules that will be understood and followed by your students. You should emphasize that violations of the rules endanger everyone and can lead to dismissal from the class. A set of basic rules developed for a laboratory is given in the table; these are offered as guidelines for you to use in formulating your own rules.

A Sample List of Laboratory Rules

- Come to lab prepared.
- Bring any necessary equipment or information, including lab procedure, notebook, and goggles.
- Pay careful attention to detail in directions; when in doubt, ASK!
- Keep work area clean, organized and uncluttered.
- Note all observations in a laboratory notebook.
- Keep communal areas clean.
- Dispose of waste properly; never pour chemicals down the sink!
- Be observant and then try to formulate explanations.
- Be safe; notice your surroundings; be ready to help others.
- Think about what you are doing.

Securing Supplies and Equipment

As laboratory instructor, you may be responsible for ordering supplies and checking to see that equipment is in working order. Additional administrative responsibilities of laboratory instructors often include the following.

Purchasing Lab Supplies and Equipment If you will need to purchase experimental supplies such as specimens, chemicals, glassware, and perhaps major pieces of equipment, be sure to plan ahead. Find out who is authorized to order on your departmental budget; it may be you, your department chair or your purchasing agent. Whether you order supplies or a department purchasing agent handles the orders, you must generally select the items.

Most equipment manufacturers are happy to send out catalogs free of charge; larger equipment and chemical suppliers have toll-free numbers and technical specialists who will give you referrals for specialized equipment. Scientific meetings and expositions offer good opportunities to visit manufacturers while they are displaying their wares, and most institutions have a library of catalogs.

Consider the costs when selecting items: compare catalog prices, ask about institutional or educational discounts, find out about shipping and handling costs and delivery deadlines. Ordering for the laboratory is the same as ordering for your home: you desire the best price and the most efficient delivery of merchandise. It is generally a good idea to order the least amount necessary: large containers are difficult to store, chemicals can deteriorate if held for too long a time, large inventories are difficult to maintain, disposal costs are high, and buying a five-year supply is inadvisable since the laboratory exercise might be performed only once. Also ask about the cost of delivery; for some hazardous materials, the delivery costs more than the product itself. Some companies will deliver exactly the amount of chemical you need for one experiment, so that there will be no leftovers.

Payment Arrangements Most institutions and businesses use a purchase order format. The purchase order system depends on the fact that the company will send you the order before you have to pay the bill. The vendor generally requires a purchase order number when the order is placed. The purchase order is the paper that details the specifics of the order. It is important to note on the purchase order, the date and time that order was placed, the person taking the order and the expected date of delivery. You will need to refer to the purchase order when the order is received and the bill is authorized for payment. Whether you place the order yourself or someone else does it for you, it is important that all the specifics are noted because any mistakes will delay the prompt delivery of the equipment or other material you ordered.

Receiving the Order Delivery is generally to a central receiving area, and you must retrieve your order from receiving or request that it be delivered to you. For this reason, it is important to have your name on the purchase order form. You should check the order immediately upon receipt, so that if anything is wrong you can return the materials in a timely fashion. To return items, call the company to get a return order number; in this way the company expects the return and can accord proper credit to your account.

Inventory and Storage All receipts should be inventoried and catalogued. At many institutions equipment is labeled with the school's name and with an inventory number; expendable materials are dated. Storage sites are labeled on the inventory list and a simple spreadsheet program, such as Microsoft Excel, may be used. Specific programs designed for inventory purposes such as Chem-Stock (Sci-Tech, International, 1996) may be purchased.

If any materials are hazardous, radioactive, registered drugs, corrosive, toxic or flammable, they should be stored in safety cabinets

199

or containers as required; these containers should be labeled according to Fire Protection regulations. It is particularly important that hazardous materials be stored in an area under lock and key. Corrosive chemicals are also considered hazardous and care should be taken in their storage and handling. If it is necessary to maintain large quantities of these chemicals, they should be stored on low shelves with lips or bars to help prevent accidental breakage; large bottles of corrosive chemicals are usually clearly marked and have a thumb ring requiring that two hands be used when lifting or pouring.

Disposal of Waste Materials

Virtually all chemicals used in laboratories have clearly defined protocols for disposal. Every institution should have a procedure for handling wastes; consult your institutional safety officer for specific procedures. Generally, you may collect wastes in one or more bottles, being careful not to mix materials that might be incompatible. Wastes are generally segregated into biohazards, heavy metals, volatile organics, water soluble but neutral salts, and any other specific category such as polymers or halogenated hydrocarbons. Solid wastes should be placed in plastic bags and carefully labeled. Once a bottle is labeled as waste, specific procedures must be followed. Generally, there is a manifest which lists all the chemicals in a waste bottle. Companies that specialize in disposal are contracted to dispose of waste; it is often true that the expense of disposing of wastes may be double or triple what was paid for the original chemicals!

Maintenance of Equipment

Generally, the person in charge of the laboratory is the one responsible for the maintenance of the equipment. All instruments and computers should be checked on a regular basis to be sure that they are operating properly. Manuals and directions should be kept in a clearly marked place that is easily accessible.

Conclusion

Teaching science requires teaching laboratories which model the way science is done in the real world. At its best, the instructional laboratory exposes students to the challenge and excitement of science. It offers students the opportunity of scientific inquiry into unknown areas and may motivate them to continue their studies in science. At the very least, laboratory work teaches observational skills and the way in which science is done.

As laboratory instructors, we must be especially concerned with safety issues and administrative details. Our responsibilities include:

- adequate planning for experimental work;
- keeping students safe while in the laboratory;
- updating experiments to keep the program relevant;
- ensuring that adequate supplies are available; and
- maintaining necessary equipment in working order.

The laboratory is the model for the real world of science. It is the ideal place for students to learn how to do hands-on experimentation, for it is here that they learn to question nature and to marvel at its wonder.

References

American Chemical Society (1993) "Safety in the Elementary(K-6) Science Classroom," Committee on Chemical Safety, American Chemical Society, Washington, DC.

American Chemical Society (1994) "Safety in Academic Chemistry Laboratories, 6th Edition," Committee on Chemical Safety, American Chemical Society, Washington, DC.

Caprio, Mario C. (1993) Cooperative Learning—The Jewel Among Motivational-Teaching Techniques, *Journal of College Science Teaching*, 22, 279-281.

Cooper, Melanie M. (1996), *Cooperative Chemistry Laboratory Manual*, McGraw-Hill Companies, San Francisco, California.

ChemFinder. (1977) "ChemOffice," Cambridge Scientific Computing, Cambridge, Massachusetts.

Dodd, Janet S. (1985) *The ACS Style Guide: A Manual for Authors and Editors"* , American Chemical Society, Washington, DC.

Emerson, Ken *et al.* (1996), "Handbook for Teaching Assistants" *Journal of Chemical Education*, ISBN 0-910362-29-7, Book Order Dept., Mack Printing Co., 1991 Northhampton Street, Easton, PA 18042. Institute for Chemical Education, University of Wisconsin, Department of Chemistry 1101 University Avenue, Madison, Wisconsin.

Isis (1997) Molecular Design Limited, San Leandro, California.

Kanare, Howard M. (1985) *Writing the Laboratory Notebook*, American Chemical Society, Washington, DC.

Kaufman, James A. (1994) *Laboratory Safety Guidelines*, The Laboratory Safety Workshop, 192 Worcester Road, Natick, MA 01760. For a free copy, fax at 1-508-647-0062.

Lysakowski, Rich (March,1997) Electronic Laboratory Notebooks: What do Scientists Want? *Scientific Computing and Information*, pp 12-14. Gordon Publications, Morris Plains, New Jersey.

National Research Council. (1995) *Handling, Storage and Disposal of Chemicals in Laboratories*, Committee on Prudent Practices, National Academy Press,Washington, DC.

Nurrenbern, Susan C. (1995) *Experiences in Cooperative Learning: A Collection for Chemistry Teachers*, Institute for Chemical Education, ICE Publication 95-001, Madison, Wisconsin.

Poruch, David (1995), *A Short Guide to Writing About Science,* Harper Collins College Publishers, New York, New York.

Sci-Tech International (1996) , "Chem-Stock" Chicago, IL, 800-622-3345

WWW-MSDS (1997) sites that have MSDS forms:
    http://www.chem.uky.edu/resources/msds.html
    http://www.phys.ksu.edu/~tipping/msds.html
    http://www.library.wisc.edu:80/Biotech/guide/msds.html

WWW-Safety, (1997) sites that have general safety information
    http://www.rtk.net/
    http://turva.me.tut.fi/~oshweb/

Young, Jay A., Ed. (1987) *Improving Safety in the Chemical Laboratory, A Practical Guide,* Wiley Interscience, John Wiley & Sons, New York NY.

IV

Management Issues

Introduction

MANAGEMENT ISSUES

Earlier units of this book have touched on management issues that are critical to the success of any course. Management is particularly important in large classes and in laboratory work where hazardous materials are involved. However, some management issues surface in every course you teach. Three crucial issues are considered in Unit IV: the selection of instructional and learning support materials; creating a course syllabus and assigning grades. The decisions you make about these three issues need to be supportive of your course objectives. But how should you begin to choose a text or draft a syllabus? Even if you are experienced in these tasks, this unit has useful information for you. It provides a comprehensive set of considerations for making these decisions.

In general, students will spend more time reading the textbook and other instructional materials you recommend or require for the course than they will spend with you. Most importantly, textbooks are used for a very large portion of learning by most students; this means that textbooks must be carefully chosen to complement your educational philosophy, not to be at crossed purposes with your approach to subject matter, and to provide material clearly directed to a diverse group of learners. Chapter 18 discusses a series of criteria to consider in selecting course materials as well as the need-to-know information about publishing companies.

Chapter 19 considers the course syllabus and its role as a contract between you and the student. It also serves an important role as a road map for students, outlining what they will need to know and demonstrate in order to be successful in your course. Information that must be *included and information that should be included are explained to help you construct a document that will serve you and your students well. One important section of information on your syllabus is a clear description of your grading policy.*

Chapter 20 discusses many important considerations that go into the development of a grading policy. It also considers the dual meaning of grades: they are both a motivating force and a measure that represents achievement. Should you curve your grades? Should you grade on attendance and participation? And what implications do the answers to these questions have on the motivation of your students? Even experienced instructors should re-evaluate grading policy from time to time—as we rethink our course objectives, teaching strategies and assessment instruments. Chapter 20 has helpful discussion and suggestions to help guide your thinking.

Carri M. Lyda

Chapter 18

SELECTION OF COURSE MATERIALS

In-class presentations and activities comprise the heart of most introductory science courses, but students will likely spend more time studying the text and ancillary materials than attending class. As instructors we have important decisions to make regarding the resources our students will study.

The market is overflowing with introductory-level science course materials. Publishers produce packages for introductory science courses which include a text and many ancillary support products. For students, the offerings include textbooks, laboratory manuals, study guides, interactive CD-ROM programs, student solution manuals, art-notebooks, supplemental skills books, resource web pages, and on-line e-mail assistance with problem solving. And to serve the instructors, publishing companies offer annotated instructors' editions, test item files—in hard copy and on disk—custom compiled, printed, and faxed exams, instructor solution manuals, instructor course manuals, overhead transparencies, and weekly electronic provision of current newspaper article synopses.

Instructors must decide whether to choose from this array of commercially published materials or prepare their own. If you are a beginning instructor, time constraints will likely require that you adopt a text for at least your first year. And if you are teaching a standard introductory science course, the enormous task of preparing one will understandably encourage you to continue to adopt commercial texts for years. For these reasons, most instructors utilize a commercially published textbook to supplement class presentations in their introductory science courses.

Carri M. Lyda

Our students will spend many more hours reading and studying the text and ancillary materials than learning directly from us. According to Young and Reigeluth (1988), textbooks are responsible for 75% to 90% of the information students will learn on a given subject. Clearly, instructors have pivotal decisions to make regarding the materials our students will study. Considering the vast array of choices available, where should the selection process begin? Which selection criteria weigh most heavily?

Reviewing Materials

Not surprisingly, the task of selecting course materials begins with reviewing the offerings. Because there are so many possible choices, consider asking a group of introductory level students assist you in reviewing materials. I recommend beginning the review process with the text; once you have decided on a text that seems to be the best choice, consider the ancillary support materials available. It is important to narrow the choices by selecting a relatively few texts for closer scrutiny. Some general guidelines to help you decide which books to examine are:

> *Check the authors' names and credentials.* Ensure that the books are written by scholars in your area rather than as "managed books"; although the latter are superficially attractive, they are written in a publisher's office by someone who may not know the field well (McKeachie 1986).
> *Check the names and credentials of subject-matter reviewers.* These names listed in the front of the book may also give some indication of the content accuracy.
> *Read some critical reviews of the textbook.* Journals often publish reviews of texts. Although reviewers' comments are no substitute for your own careful deliberation, they can be helpful in flagging severe problems (Robinson 1994).

Guard against selecting your text based on the persistence, personality, or customer service of a publisher's sales representative.

Some instructors choose their course materials at professional meetings and conventions. In the exhibit halls of these meetings, nearly all the major publishers of texts in your discipline will be displaying their offerings. Standing in publishers' booths seldom allows for an adequate review of the choices. A thorough assessment of the text organization, treatment of diversity issues, and other criteria described below requires careful scrutiny.

Because the textbook industry is competitive—especially at the introductory course level—publisher representatives will gladly provide you with complimentary examination copies of the text and most of the supplemental materials for your consideration. If you attend a professional meeting, ask the publishers' representatives to send you examination copies of texts that appear promising. You also may hear from publisher representatives offering to send them to you, or you can call and request the books. Your bookstore has addresses and phone numbers for most publishing companies. When you do call, ask to speak to the representative assigned to your discipline or institution; otherwise you may not get the best service.

Since we carefully plan our courses and laboratories to maximize their synergy, the text should be a supporting partner resource for the total course learning experience. Through careful consideration and weighing of selection criteria, an effective set of commercially published course materials can generally be found. This chapter provides a discussion of possible selection criteria for consideration when choosing texts and supporting materials. Our goal should be two-fold: *that our students will learn from their course materials while enjoying them.*

Because the textbook will likely be the main instructional aid to your students, the discussions of this chapter focus upon criteria for textbook selection. These criteria include answering the following questions:

1. Does the text match or complement your course objectives?
2. Will the text serve as a primary or secondary source of information for the students?
3. Is the organization of text material suitable for your presentation?
4. Is the text readable and clear for your average students?
5. Does the text portray people of diverse backgrounds equitably in its narrative and in its figures?
6. What learning aids are built into the text organization and format?
7. What ancillary and supplemental materials are available from the publisher?
8. After using this text, do you still consider it a good choice? (Carry out a post-course text evaluation.)

Other selection criteria examined are such practical considerations as cost, availability, and weight.

Course objectives

The first criterion involves determining how the text matches or supplements your course objectives. This means that before beginning to review texts, the course objectives must be specified (Chapter 12). With the course objectives in mind, we can consider texts based on whether they support and further the course outcomes. For example, three objectives of my introductory science courses are:

1. *The students will recognize that the course material pervades their own physical world and is relevant to their lives.* Therefore, I am particularly interested in a text that offers explanations, evidence, anecdotes, and exercises that relate directly to the life of an average student.

2. *The students will understand the importance of the subject to their individual major courses of study.* Because my course is a requirement for agriculture, pre-nursing, education, and physical education/health, finding a text to offer such diverse material has proven to be difficult.

3. *The students will acquire skills in solving scientific problems, and to then be able to predict and interpret the physical world.* I, therefore, look for a text that provides numerous and varied word or thought problems, rather than the more common numerical problem just requiring the use of some formula and a bit of algebra.

In addition to comparing text "fit" to your specific course objectives, consider your preferences regarding the presentation, cross-linking of topics, and any controversial aspects of the course content. With these preferences in mind, survey the texts to find whether they share your views. Students tend to be confused and annoyed when instructors disagree with the text (McKeachie 1986).

Role of Textbooks

Another important thing to consider in selecting a text is whether it will serve as a primary or secondary source for course information. Some instructors choose a text and follow its order and content; in this case, the text *is* the curriculum for the course. Although this method at first might seem undesirable, it can work well. After all, we all seek the ideal textbook that follows our preferred paradigms, theories, organization and content. Likewise, one might write the book oneself in order to perfectly suit the needs of the course. But one danger that accompanies this method is that students begin to see the text as the director of the course, and see the instructor as one who merely speaks from the text, reiterating the same examples. For this and other pedagogical reasons explained in Unit I, the instructor must ensure that class time provides reflection, extensions, and practice in problem solving.

Using the text—or even more than one—as a reference has the advantage of showing students the value of gaining knowledge from a variety of sources. Indeed, as scientists we augment the understanding of a concept by accessing a variety of our favorite references; we would not expect one particular book to provide everything we need to know about a topic. By using one text as a reliable source to complement—but not dictate—course content, we can better provide students with the opportunity to assimilate course material and form connections with the text's content. By considering the text as just one resource, the instructor models for the students the thoughtful scientist who compiles information from different sources, ponders, organizes, and then reexamines the information.

Many introductory science texts are encyclopedic, perhaps reflecting the immense amount of material some courses attempt to cover. These books also represent an attempt to include the favorite research area of every instructor potentially adopting the text. Consider whether you seek such coverage in your course; for most introductory courses, such encyclopedic coverage attempts are not advised (Robinson 1994). These texts might be useful as reference tools, but your students will likely resent the cost for just this purpose.

Organization of Content

Many instructors, particularly experienced ones, have established a preference for the order in which introductory and fundamental scientific concepts are developed. This preference should be a factor considered in textbook selection. But before reading the tables of contents for the texts you are considering, take some time to think about the course content and how it might be organized in new ways.

> *List the topics you believe must be covered in your course. Now add the topics that you will also include as time permits. Talk to your colleagues who teach subsequent courses to learn what content they feel is necessary in the prerequisite. Draw arrows between topics that you believe have important relevance to one another. Think about the order you prefer for these topics to be developed.*

The purpose of this exercise is to get away from simply teaching your course "the way it's *always* taught" and to consider new approaches. While a full view of one topic might need the complete understanding of another, in many cases their order can be reversed or interspersed for some cognitive advantages.

For example, in introductory chemistry, the concept of molecular polarity is usually taught early in the course with examples of small molecules. But most students have far more experience dealing with the immisibility of fat in water than small molecule examples like methane and nitrogen dioxide! Typically, not until months later do students get to apply this previously intangible concept of polarity to the immisibility of fat and water. The common reasoning is that large molecules like fat are too complex for early in the course. But it can never be too early to introduce familiar examples. Why not include some of these important, real-world examples in the original discussion? In my course, I introduce this and other examples, and thereby deviate from the typical text content order. And so I look for a text that can offer this integrative approach.

Also prior to reviewing the tables of contents, decide whether you want your chosen text to follow your preferred topic order, or whether you are willing to "jump around" in the text. Is the text adaptable to your preferred order? As was discussed in the previous section (*Role of the Text*), there are some advantages to course topic order not matching the text topic order.

As you review the tables of contents and compare them to your organizational ideal, consider which topics are grouped or treated individually by chapters. Consider the order of the chapters. Consider whether the text draws on content and examples from later chapters in a manner helpful to students constructing their understanding.

Readability and Clarity

Many students attending college do not have college-level reading skills; for them, studying the book is more of an exercise in reading than in learning the subject at hand. Herbert Spencer's quote of 1852 aptly describes the importance of readability, "...the time and effort spent devoted to decoding words would be subtracted from the energy left to consider the meaning" (Harris and Jacobson, 1979). Indeed, the consideration of readability is a highly important aspect of textbook selection.

Several formulae are available to help instructors predict the readability of a text; these focus upon various measures of writing, such as sentence complexity, vocabulary difficulty, sentence length, and line length (Mitchell-Beard 1990). Most publishers can provide an assessment of the reading levels of their textbooks (Robinson 1994). A limited study indicates that college instructors are fairly accurate in their estimation of readability of text books *when they take the time to estimate such* (Mitchell-Beard 1990). This implies that we must remember to consider readability in our list of considerations; as high level readers, we might easily not recognize text writing that is difficult for our students to read. Further, can we also correctly estimate the reading level of our particular population of students? And do we seek to exercise their reading skills, or do we seek to expand their scientific knowledge and thinking skills, or do we seek both? Each instructor must decide the answers to these questions based on their course objectives and their student population. My recommendation is to choose writing that is closely matched to the reading level of your average student. Since science courses often have the distinction of being the most feared courses in college-degree programs, why not leave the improvement of reading ability to the humanities courses?

Some books are written in a readable style, but they assume that the reader will have some basic knowledge of the subject. Our introductory students often have no prior knowledge of the subject! But as scholars in the field, it may be difficult for us to recognize these flaws. We must remember to consider this criterion, and attempt to detect any assumption of prior knowledge. The opinions of one or two introductory level students could be quite helpful here.

As experts in our fields, it is also difficult for us to assess the clarity of a text. Try choosing some diagrams, figures, and tables at random throughout the text. Without noticing the particular chapter, examine an illustration. Is its meaning clear? Is it adequately labeled? Does the caption direct the reader toward the important points? Is it located near the corresponding discussion? Try to imagine that you don't know the content well, and then notice what is not obvious in the figure.

Diversity and Equity

As discussed more fully in Chapter 14, we must provide an atmosphere that is conducive for learning for all students. Since all people of color, and white women have fewer role models than do white males, and since these groups also tend to have more difficulty envisioning themselves as scientifically capable, all of our course materials must be inclusive of them.

213

We need to pay attention to the diversity represented by the content material and by the illustrations. Scientific content tends to be applicable to all, so the content itself is usually not problematic. Regarding the history of the discipline, look for gender balance in the accounts of great discoveries. Despite the popular examples used in each field, there are women who can be included. Illustrations depicting mostly white males conducting experiments, operating technical equipment, and generally being the active subjects give the subliminal message that most scientists, technical equipment operators, and active participants in science are white men. Some texts also include white women, but usually showing them only as passive subjects displaying the wonders of science, such as through the cosmetics they are wearing. In one instance, an African woman and her children were included, but only as famine victims. In another example, a Phillipino man appeared, but as a sugar cane laborer (Middlecamp 1996). In illustrations men and women, white and non-white, all need to be depicted being active, scientific, technical, and capable.

An example of a more subtle and therefore more insidious example of gender bias is described by Young and Reigeluth (1988):

> *What may linger is a more subtle bias reflected by a photo caption such as, 'This woman is employed in a factory and does all the work expected of men doing the same job."*

Remember, the course materials you use will determine the message you send to your students, and the message is:

> *Every citizen of the world is enriched by science; and science is enriched by the contribution of all.*

In order that your course be inclusive, Jerry Krockover (1997) suggests referring to the following questions as selections of text and other resource materials are made.

- Do the materials provide concrete experiences for the science being taught?
- Do the materials provide in-depth experiences over an extended period of time?
- Do the materials relate science experiences to everyday life?
- Do the materials encourage students to access their prior knowledge and experiences?
- Do the materials provide opportunities for students to meet in small groups to defend their own evidence and express their results in a variety of ways?
- Is the content included in the materials free of bias? Are the photos used diverse and equitable in their portrayals?
- Is the science represented connected to a global society?
- Are the materials free of ethnic, cultural, racial, economic, age and gender bias?
- Do the materials provide appropriate strategies to meet the special needs of a diverse population?

Certainly, my discussions and my groupings such as those shown in the table that follows are anglocentric; however, considering the low to moderate level of awareness of these issues in the scientific community, we will do well to achieve this level of diversity in all texts. We look forward to the day when textbook discussions and portrayals are representative of all peoples and cultures.

This is perhaps the most easily quantifiable portion of your review process. Survey the historical figures included in the text. Survey the artwork of all of the course materials you are reviewing. Choose a chapter at random and look at the illustrations. Compare the numbers of pictures of each group, and also compare the type of depiction. Be sure to include hands, as they are often associated with one group or another. You can construct a table to tally the data; a sample is given on the following page.

Learning Aids in the Text

Texts that present difficult material in several different ways enhance student comprehension; the use of written explanations combined with two-dimensional displays—*e.g.* concept maps, flow charts, tree charts—are examples (Robinson 1994; Uno 1997). Special formatting which distinguishes the main points and ideas is also helpful for students (Young and Reigeluth, 1988). Other useful information in the text chapters includes:

- *Chapter summaries*, which provide students with an overview to help them understand the broad view of the material.
- *Sample applications* embedded in the text reading, which helps students put the reading into context.
- *End-of-Chapter exercises and problems*, which provide a wide array of opportunities for students to evaluate and extend their understanding.

Sample Table for Textbook Review

Item being reviewed:						
Number of illustrations of each type:						
Women of color, technical:						
Women of color, non-technical:						
Men of color, technical:						
Men of color, non-technical:						
White women, technical:						
White women, non-technical:						
White men, technical:						
White men, non-technical:						
White, gender not obvious						

Glossaries are crucial for introductory students, and of course, an *index* is assumed. Does the text you are reviewing have these features. If so, how well are they crafted? Read the chapter summaries—one from each of the texts being considered and note whether it provides a helpful overview or merely lists the content in an abbreviated manner. Do you agree with the overview it provides? Try the index. Look up some topics, especially those that may have synonyms; are they cross-referenced? Does the glossary also include page numbers where the students can find an expanded discussion of the entry?

Consider the end of the chapters questions and problems, as well as those within the chapters. Do they require thought and the integration of information, or do they ask for one-word answers and definitions found easily in the chapter? Do they simply require the location of a formula, an algebraic manipulation, and a calculation, or do they cause students to predict qualitatively the nature of the physical world? Do they help students apply their knowledge to new situations (Uno 1997)? Are there sufficient numbers of them?

Other Practical Considerations

Issues of cost, volume, mass, and availability are also worth consideration. Cost is virtually always an important consideration to our students, and should be a factor in text selection. Textbook prices are often not published in advertising pieces and will not be obvious; you should determine the publisher price and then the markup added by your bookstore.

Also consider whether the book will be used for future courses in the sequence. I recently taught a course that was cross-referenced between two science disciplines. Although the students from my discipline do not continue in a sequence, students from the other discipline do continue. Because I did not consult with the instructor of the next course in the sequence, the text I chose did not contain the content for the second portion of their course. These students then had to buy what appeared to them to be an extra book.

Many students live some distance from campus and some campuses are large: so know that the volume (and mass) of the text will be inversely proportional to its utilization. Some instructors ask the publishing company to provide the instructor with two copies for his or her own use: one for the office and one for home. Consider the implication: "The book is too heavy or bulky for me to carry back and forth" and then extend it to the students! They won't want to carry it either, and therefore will use it less than they would if it were smaller.

Custom publishing is one way to reduce the volume. Some publishing companies will print a special version for your students with only the pages you use being included. Contact your publisher representative to determine whether this is possible for the text you are considering. Again, be sure to ask about the cost. Keep in mind that this strategy will reduce resale value of the book, usually to zero and that few, if any, used copies will be available to reduce initial cost. Where students sell books back after the course, the real cost of using the text is the difference between the purchase and buy-back price.

Ancillary and Supplemental Materials

Once you have chosen the textbook, consider the each of the ancillaries. The most common ancillaries for students include solution manuals, study guides, interactive software and CD-ROM's. Use the same criteria described above for textbook selection. Consider whether the products are worth the extra money. If possible, ask introductory level students for advice. Are the computer programs user-friendly or problematic? Would a computer program be worth the extra price? If you are considering requiring the purchase of a supplemental book, CD-ROM, or model kit, ensure that you build its use into your course. Students are generally willing to purchase extra items, but they also want to make good use of them. Most instructors order fewer copies of optional materials than of the required texts for obvious reasons.

As supplements, consider the adoption of a novel, magazine articles, or short stories to enhance and provide context to the main course content. Magazine articles and short stories can be duplicated and sold for the cost of permission and duplication at your campus bookstore. Model kits or other hands-on learning aids can also be useful. I require my introductory students to purchase chemical model kits to provide three-dimensional views of molecules.

As soon as you have settled upon your choice of textbook and ancillary materials, contact your department chair or campus bookstore to fill out the proper order forms. Soon after, call the publisher representative and request all the instructor materials. With an annotated instructors' book, instructors' guide, text question banks, and overhead transparencies in hand, you can better begin to plan your classroom activities.

Post-use Evaluation of the Text

As your course progresses and after it has ended, you are well prepared to reevaluate your choices. Reconsider each of the text selection criteria described in this chapter: match with course objectives, role of text in the course, organization, readability and clarity, diversity and equity, learning aids, and ancillary materials. Did you and your students' detailed use of it reveal unforeseen problems or mis-matches? Consider the number of typographical and content errors, omissions, and misinterpretations. Did your text serve as you expected it would?

Most of us who now teach college science courses never thought of selling back our science books; indeed, many of us still treasure the text from that survey course that clinched our decision to become an earth scientist, geologist, chemist, physicist, or biologist. But clearly, most of our students are not going to become scientists. Many of them will sell their book back for the money, even if they did enjoy the course. For this reason, among others, many instructors repeatedly choose to use the same textbook. I encourage you to reconsider your selection of course material, particularly after the first usage. Weigh the importance of book resale value against the importance of an excellent text. Although your bookstore may not buy the used texts from your students, used book wholesalers will do so at a lower price. More importantly, a book that is not serving your students well simply does not warrant readoption!

Conclusion

Your course materials will have significant impact on the learning experiences of students in your courses. The importance of these materials and the message they send deserves attention. Your responsibility is to conscientiously review and judge the appropriateness of textbooks, as well as all ancillary and supplemental materials you use. Let the learning resource materials used support your course goals and lead your students to new discoveries.

References

Harris, A. J. and Jacobson, M. D. (1979) A framework for readability research: moving beyond Herbert Spencer. *Journal of Reading 22*, (5), 390-8.

Krockover, Gerald. (1997) Personal communication.

McKeachie, W. J. (1986) *Teaching Tips: A Guidebook for the Beginning College Teacher*, Eighth edition. Lexington, Massachusetts: D.C. Heath and Company.

Middlecamp, C. H. (1996) *Images of women (or lack thereof).* Oral presentation at the 211th American Chemical Society National Meeting, March 26, 1996, New Orleans, Louisiana.

Mitchell-Beard, B. (1990) *Textbook Selection Criteria and the Importance of Readability: The Judgment of College Instructors.* Dissertation: Southwest Missouri State University.

Robinson, D. H. (1994) "Textbook Selection: Watch Out for 'Inconsiderate' Texts", chapter. 32, in *Handbook of College Science Teaching: Theory and Applications*, Prichard, K. W. and Sawyer, R. M., eds. Westport, Connecticut: Greenwood Press.

Uno, G. E. (1997) *Handbook on Teaching Undergraduate Science Courses: A Survival Training Manual.* Norman, Oklahoma: University of Oklahoma Printing Services.

Young, M. J. and Reigeluth, C. M. (1988) *Improving the Textbook Selection Process.* Bloomington, Indiana: Phi Delta Kappa Educational Foundation.

Chapter 19

THE COURSE SYLLABUS

Recently I drove from my home in Dover, Delaware to an important conference in Atlanta, Georgia. Prior to my trip, I visited my local motor club to obtain a detailed map of the route I would take. In addition to the map, however, I was given information on road construction, potential speed traps, service areas and scenic overlooks that would make my trip more pleasant. The journey was, as I expected, arduous in terms of the distance traveled; however, cognizant of the value of the destination and armed with the essential details of the path I would take, my ride was a successful experience.

Similar to my story above, learning is both a destination and a journey. Students come to college to learn a body of knowledge and skills from professors in whose courses they enroll. They are more likely to be successful in a course if they know, in advance, the nature and scope of the material they are expected to learn and the rules of the road over which they are expected to achieve this knowledge. The mechanism through which this best can be accomplished is the course syllabus.

The course syllabus is an outline of a course of study. It is a written document, distributed to each student, designed to communicate essential information about a particular course. A syllabus can inform and motivate student performance. Since it serves as a contract between the instructor and the student, it should be thoughtfully written and contain certain essential components.

The purpose of a syllabus is to show to students the path they must follow to reach successfully their learning destination. It clearly should define what students need to know and be able to do to successfully complete a course, and it must guide students to the resources required to achieve this task. Because the syllabus constitutes a legal covenant between faculty members and students (Altman 1990), it should define both student and teacher responsibilities. A quality syllabus shares not only the expectations the instructor holds for his or her students but also communicates, to the learner, the standards to which the student can hold the instructor accountable as well. Some may find this level of accountability disconcerting. Some may argue that the level of specificity detailed above takes away from the spontaneity one might bring to a course. In reality, instructors still are free to discuss the contemporary issues and new discoveries they deem relevant. The specificity in the syllabus, however, reduces the chances of miscommunication and reduces potential problems students may have with classroom procedures and decorum. For example, students who have a clear understanding of the grading parameters and see these parameters as fair, tend to argue less about their final grades. Similarly, it's easy to see how clearly defined long term assignments not only result in fewer complaints about workload but also encourage students to practice long-range planning skills and submit better quality work.

Of course, you may need to make changes in the syllabus after the course begins; tests may need to be postponed or assignments changed to improve the students' experiences. Since the syllabus represents a contract between teacher and student, any deviations from the original document should be communicated in writing and distributed to every student. Changes should be considered carefully since, particularly in very large classes, this can become quite unwieldy.

The syllabus can also serve to communicate elements of style and tone that give students additional insights into the disposition of the professor (Erickson and Strommer, 1991). Tone can be upbeat and positive and communicate to the students acceptance and encouragement from the instructor. It can also be negative and send a fear through the hearts of students during those impressionable first days of class. It is only natural that students feel defeated before the first class when they see a phrase like "only 30% of you will pass this course." Style refers to the presentation of the document in a manner students can readily understand. A syllabus with good style is error free, legible, and easy to read.

Good syllabi have common elements that serve to communicate essential information about the course. This information can be organized in many ways but should contain the essential components below.

Course Information

A syllabus generally starts with a cover page that may offer the following information: the course name, course number, credit hours, instructor's name, department, office number, instructor's office hours, campus phone number and e-mail address. Every effort should be made to include office hours and phone numbers as early in the semester as possible as this demonstrates to students your willing accessibility (Matejka and Kurke, 1994). Be sure to arrange office hours that are compatible with students' schedules and consider being available by appointment as well.

Introduction to the Course Content

The introduction should summarize the scope of the course content under study, the important skills students are expected to acquire and the reasons why these skills and content are worth studying. I find that many students entering my *Introduction to Physical Science* course have no preliminary idea of what the course is about. Although it is obvious to the instructor, course titles such as Earth Science, Geology, Physics, *etc.* do not convey the breadth and depth of the content to be covered. A statement of major course themes offers students an organizing framework upon which to hang future concepts.

We probably all perform better if we value the task in which we are engaged. Similarly, students will generally perform better if they are convinced the course in which they are enrolled is worth studying. While the worth of something is subjective, a good instructor points out potentially relevant aspects of a course and communicates, in writing, enthusiasm for the content.

Course Goals

Course goals are broad statements that tell students what they should know and be able to do by the end of the course (Chapter 12). Goals can be cognitive and stress the acquisition of knowledge but they also can define physical and intellectual skills students are expected to learn. Students should know, for example, whether the acquisition of inquiry or problem solving skills are important course goals. Course goals might include the following:

> *To develop inquiry processes that contribute to the ability to critically evaluate and investigate scientific problems and conundrums.*

> *To develop a knowledge of scientific facts, concepts and principles with which one can better understand the world in which one lives.*

Student Expectations

The information in this part of the syllabus is designed to inform students of your expectations and the consequences for failure to adhere to these expectations. Put a different way, you are telling students you expect them to exercise choices that, in your opinion, position them to succeed in your class. You are also communicating the consequences that will take place if their choices do not conform to your expectations. This interplay of expectations, choices and consequences is an everyday part of life and need not connote negativity. The expectations should be written in clear, concise terms to avoid future misinterpretations. Students, at the beginning of a course, should know your position on such issues as

> *Attendance:* Do you expect students to come to class everyday? Why? What will happen if they cut class? What will happen if they are chronically late for class?
> *Missed tests and quizzes:* What defines an excused absence? Under what circumstances can students make up missed tests and quizzes?
> *Lab experiments:* Can missed labs be made up? Under what circumstances? When do lab results need to be turned in to the instructor? What happens if they are late? What is the difference between collaboration and plagiarism? Can results/conclusions be shared among a lab group?
> *Incomplete:* Under what conditions will an incomplete grade be given?
> *Academic Honesty:* What are the consequences for cheating, plagiarism or other forms of academic dishonesty. What actions, by the student, constitute academic dishonesty?

The above suggestions may, at first glance, seem unwarranted for college-age students. However, students appreciate structure and forthrightness and, if expectations are clearly communicated, they are more likely to respect your requirements. Experienced instructors have come to appreciate the necessity of including these topics.

Learning Activities and/or Projects

This part of the syllabus describes activities, field experiences, projects, and papers for which students will be responsible. No student wants to be surprised with a major assignment after the course starts. Good students plan ahead and budget time to study for tests and complete long-term projects. To accommodate these students, the instructor should provide synopses and due dates for each assignment. Details may be provided later but students should be given enough information so they can begin working on the assignment soon after the semester starts. Students should be given ample notice so they can plan to participate in field experiences.

Texts/References

It is appropriate, in this section, to provide a bibliographic citation of the course texts and supporting materials. In addition, a list of up-to-date references should be included, as optional materials, to introduce students to important readings in the field. Classics and seminal literature should be noted as such.

Evaluation of Student Achievement

Evaluation refers to the mechanism by which a student will obtain a final grade. It includes the methods of evaluation, the relative percentages assigned to each method, and a description of what students should expect to encounter in each situation. Evaluation can take the form of tests, quizzes, final examinations, laboratory assignments, performance assessments, collaborative assignments, *etc.* (see Chapter 20). Since students typically study what they feel they will be tested on, it is important to carefully plan an evaluation scheme that mirrors goals and anticipated learnings. For example, if one goal is to increase student problem solving ability, then provisions must be made to evaluate the degree to which that goal was reached. Typically, students perform better in a course that has evaluations spread evenly throughout the semester. A good computer assisted grade program, or spread sheet can allow instructors the flexibility of offering, to the student, regular printouts of grades to date. Below is an abbreviated example of a format with essential information.

Final Exam   20%
A 30 question essay exam that is cumulative in nature and requires the student to synthesize and apply knowledge.
Collaborative Problem Solving   10%
Problems, the answers to which will emerge by analytic thought over a period of time, will be given. Problems may be worked on in groups, but every participant will be accountable.

Grading Scale

The grading scale defines the level of accomplishment required to obtain a specific grade (see Chapter 20). Some instructors who convert grades into percentages might have a scale like the one below; this conversion varies among instructors, depending on how their assessment tools have been designed. The scale should be adjusted accordingly if your institution uses plus/minus grading.

A=90-100%   B=80-89%   C=70-79%   D=60-69%   F=< 60%

Another option might be to keep a cumulative point total. For example, if 550 points are possible throughout a course, grades might be assigned as follows:

A = 451-550 points   C = 251-350 points
B = 351-450 points   D = 150-250 points
                F = < 150 points

You should check to see whether any institutional policy exists that would supersede your criteria.

Course Schedule

The course schedule provides a list of topics and the approximate dates they will be covered. The list of topics provides a more specific overview of the course than the goals. The syllabus also provides a list of class meetings, holidays, suggested readings and due dates for quizzes, tests, exercises, homework assignments, *etc.* This feature enables students to see a sequential picture of the topics that make up the course. If students are absent, they can easily find out what material they missed and what text pages to read to catch up. The testing dates allow students to schedule time for studying. A typical course schedule might look something like this shortened version:

Date	Topic	Text Pages
September 12	Measurement; Speed; Velocity	5-25
September 14	Vectors; Acceleration	26-32 & 314-315

Some syllabi provide for more flexibility by listing weekly topics.

Conclusion

Professors who give attention to the essential components above, share with the students the anticipation of the destination and the inspiration to savor the journey. If indeed the journey is arduous, the road you pave early will show rewards of both student appreciation and achievement.

References

Altman, H.B. (1990) Syllabus Shares "What the Teacher Wants". in *Teaching College: Collected Readings for the New Instructor"*, Madison, Wisconsin: Magna Publications.

Erickson, B. & Strommer, D. (1991) *Teaching College Freshmen.* San Francisco: Jossey-Bass Publishers.

Matejka, K & Kurke, L. (1994) Designing a Great Syllabus. *College Teaching* 42(3): 115-17.

William J. McIntosh

Chapter 20

ASSIGNING COURSE GRADES

There are many reasons for giving grades but the primary one is to communicate the extent to which a student has met course objectives. The potential use of grades encumbers us with the added responsibility for assuring our procedures accurately represent student work. In fact, the grades we give our students often have high-stakes consequences with the potential for affecting life decisions.

Instructors, in an effort to arrive at a fair evaluation of student performance, typically compile and analyze, according to a prearranged procedure, the results of a variety of both objective and subjective measurements. Grades, which are the results of these analyses, may have far reaching implications; for example, they can serve to limit entry into major programs, graduate schools or jobs, or decide scholarships and awards.

Grading policies and procedures deserve our careful attention. The sections below pose questions instructors should consider as they develop their own grading procedures. The responses to these questions are designed to address the issues, stimulate thought, and inform decision making in this important area.

What Evaluation Instruments Should Determine a Final Grade?

It is an extraordinarily difficult task to accurately measure student achievement. Because of this fact, the general rule of thumb is that a final grade should be determined by evaluating evidence of course mastery drawn from different contexts and a variety of student experiences. Traditionally a combination of tests, quizzes, laboratory reports, and perhaps a research paper have provided sufficient information by which instructors assigned a final grade. However, many professors have been using alternative assessments to better measure student achievement of course objectives (see Chapter 12). Alternative assessments may be used to determine student achievement in areas not readily addressed by standard measures such as those mentioned above. A performance assessment, for example, typically requires students to submit a product that demonstrates applications of concepts, problem solving skills or critical thinking. A colleague of mine, for example, asks students in his physical science class to design a way to protect an egg dropped from a high place on campus. Students present their results (and their egg) at a poster session that is evaluated, with a set of common criteria, by a panel of faculty judges. Other examples of alternative assessments might include student research projects, collaborative problem solving tasks (McIntosh 1996), and portfolios (Slater and Astwood, 1995).

The decision about which combination of the above evaluation instruments to use should be informed by careful consideration of course objectives. If objectives define what students should know and be able to do at the completion of a course of study, then evaluations should be constructed to establish the degree to which those objectives have been met. If a course outcome is that students are able to debate risks and benefits of chemicals in the environment, then a performance assessment might be more appropriate than a paper and pencil test.

It is important that all the evaluations we use be fair and quantifiable. They are fair if they allow students equal opportunity for success and if they equitably evaluate what has been covered and emphasized in class (see Chapter 14). Tests or test questions that are biased towards any group of students are clearly not acceptable and can unfairly skew final grades. Similarly, one should not place on a test a high number of questions about concepts that were minimally covered in class. Evaluations that are not quantifiable allow too much room for interpretation and should not be used for determining a final grade. While it may be very appropriate to share written or oral comments about a student's commitment, cooperation or attendance history, a fair policy would not calculate these factors into the final grade.

Some instructors would argue that attendance should be part of a final grade. The argument against this is that, while attendance should be encouraged, it does not measure mastery of course material. If attendance is required to attain non-content objectives such as critical thinking skills, then the acquisition of these skills should be formally measured by the appropriate instruments. Class participation also should not be calculated into the final grade since it does not represent student achievement. An alternative would be to record and use information about attendance and class participation for use when deciding borderline cases. This procedure eliminates the less defensible option of using one's own judgment to assign grades in these special cases.

How Many Evaluations Should I Use to Achieve a Final Grade?

Because the final assessment of a student's work becomes more reliable when the number of varied experiences increases (Ory and Ryan, 1993), it is recommended that you evaluate often using multiple instruments. One might use, for example, scores on 3 tests, 4 quizzes, 10 lab reports, a final examination, and 3 cooperative problems to arrive at a final grade. Your situation of course will vary with the nature of the course you teach. Evaluations often provide students with a tool for learning or serve as a study aid for future examinations. Evaluations should be returned to the students within a reasonable time so they can reconstruct their thinking and keep track of progress to date. Even then, students may fail to account for grading components having different weights and arrive at an inaccurate picture of current performance. A good computer grading program can print out progress reports that show student grades at regular intervals throughout the course. This practice supplements the common mid-term deficiency notice.

Should I Curve My Grades?

Let's examine what it means to curve any grade. Curving means students are compared to each other and are ranked according to their relative position among other students in the class. One way to achieve this ranking, when grading a test, is to calculate the mean and standard deviation of a set of test scores. The standard deviation then becomes the cutoff for grades. For example, a score two standard deviations above the mean might be considered an " A" while a score one standard deviation above the mean might be a "B" (Blommers and Lindquist, 1960). Other variations utilize standard scores, frequency distributions, *etc.* to arrive at a rationale for establishing grade ranges and cutoff points. Curving tests or final grades is a common practice that, on the surface, seems to be advantageous. There exists a clearly defined mathematical procedure that students can easily understand and appreciate. By its very nature curving guarantees some students will receive "A" grades no matter how hard the course might be; teachers may find solace in that at least some students are performing well in their class. Of course, it also guarantees some students will receive poor grades which in actuality may or may not be the case in an uncurved environment.

In spite of the advantages however, there are fundamental problems with this approach that should deter instructors from using it. The procedures described above are based on the normal curve which describes a predictable distribution of scores within a population. An assumption of the normal curve is that the greater the number of scores, the more likely the population will reflect the classic distribution. The method is hard to justify since the validity of the normal curve is severely compromised using the small number of students in typical classes. Even large classes, with hundreds of students, jeopardize the model. This approach is also inconsistent with our stated purpose for issuing grades: that is, to quantify the extent to which that student has met course objectives. A student could know only half of the answers on a test yet conceivably merit an "A" grade. In this case, the "A" grade does not reflect content mastery—rather it indicates a limited understanding of course content among a class of equally poor performers.

The alternative approach is to use a grading scheme that measures the degree to which a student masters predetermined standards. In this scenario, the instructor needs to communicate what students need to know and be able to do in the course, and then evaluate according to these standards. It is possible, although it may not be likely, under these conditions for all students to achieve an "A" in the course. It also allows, in some cases, for a large number of students to fail the course.

Instructors sometimes feel pressure from students and the institution not to fail large numbers of students and therefore revert to curving grades. This procedure does not result in increased student knowledge and may over time actually hinder performance by lowering student motivation and personal expectations. Students quickly modify their behavior when they discover that good grades can be achieved with a minimum amount of work. If we reward mediocre performance, we discourage excellence, contribute to grade inflation, and put the value of higher education in doubt with the public. A final reason to consider criterion-referenced grading is the opportunity to foster valuable cooperative experiences that are difficult to achieve in the more competitive "curve" environment (see Chapter 2).

Student failures, while cause for alarm, should be addressed by troubleshooting course components over which the instructor has control. If you are the instructor,

First, critically evaluate the testing instruments. Are the testing instruments adequately measuring what students are expected to know? Are the questions unambiguous? It seems obvious that the tests should measure accurately course content; however, some instructors rely on publishers' test banks which, in fact, may measure book content rather than course content. Test questions should be stated so both the instructor and the students have a common understanding of their meaning.

Evaluate your teaching methods. Careful introspection of teaching practices could identify areas for improvement that could result in gains in student achievement.

Investigate an alternate policy for accepting work. Of course, sometimes in spite of our best efforts students fail because they don't study or complete assignments. Some students care but turn in substandard work. The latter group of students can learn and succeed if we adopt a resubmit policy. Laboratory reports and research papers, for example, can be returned with comments and an offer to accept them again if the comments are addressed.

What Weights Should I Assign to Each Evaluation?

Weights refer to the percentage each evaluation component contributes to the final grade. While a test is usually worth more than a quiz it may be debatable that it is worth more than a performance assessment. While an instructor will want to weigh each component according to its importance toward determining a final grade, there is no agreement as to what the "correct" distribution should be. When assigning weights, instructors should compare their own judgment about how much a specific component is worth with the amount of time a typical student might spend completing the task or preparing for it. The instructor, for example, may feel it is very important that students know the content of a particular course and accordingly weigh tests heavily. This same instructor decides that decision making is viable but a low priority. The dilemma occurs when the performance required to assess the decision-making outcome is weighted low but the amount of student time required to complete the assignment is comparatively high. Knowing that student efforts are likely to be proportional to their perceived reward, the instructor may have to re-evaluate his or her assigned weights.

How Do I Arrive at a Final Grade When My Evaluation Components Have Different Weights?

There are two main methods of computing a final grade that accounts for different weight assignments. The choice of these methods depends on whether students are graded on a curve or with reference to a set of standards. The former, which we will not elaborate upon here, requires the use of standard scores. A criterion-referenced grading system, however, may account for different weights according to the formula below. The final grade will be expressed as a percentage that, by referring to a predetermined grading scale, can be converted to letter grades (Nitko 1983).

$$\text{Final Grade} = \frac{\Sigma \ \underline{\text{(weight given to a component)(percent score on a component)}}}{\Sigma \ \text{percent score on a component}}$$

A sample calculation appears below using grades for a single student.

	Raw Score	% Score	Weight%	Score X Weight
Test Average	75	75	3	225
Quiz Average	60	60	1	60
Lab average	93	93	2	186
Final Exam	112	80*	3	240
TOTAL			9	711

Final Grade= 711/9 = 79

*calculated as a percentage of a total possible points of 150.

While this procedure would seem to take more work than simply averaging the percentage scores, it more accurately weighs the importance of each component. Note that by taking the mean of the scores, the final grade would be 77%. The above calculation is easily programmed into a computer spreadsheet. Also, most grading programs take into account the effects of using different weights.

Should I Give Extra Credit?

Extra credit that extends and refines students' knowledge of the subject and is offered to all students at the beginning of the course may be appropriate. If extra credit is given, students should know the procedure for obtaining the credit and how it fits into the grading scheme. Often students request extra credit occurs at the end of a semester when they realize they are performing poorly in class. This is an inadequate reason for giving extra credit. This scenario typically sets up an unfair situation where only a few students are aware of the opportunity to improve their grade. Also the typical assignments tend not to provide adequate evidence of the extent to which students met course objectives. A good extra credit assignment, for example, might be to design and conduct, for presentation at an honors day forum, an experiment germane to the course of study. Students would be given grading parameters and a clear direction how the project becomes part of their final grade.

A Final Word

Faculty use grades to serve a number of purposes that go beyond the scope of this chapter. Grades can be used to motivate students, to provide feedback and improve learning, to reward hard work, to punish indifference, to rank achievements, or to maintain academic standards (Erickson and Strommer, 1991). These reasons, some of which are quite legitimate, should not obscure the primary purpose of assigning grades: *to communicate the extent to which a student has met course objectives.* Although the procedures for determining grades are admittedly imperfect, the potential consequences of these determinations should stimulate careful thought about the grading policies and procedure you employ.

References

Blommers, P.J. and Lindquist, E.F. (1960) *Elementary Statistical Methods.* Boston: Houghton Mifflin Co.

Erickson, B. and Strommer, D. (1991) *Teaching College Freshmen.* San Francisco: Jossey-Bass Publishers.

McIntosh, W. (1996) "Assessment in Higher Education," *Journal of College Science Teaching.* Sept./Oct.: 52-53.

Nitko, A.J. (1983) *Educational Tests and Measurement an Introduction.* New York: Harcourt Brace Jovanovich, Inc.

Ory, J.C. and Ryan, K.E. (1993) *Tips for Improving Testing and Grading.* Newbury Park: Sage Publications.

Slater, T.F. and Astwood, P.M. (1995) "Strategies for Using and Grading Undergraduate Student Assessment Portfolios in an Environmental Geology Course," *Journal of Geological Education.* 43 (May): 216-220.

V

Measures of Success

Introduction

MEASURES OF SUCCESS

In the final unit of this book we consider how to measure success in your chosen academic career—which includes teaching undergraduates in science. How well have you have met your own expectations? How well have you fulfilled the expectations of your students? And how well have you met the expectations of your institution? You will have some indication of how well your own expectations have been met as you evaluate student achievements in light of your course objectives. If the students met your course objectives as desired, then you may well be satisfied with your teaching experience. If some (maybe one) students have changed to a science major or simply have begun to wonder—ask, observe and seek explanations—about the workings of nature, then you may judge your course a genuine success!

The feedback from students on the course experience is sometimes gratifying and sometimes very disappointing. Remember that a student's perspective is clouded by the pejorative grade and what it might mean to his or her academic or career plans.

The feedback from the institution is important, especially because such measures are used in making employment and/or promotion decisions. The criteria by which the institution judges your performance generally goes beyond how well you teach. Other standards used in making decisions on rehiring and/or promotion will vary by institution type, size, and mission. However, additional criteria may include research and scholarship, college service (read committee work, here!), professional activity, public service, and faculty rapport. At institutions which value undergraduate teaching, the two most universal criteria used in faculty evaluation are teaching competence and collegiality.

239

In Chapter 21, some of the ways in which teaching competence is measured are discussed. While the standards may be quite clear on teaching excellence (by reference to command of subject, continuing scholarly growth, effective pedagogy, classroom management, rapport with students, communication skills, etc.), often the way in which achievement of these standards is measured leaves room for ambiguity and some concern. The author suggests ways in which you can become an active participant and maximize input into the evaluation process.

Finally, the editors, with input from the authors of this book, address the special characteristics of a community of academics at institutions of higher education. In Chapter 22 we consider what makes the academic community unique, what expectations this places on each academic member of the community, and how these expectations may be met. Faculty must work, reason and debate together. The best faculty support educational excellence and integrity and are committed to the mission of the institution. Thus, as discussed in Chapter 22, faculty rapport and the ability to work with other faculty, administrators and staff are important factors on which you will be judged.

Eleanor D. Siebert

Chapter 21

INSTRUCTIONAL EFFECTIVENESS

Teaching is a part of your job, and you will be held accountable for how well your students learn—presumably an outcome of how well you teach. But student achievements are only one measure of your instruction and an imperfect one at that. Other measures come from subjective student, peer and administration evaluations. In this chapter we discuss how to maximize your input in the evaluation process and how to increase your awareness of what criteria are used.

While certain characteristics of the instructor do have a special significance in determining whether a student learns, the instructor is not the only and maybe not even the single most important determining factor in the learning process. Many factors affect the students' learning experiences; in addition to the instructor, there are obvious inputs from the individual students and the course structure. Important student characteristics that impact learning include individual student interests, ability to meet course responsibilities, *etc.*; influential characteristics of the course structure include the text used and perceived value of any supplementary materials, the time the class is taught, *etc.* In evaluating instructional effectiveness, it is difficult—if not impossible—to separate the influence of student, course and instructor characteristics. The evaluation looks at the total learning experience, a blend of many factors over which the instructor does not have equal input and control.

Examples of course factors over which your control is limited begin with the description of your course in the college catalog; you probably did not have a role in drafting it. Although these descriptions are intentionally vague, an outline of the material to be covered is defined.

Indeed, the course may be designed as a part of a degree program in which certain objectives, determined by the department or school, must be met. If you are teaching a course in which there are multiple sections or if you are part of a teaching team, the course outline and textbook were likely determined by committee. Your input into selection of course materials may be limited. Nevertheless, you will be held accountable for the outcomes of your course. As instructors, our job is to teach effectively and to maximize input into the factors that influence instructional outcomes and, ultimately, the assessment of instruction.

When Assessment Takes Place

There are two common categories of evaluation: formative and summative. *Formative evaluation* takes place early during a course and at a time when you can respond to suggestions for improvement. This type of assessment is often part of a faculty development program, and your institution may have a Faculty Development Officer whose job it is to respond to requests for formative assessment. In general, you must take the initiative to ensure that evaluation is carried out early and in a manner that allows you to respond to suggestions and to improve your teaching. *Summative evaluation* takes place at the end of the course and is helpful to you only in future teaching. At many institutions a summative evaluation is automatic, with the primary purpose of summative evaluation being generally to determine whether or not you will be rehired or promoted. A *formal evaluation* is one that may be entered into your record, while an *informal evaluation* may be accomplished through conversation and observation.

Criteria Used in Assessment

The detailed criteria used for assessing teaching effectiveness varies among institutions, depending on the mission of the institution, its programs and student body. There are, however, some general areas which are nearly always probed. For example, questions that probe characteristics of the course, the instructor and some information about the student may be included. You, of course, have the most control over yourself as instructor. The following criteria over which you have primary influence and control are common to various assessment tools:

Personal Characteristics:
    Enthusiasm for subject *and* for teaching
    Knowledge of subject matter

Preparation for class
Encouragement of independent thought
Interest in and respect for students; friendliness
Availability and helpfulness
Preparation for course:
Organization of course
Syllabus with clear course objectives, requirements, grading criteria
Value of required course materials
Value and availability of supplementary materials
Presentation:
Elocutionary skills
Sensitivity to and concern with class comprehension and progress
Classroom management and effective use of time
Classroom atmosphere; openness to questions and discussion
Individualization of teaching
Pursuing and meeting course objectives
Stimulation of interest in the course and its subject matter
Motivation of students; high standards
Assessment:
Fairness and quality of exams
Impartial evaluation of students
Variety and frequency of student assessment
Frequency of feedback from teacher to students

You should be fully aware of the criteria used in evaluating your teaching effectiveness. They are articulated in your Faculty Handbook or in your contract. If you have any questions, do not fail to consult your teaching supervisor or department chair as soon as possible!

Who is Assessing—and How?

Next we consider who evaluates whether these criteria have been met and how. Both formative and summative assessments usually come from multiple perspectives. The most common perspectives are provided by yourself, informally by your peers, formally by an administrative representative (*e.g.*, your department chairperson), and by your students.

Self Assessment This is probably the most valuable mode of assessment, primarily because you can continually evaluate how well you are doing throughout the course. Are you meeting your course objectives in a timely fashion? Do the students give evidence of learning? Are students meeting the expected performance standards? Conversations with students, or anonymous, short in-class evaluations will provide additional dimension to your self assessment. This type of assessment is formative, because it puts you in a position to alter your teaching immediately when the feedback is negative and to build on your strengths. Some institutions have the staff and equipment required for videotaping class sessions. These sessions may be a bit unsettling to the class (and to the instructor), but it is useful to see yourself as others do. Mannerisms that deal with presentation, facial expressions, reactions to student questions, class participation, *etc.* are really seen in a whole new light. Some institutions even have Development Personnel who will analyze a tape and suggest ways to improve teaching and learning.

Informal Peer Assessment Peer assessment can be carried out in several ways—through classroom visits, viewing videotapes of your teaching, *etc.*—and by various peers. One of the most common ways is through classroom visits. In this approach you select a colleague to visit your class—someone by whom you do not feel professionally threatened, and it should be someone you respect as a teacher. Peer visitations, when they are planned and focused on evaluating a particular aspect of your teaching, can be a powerful aid to professional development. Caprio (1997) recommends the following process.

> *"To make the class visit as useful as possible, you need to decide on one—or perhaps two or three, but no more—questions you would like to have your colleague address: How am I handling student questions? Do I convey the enthusiasm I have for my subject? Am I using visual aids as well as I can be? Do I treat all students equitably—regardless of age, gender and special needs?*
>
> *Plan to have a pre-observational conference with the observer, explaining the questions you have and, maybe, why these questions have come to mind in the first place. Tell your colleague the general lesson plan for the class session he or she will be observing. Plan on ending the session a little early so your colleague can talk with the students privately for a few minutes; perhaps you should prepare a list of questions you'd like to have your colleague ask the students. Make them as specific as possible. Questions like, "How are Mr. Jones's classes?" are almost useless. "Does the pace of Mr. Jones's class allow you to take notes?" might be one of a whole string of more specific questions that would be needed to learn about class quality.*
>
> *On the day of the classroom visit, you will be nervous; but you will not be as stressed as you would if there were no pre-observation conference and if this were not an informal evaluation. Your students will notice the visitor. It's perfectly all right to acknowledge the*

person; it is polite to introduce your visitor to the class and tell the reason you've invited him or her. You need not explain the particular questions you've invited the visitor to address, but you could. It is good for students to see that part of professional behavior includes taking the initiative for personal professional development. If the observer will be staying to chat with the students after you leave, tell them about it. And, you may want to thank the students in advance for participating in this project.

At the post-observational conference, you will get some answers to your questions, some answers to questions you didn't think to ask, and you will think of some new questions. Understand early on that excellence in teaching is an ephemeral thing: it is approachable but, for the truly conscientious teacher, it may never really be attainable. As you approach excellence, you will find that you redefine it and place it on a higher level, keeping it just out of reach. It is a quest.

The next time you meet your students you may want to share with them some of what you learned, and you may want to talk to them about some changes you plan to make. This is not necessary, but I find including the students in my growth process helps them to become more committed members of the teaching-learning partnership.

Formative evaluations of this sort are best done just before midterm. By then you are comfortable enough with the students for an observer to be able to see the "real" you, and there is still time to practice the changes you want to make while the problems are still before you. But keep in mind that this will not be your last semester. If the observation is later in the term, it will still improve your teaching. There's no rush—there is time to learn and grow. This is indeed fortunate, because teaching is an enormous challenge and will take all the time you can invest in it. As is the case for students, assessment and learning go hand-in-hand. Arranging your own assessment in ways to optimize its effect on your professional growth is important."
(Caprio 1997)

Formal assessments Some institutions have administrative officers who are a part of the formal evaluation process. If your institution has a strong faculty development program, there may be Development Personnel who will carry out an assessment of teaching. Development Personnel are generally less threatening than a Department Chair, members of the Administration, or others who will eventually make a decision on whether you will be rehired. The closer an evaluator is to being a current classroom instructor, the more helpful and understanding they generally (but not always) are to the anxiety and peculiarities of the evaluation process.

Classroom visits Your department chairperson or other administrative evaluator also may assess your teaching by visiting a class session. An official evaluation that may be used for re-hiring decisions is sometimes difficult to confront. As a teacher, you know that this is just one class session. It may be the worst lesson you've ever presented, but that still doesn't mean you've done a poor job for the whole semester. You will probably be a little tense about the process: apart from wanting to do a good job, whether or not you have a job to do may depend on the outcome of this one class, and those are pretty high stakes. It may, however, be possible to take some of the sting out of the experience.

As a result of your own self-assessments, you may already have some ideas about your weaknesses. Caprio (1997) recommends that you take a more active role in the formal evaluation process:

> "Consider making an appointment for a pre-observational conference with the evaluator. Discuss your concerns and identify them as areas in which you are seeking to improve during this academic year. (It is generally better for you to bring up the weaknesses and let the evaluator discover the strengths.) Develop some specific questions on which you would like your evaluator to report back to you. (Get them working for you.) This conference might be a good time to present the evaluator with your portfolio relative to your course. Exams you have given, written assignments, copies of exemplary student papers you've received, the course syllabus, and maybe even a statement of your personal growth plan for the semester: this will provide a context for the observation and a view of you as a serious professional. (Most people don't do this—it will be a pleasant surprise and mark you as an astute professional.) Before you leave the conference, perhaps you can schedule a post-evaluation meeting to discuss the evaluation and receive the answers to the questions you asked; it is better that you bring this up than to wait for it to come to you. The sooner this meeting comes after the observation, the better it will be for you." (Caprio 1997)

During the classroom visit, what will your evaluator be looking for? He or she will assess your apparent enthusiasm and interest in the subject and in teaching, your general classroom management and your rapport with students. For example, the evaluator will note whether or not your use of class time is effective, whether your presentation is organized and coherent, and whether your presentation stays "on track." In assessing rapport with students, he or she will note whether the classroom atmosphere seems comfortable and pleasant, whether you encourage or are open to questions, and whether you are able to answer questions. Of course one or two classroom visitations provides only a snapshot of the entire course experience, and most evaluators recognize this. But remember that an outsider's perspective can be valuable to your professional development.

Becoming an active partner in your own evaluation will provide you with a more useful outcome. By directing the evaluator to items of real interest, you are setting the process up to be a constructive one. And by assuming some of the responsibility in the process, you are relating to the evaluator on a more collegial level. You are also telling the person that they are doing more than assessing, they are playing a role in your professional development. Surely, they are going to want you to be around next semester to see how well they are bringing you along! (Caprio 1997)

Student Assessment Student input into the formal evaluation process usually comes from formal interviews or from written evaluations.

Student Interviews In addition to classroom visits, the Department Chair or evaluator will sometimes arrange to interview students who are in your classes. Evaluators try for a random sample or cross section of students. Any interviewer should determine at the outset of any meeting with a student to determine to what extent the student participates in meeting the requirements of the course. If you have been open with students in asking for comments about your teaching and the course, hopefully they will not tell your supervisor anything you don't already know. Sometimes you will know that one or two of your students are angry—often because they have not seen the results of their efforts reflected in a grade they feel they deserve. Fortunately, the comments of one or two disgruntled students are fairly transparent and easy for evaluators to recognize; and because virtually all instructors have encountered the unhappy or problem student your peers are aware of the anger that can be expressed.

Written evaluations Many institutions require written student evaluations of each course. These evaluations may be administered by the instructor, but may be submitted directly to the department or office responsible to the committee on faculty performance evaluation. There are many types of forms, many of which give a numerical scale and a space for student comments. Some forms attempt to separate the evaluation of the course from the evaluation of the instructor, and which attempt to determine how well the student evaluator participated in meeting course requirements. However, other forms do not ask for student information and thus any failure in learning is held to be the responsibility of the instructors; students, who are an integral part of the contract, are not held accountable for upholding their responsibilities in meeting the course contract. There are additional cautions in interpreting student evaluation forms: first, students are often not in a position to be able to judge answers to the questions being asked, and second, student perceptions of instructor effectiveness are strongly colored by their own course performance (grade). If the evaluation form asks students to judge the professional competence of an instructor, students may respond to how authoritative the instructor sounds in presenting answers to questions. When asked whether the instructor effectively communicates course content, the way in which a student responds is largely determined by whether the student comes to class prepared—or even comes to class. If the student is asked to evaluate whether the instructor utilizes class time effectively, students may judge that time spent on oral student reports or group work may be an ineffective use of time. Instructors, however, may consider such activities essential to meeting the learning objectives of the course. To circumvent ambiguous answers, some institutions have pared down the questions to a minimum in which the student is asked to evaluate (1) the course, and (2) the instructor. For example, the University of California, Berkeley asks its students to rate the intellectual challenge of the course and the teaching effectiveness of the instructor. There is, however, no attempt to correlate these answers to how much effort the student put into the course.

A Grain of Salt

Inevitably, a student's educational experience is a combination of the course, the instructor, the student's personal interests, *etc*. Often students are not in a position to be able to evaluate the separate components—if, in fact, they can recognize the differences. It is easy to get an idea of how variable student responses are when reading the comments on these forms. Forms which supply a numerical rating scale facilitate analysis and are used in many institutions; however, a troublesome point on these forms is that the numerical scale tempts an institution to impart more objectivity to the responses than warranted. The average for each item, the median, a comparison to other courses evaluated in the department and the college, all provide a convenient set of numbers which become endowed often with great significance in evaluating faculty teaching performance. Often a careful reading of the forms shows a large range of numerical values recorded for each item.

Does this discussion mean that the students' perspectives are of no value? *Of course not!* Perceptions are the students' reality, and often they provide insight to problems which you and your peers may not recognize. It does mean that student evaluations are only one part of a total assessment of instructional effectiveness and should not be granted "favored status." Fortunately, multiple perspectives, yours included, are nearly always an important part of a total teaching assessment.

A sobering thought emerges in a review by Feldman (Feldman 1989) comparing the overall ratings of instruction effectiveness as reported by current and former students, peers, administrators, external observers, and of teachers themselves. Where data are available, the greatest similarity among ratings of instructor effectiveness was found when the ratings of current students were compared either with the ratings of peers or administrators; the least similarity was found between self-ratings of the teachers with that of their peers. In fact, ratings of current students were most similar to all other groups, but self assessments were most dissimilar to those of other groups of assessors. So who can you believe, if not yourself? Feldman's work suggests that current students provide good insight.

How to be in Charge

Be proactive. Show that you care about teaching and value the opportunity to become even more effective. Prepare a teaching portfolio that illustrates exemplary work of your students as well as the type of assignments and learning assessments you give; include a professional growth plan, and an up-to-date *curriculum vitae*. Work *with* your evaluators and treat every evaluation as an opportunity for professional growth.

Assess informally early and often; every class is different. Even after more than twenty years in college teaching, I find this observation to be true—and thankfully so. It keeps teaching interesting—even when teaching the same course in the same program at the same institution for many years!

Engage your students in evaluating how the class is going; be open in your conversations with them. Do not become defensive when they tell you things that are counter to your philosophy of teaching or things that are uncomfortable to hear. Maintain student rapport: be consistent and fair in your dealings with them; treat each one with respect and a dose of skepticism. Expect and require that they treat you the same.

Eleanor D. Siebert

Ask peers to observe your classes and offer suggestions. Visit the classes others teach to see how they behave in the classroom. Remember that you must be comfortable in the way you teach, and that techniques used by others may not work for you. For example, some instructors have a great deal of showmanship. This approach doesn't tend to work well for me, but I can usually take something from the approach of any peer to use in my own classes. Maintain rapport with your peers (as well as with your students)—as peers you share a common mission:

to educate students to maximum potential, so that each may participate actively, ethically, and productively in society.

References

Feldman, K. (1989) "Instructional Effectiveness of College Teachers as Judged by Teachers Themselves, Current and Former Students, Colleagues, Administrators, and External (Neutral) Observers," *Research in Higher Education*, Vol. 30, No. 2.

Caprio, M. (1997) Personal communication.

Chapter 22

PEER RELATIONS AND COLLEGIALITY

Collegiality: shared authority among colleagues

In the academy, all faculty have undertaken advanced study in at least one discipline and have been trained in scholarly pursuits of knowledge. This common background results in an academic community in which faculty are roughly equally empowered members, a community in which "authority is shared." (Weeks 1996) This means that peer relations in the academy require more than civil working relationships; these relationships require the sharing of authority and decision making in a way that is not common in many workplaces.

Ideally, academic decisions are made by a thorough analysis of options, honest debate and finally, consensus. Of course, ideality is often not reality, and interpersonal relationships in the academy suffer from many of the difficulties found in all workplaces: among them, personality differences and political differences among peers. The American Association of University Professors (AAUP) frequently refers to the importance of peer relations in its documents. For example, in its statement on professional ethics, AAUP outlines collegial responsibility in terms of personal obligations derived from membership in a community of scholars; faculty are obligated to be

    objective in the professional judgment of colleagues;

    active in the defense of academic freedom; and

    duly respectful of the studied opinions of colleagues.

In some institutions, the criterion of professional competence includes demonstrated professional and ethical relationships with colleagues and administrators.

Why is Collegiality Important?

Collegiality and the ability to work with colleagues is a factor in any employment decision—and with good reason. Collegiality is important to the effective functioning of an educational institution; it critically affects the performance of instructors, the coordination of curriculum within academic programs and the overall health of the institution. In cases where unpleasant and abrasive working relationships exist, productivity of individuals is affected, student learning can be negatively impacted, the curriculum may become disjointed and fractured as individuals promote different philosophies and expectations of students. In extreme cases, where an institution fails to meet its obligations to provide a learning environment for students, the institution may be held legally liable.

Establishing a Collegial Relationship

In a college or university setting, the number of colleagues you have contact with might be quite limited. On a smaller campus, you may be able to establish collegial relationships by serving on college-wide committees, but on larger campuses, your world may extend no further than your department or division. And if your department is located in several buildings on campus, it will even be difficult to maintain a community at the departmental level. On a daily basis, your circle of colleagues may extend no farther than those who have offices near yours, those with whom you teach, or those with whom you share a table at lunch. If collegiality is important, how can you establish those collegial relationships while attending to your teaching and professional responsibilities and student needs?

Faculty Commons Many colleges and universities have faculty centers, places where faculty can meet to discuss issues of common interest. These centers go by different names on different campuses: faculty resource center, teaching center, teaching and learning center, faculty center. In almost all cases, they began and still function as professional development centers; typical goals of a successful teaching center (see Table 1) demonstrate that its efforts are heavily weighted toward developing collegiality.

```
+-----------------------------------------------+
|  Typical Goals of a Faculty/Teaching Center   |
|                                               |
|         Connect Human Resources               |
|          Sponsor Faculty Learning             |
|       Coordinate Educational Resources        |
|            Information Exchange                |
|        Promote Classroom Research             |
|           Showcase Achievement                |
+-----------------------------------------------+
```

Table 1

And the kinds of faculty development programs and workshops these centers sponsor (see Table 2), not surprisingly, foster this same end.

At most schools, these centers are operated by the faculty and are, therefore, extremely sensitive and responsive to faculty needs. In addition to being a place for workshops, the center usually has the coffee pot fired up and a refrigerator loaded with snacks: it seems that in order to function, collegiality requires this kind of fuel as well as open minds and professional attitudes. When special programs are not taking place, this is a neutral ground where faculty can meet their counterparts from other buildings and talk.

You might want to look for the faculty center on your campus. Once you locate it, drop in and ask about its programs. If you are new there, know that there is no need to feel self-conscious: you definitely will be welcome!

Faculty Forums Some institutions or departments are proactive in providing an opportunity for faculty to come together and participate in shared decision making. In many of these institutions, these programs and meetings are held in the faculty/teaching center. In smaller institutions, the entire faculty may assemble to consider governance or policy issues over the course of one to two hours. There may even be full- or half-day convocations where faculty consider strategic planning or issues in teaching; some institutions have such a meeting at the beginning of each semester. When faculty gather, several objectives are often accomplished. For example, a meeting to develop institutional objectives also usually results in improving the collegial atmosphere at the institution.

At larger universities, such meetings may occur less frequently and may include only department or division faculty. But whenever a special time is dedicated to working together on one or more issues that critically

253

affect the entire group, teambuilding also occurs. Academic issues that involve goal setting, curriculum, teaching excellence, grading, *etc.* are all good topics on which the faculty work together. When you learn to put names with faces of fellow faculty, when you hear colleagues give opinions, ideas and suggestions, when you work in small groups on focused issues, a real community of scholars can emerge! (Lumsden 1997) Typical of programs held at the faculty/teaching centers are listed in Table 2.

Faculty Center Workshops[1]

- Yes and No: How to Disagree Without Being Disagreeable.

- Demystifying Computer Applications Presentations, Windows 95 (Tutorial Group)

- Panel Discussion on Classroom Environment - Strategies to Improve Student/Faculty Interaction and Classroom Management

- Panel Discussion on Pedagogical Implications of Internet Applications and Other Computer Technology

- Conference Day - Overview of Past, Present, and Future Teaching and Learning Center Workshops.

Table 2

Barriers to Collegiality

We won't dwell on this topic except to mention that institutions, departments and individuals generally have to work at maintaining collegial environments. The main barriers to building an inclusive team of colleagues include: size of the community, geographical boundaries, personalities, habits, politics, and genuine differences of opinion. An academic community is not much different from society-at-large in that personalities and political agenda determine much of what is done and said. Bias and harassment based on gender, race, ethnicity or culture are evident in too many academic settings. In its ideal state, however, the academy should be able to resolve these issues. The academic should be

---

[1] Teaching and Learning Center, Suffolk Community College, New York.

well prepared to participate (be active), examine issues (make observations), collaborate (work together), analyze alternatives (think critically) and synthesize new approaches (construct new knowledge). This is how we want our students to solve problems; it is what we what hope to teach; it is what we should model.

Introductory Science Courses

For instructors of introductory science courses, there are frequently conflicting ideas in the academic community on *what* should be taught in the introductory science course, *how* the content should be taught and *when* it should be taught. Less frequently is debate engaged on standards of competence—of students and faculty. In the broad view, diverse opinions are healthy and an expression of differences of opinions and views opens areas for discussion that might never be explored in a homogeneous community of scholars. If your ideas are in conflict with other departmental faculty, there must be opportunity for discussion, debate and an opportunity for consensus. Unfortunately, consensus does not always result from academic debate, but all members should emerge from such discussions with professional respect for the opinions of others. *Do not confuse collegiality with conciliation.* Collegiality implies that there will be respect for opinions of others expressed in academic debate; it does not mean that you must teach the same material and in the same way as your colleagues. It does mean that you need an informed rationale for your own approach—that your ideas are based on good theory and practice and that you are aware of the research and resources in science education. In addition, your ideas as well as those of others must be open for debate and scrutiny by your colleagues. You should indicate a willingness to collaborate on developing better ways to teach and an interest in continuing scholarly development.

Common Problem Areas for Creative Faculty

Faculty who are new to a college or university, or those who wish to try new methods of teaching may experience differences of opinion with more established department members. Unfortunately, teaching assistants, new and/or part-time instructors are all in a tentative situation. Contracts are issued either for a term or for an academic year; even for new instructors on a tenure-track, there is always a probationary period. During this time, the faculty member is continuously evaluated in terms of teaching effectiveness and, for those in more permanent positions, the evaluation includes an assessment of research productivity and service to the academic or professional community. In addition, there is always a stated or unstated criterion that considers how well the probationary faculty member works with other faculty and administrators. The courts have upheld employment decisions that cite lack of collegiality, even when collegiality is not included explicitly as a requirement for continued or renewed employment. (Weeks 1996)

There are some areas that surface again and again where new or innovative teachers are at odds with the "establishment." Some of these areas include the expectations that you will:

- Teach a course that is driven by the mandated text—and one that may not accommodate easily to your teaching style or philosophy;
- Teach in a way that is at odds with research on teaching and does not enhance learning—such as setting an authoritative classroom environment in which questions do not seem to be encouraged; and
- Teach a course covering such a broad content base that little depth of concepts can be explored.

In addition to these unfortunate expectations, you may face problems imposed by a budget-conscious administration that lead to large classes, standardized tests, and grading policies that foster competition among students—and faculty. Are these insurmountable problems? Is it time to give up teaching? If you ask these questions, we hope your answer to both questions is "no", because you are exactly the sort of conscientious and reflective science educator who can promote change.

How do you promote change and teach well in the face of such constraints? There is no guaranteed recipe for success under such dire circumstances, but some suggestions are offered.

- *First, attitude and knowledge are important.* Know why you want to teach differently and produce evidence that supports a different approach in any academic discussion.
- *Be active professionally.* Keep in contact with scientists who are scholars in teaching—for information and encouragement.
- *Do not try a mass conversion of your colleagues.* Be content initially that you will teach differently. If your teaching method is successful—*i.e.*, students demonstrate equal or greater learning *and* they find your classes more enjoyable—your colleagues may become converts over time. Remember that teaching by example is one of the most powerful educational methods, and it doesn't apply only to your

students: innovative teaching by a core of dedicated faculty breeds success which draws others into the stream of change.

- *View adverse conditions as a challenge.* For example, you will find material in this manual that deals with effective ways of teaching large classes; these hints do not make the large class an ideal learning situation, but there are ways in which active student participation and deep learning (as opposed to rote memorization) can occur.

The benefits of membership in the academic community are numerous. Among them are the freedom to explore and vigorously debate new ideas, and the excitement of life-long learning as you continue to hone the intellect and craft the skills of teaching and research that ensure the future of our society.

Collegiality is a professional attribute of considerable value and one that is well worth developing.

References

Lumsden, Ann (1997) Personal Communication, Florida State University.

Weeks, K.M (1996), "Collegiality and the Quarrelsome Professor," *Lex Collegii*, 20, No. 1, College Legal Information, Nashville, Tennessee.

Appendices

Appendix A

CONTRIBUTOR PROFILES

Robert D. Allen (Ph.D., University of California, Los Angeles) is Principal Administrative Analyst, IMMEX Project, at the UCLA School of Medicine. His teaching duties have included introductory biology, physics, and training teaching assistants; his scholarly interests include development of critical thinking skills, and application of computer assisted instruction to the development of critical thinking skills.

e-mail: gkrd_allen@eee.org; or gkrd@ucla.edu

Mario W. Caprio (M.A., Hofstra University; NSF Teaching Fellow, State University of New York at Stony Brook) retired from Suffolk Community College in 1996, after teaching there for 31 years. He currently teaches biology at Volunteer State Community College in Gallatin, Tennessee. Mr. Caprio is the contributing editor of the Two-Year College Department of the *Journal of College Science Teaching(JCST)*. He serves on the Editorial Advisory Board of JCST; the Board of Directors of the Biological Sciences Curriculum Study (BSCS); and the Advisory Board of the BioQUEST Curriculum Consortium, at Beloit College. His awards include the New York State Chancellor's Award for Excellence in Teaching and the Suffolk Community College Faculty Association Award for Outstanding Service in Peer Coaching. He is a charter member of the Society for College Science Teaching (SCST), is a Councilor-at-Large on its Executive Committee and chairs its Introductory Course Committee. Developing course materials and approaches for teaching science literacy courses in biology and the professional development of teachers of those courses are his principal professional interests.

e-mail: mcaprio@blue.net

Angelo Collins (M.S., Michigan State University; Ph.D., University of Wisconsin) is currently Associate Professor of Science Education at Peabody College of Vanderbilt University. She served as the Director of the National Science Education Standards Project, the Director of the Teacher Assessment Project and as a principal investigator for Science FEAT (Science For Early Adolescent Teachers). She is a fellow of the American Association for the Advancement of Science, a member of Sigma Xi, and a recipient of the Distinguished Alumni Award from the College of Education at the University of Wisconsin. Her current research interests focus on the understandings and abilities necessary for accomplished science teaching, how this understanding and ability is learned, and how it is assessed.

e-mail: collina@ctrvax.vanderbilt.edu

Marvin Druger (M.S., Brooklyn College; Ph.D., Columbia University) is Professor of Biology and Science Education and Chairperson of the Department of Science Teaching at Syracuse University. In his 41 years of teaching introductory college biology, Dr. Druger has taught about 40,000 students. He has been active in numerous science and science education organizations, and was president of three national science education organizations: the Society for College Science Teachers (SCST), the Association for the Education of Teachers in Science (AETS), and the National Science Teachers Association (NSTA). Professor Druger has received several science teaching awards, the most recent being the 1997 Meredith Professorship for Teaching Excellence at Syracuse University. He is currently Secretary of the Education Section of the American Association for the Advancement of Science (AAAS).

e-mail: Druger@sued.syr.edu

Nathan Dubowsky (M.S., Long Island University; Ph.D., Teachers College of Columbia University) is Professor of Biology at Westchester Community College (State University of New York) in Valhalla, New York where he teaches a science literacy biology course for non-majors, microbiology, and an honors course entitled, *Life: Origin and Evolution.* In addition to his teaching duties, Professor Dubowsky serves as Chairperson of the Grants and Awards Committee of the Metropolitan Association of College and University Biologists and on editorial review panels for the *Journal of College Science Teaching*, the *American Biology Teacher*, and *Science Books and Films* (AAAS). Dr. Dubowsky's other professional activities include development of non-traditional laboratory activities for use in his non-major's course and the use of history of science to teach biology. His interest in the history of has science led to a recent publication in the *British Journal of the History of Science* detailing the fate and final resting place of the legendary H.M.S. Beagle (the ship on which Charles Darwin sailed and collected much of the evidence he later used to construct his Theory of Natural Selection).

e-mail: RedAmoeba@aol.com

George Gurria (Ph.D., Johns Hopkins University) is Associate Professor of Chemistry at Alverno College, where he is a long-time member of the Analysis Ability Department and faculty of the annual Assessment Workshop for College Educators. He is Chief Health Professions Advisor at Alverno and has served as Dean of the Natural Sciences Division and consultant to colleges in the US and Canada on outcome/ability-based education, critical thinking, and assessment.

John R. Jungck (M.S., University of Minnesota; Ph.D, University of Miami) is a Professor of Biology at Beloit College and has been involved in biology education reforms for thirty years. Professor Jungck served as President of the Association of Midwestern College Biology Teachers, he is the Editor of *Bioscene: Journal of College Biology Teachers,* has served as editor of *The American Biology Teacher*, and has been on the Editorial Boards of both the *Bulletin of Mathematical Biology* and *BioSystems.* He has participated in projects for the Pre-Service Preparation of College Biology Teachers and for the development of investigative laboratory exercises with the Commission for Undergraduate Education in the Biological Sciences (CUEBS). His awards include: an NSTA-Ohaus Award for Innovations in College Science Teaching, a FIPSE Mina Shaughnessy Scholar Award for developing "new approaches to learning from practice," and a year-long Fulbright Scholar Award as a visiting professor to Thailand (with extensions to Sri Lanka and Egypt). In 1986, with Nils Peterson, he started the BioQUEST Curriculum Consortium and became Editor of The BioQUEST Library. Dr. Jungck maintains an active research program in mathematical molecular evolution, and the history, philosophy, and social studies of biology. For the past several years he has served on the executive committee of CELS (the Coalition for Education in the Life Sciences) and several national panels devoted to examining college science education.
e-mail: Jungck@beloit.edu

Louise R. Kelly (Master of Library Science, George Peabody College for Teachers) is librarian for Bibliographic Services, Public Services and Collection Development at Volunteer State Community College in Gallatin, Tennessee. As Bibliographic Services Librarian, she is the coordinator of a one-hour library instruction course which is required for graduation from the college. The Coordinator is responsible for determining the content of the course and for writing the textbook. Professor Kelly also writes the script and narrates the video for the independent study sections of the course. Currently, she is Chair of the Tennessee Library Instruction Roundtable of the Tennessee Library Association.
e-mail: Lkelly@a1.vscc.cc.tn.us

Gerald H. Krockover (Ph.D., University of Iowa) serves as a professor of Earth and Atmospheric Science Education at Purdue University. He holds a joint appointment between the Department of Earth and Atmospheric Sciences in the School of Science and the Department of Curriculum and Instruction in the School of Education. Jerry has conducted programs to prepare graduate teaching assistants in science for more than 20 years. He has been recognized for his outstanding teaching in science by the Purdue University Outstanding Undergraduate Teaching Award, Purdue University Impact on Learners Faculty Teaching Award, National Association of Teacher Educators Distinguished Major Professor Award, and the Association for the Education of Teachers in Science Outstanding Science Educator Award. He is also cited in *American Men and Women in Science, Who's Who in Science and Engineering*, and *Five Hundred Leaders of Influence*, and has received more than $2.2 million in external funding to improve science education throughout the United States.

e-mail: xvp2@omni.cc.purdue.edu

Sandra I. Lamb (Ph.D., University of California, Los Angeles) is Lecturer and Laboratory Coordinator at the University of California, Santa Barbara. She taught for many years at UCLA where she was a full-time laboratory coordinator for the organic laboratories and initiated and managed the Departmental Undergraduate Computer Laboratory. She has also taught at Santa Monica City College, California State University, Northridge and Mount St. Mary's College in Los Angeles and has worked as a Division Manager with Global Geochemistry Corp., an environmental testing company. She is active in the American Chemical Society, holding various offices as well as being a Councilor since 1988. She has been involved in the founding of the new Los Padres section of the ACS encompassing Ventura, Santa Barbara and San Luis Obispo Counties.

e-mail: lamb@chem.ucsb.edu

William H. Leonard (Ph.D., University of California, Berkeley) is Professor of Education and Biology at Clemson University, Clemson, South Carolina, where he has taught undergraduate and graduate courses in both biology and science education. His research activities involve inquiry learning in science, science laboratory instruction, reading science text, and learning science through computer technologies. An active biology curriculum developer, he is an author of *Laboratory Investigations in Biology, Biological Science: An Ecological Approach*, and *Biology: A Community Context*. He has won university awards for both teaching and research.

e-mail: leonard@mail.clemson.edu

Georgine Loacker (Ph.D., University of Chicago) directs the Council on Student Assessment at Alverno College. As a Professor of English, she is a major contributor to the development of its ability-based education and student assessment process begun in 1973 and now recognized nationally and throughout the world. She continues to contribute to assessment theory and to design assessments of student abilities. She writes and conducts research on the process of assessment of individual students. Her publications include *Designing a National Assessment System: Alverno's*

Institutional Perspective, a paper commissioned and published by the U.S. Office of Education, 1992 and a chapter in T. Banta, ed., *Are We Making a Difference?*, Jossey-Bass, 1993. Loacker has conducted workshops and seminars on assessment throughout the country and beyond, including six weeks of them in Australia and New Zealand as a Visiting Fellow of the Higher Education Research and Development Society of Australia.

Thomas R. Lord (M.S., Ph.D., Rutgers University) is Professor of Biology at the Indiana University of Pennsylvania where he teaches general biology, environmental science, field biology, dendrology, preclinical and biology seminar. He is interested in the enhancement of instruction at the college level, effects of spatial aptitude in science learning, and allelopathic relationships in field biology.

e-mail: trlord@grove.iup.edu

Ann S. Lumsden (Ph.D., Florida State University) is a faculty member in the Department of Biological Science at Florida State University. Ann coordinates the Non-major Biology Program at Florida State which includes the non-major biology classes (1400 students) and 36 non-major biology labs (870 students). She teaches seminars and freshman biology. Ann also developed and runs the Biological Science Teaching and Learning Workshop for new graduate students and other first-time teachers. She supervises department teaching and coordinates a training lab each week for the non-major biology labs. Ann was the 1992 recipient of NABT's Four-Year College Biology Teaching Award. She received an award of service from the Florida Foundation For Future Scientists in 1994 for her work with the State and Regional Science and Engineering Fair and Florida State Science Education. Ann is active in SCST, NABT, NSTA, and ABLE and works with several local and state science organizations. She has several publications.

e-mail: lumsden@bio.fsu.edu

Carri M. Lyda (Ph.D., University of California, Santa Barbara) is an Assistant Professor of Chemistry at Eastern Oregon University in La Grande, Oregon, where she teaches introductory chemistry to non-science majors and upper division courses in chemistry. Her teaching strategies include collaborative learning experiences in the lab and large classroom, novel examples from materials science to underscore connections within the course material and among disciplines, and innovations for the science curriculum for pre-service elementary teachers. She also leads a small team of undergraduate researchers in investigations of novel syntheses of inorganic materials and characterization via solid-state NMR spectroscopy. She is a Councilor-at-Large for the Society for College Science Teachers.

e-mail: lydac@eou.edu

William J. McIntosh (Ph.D., Temple University) has been a Professor of Science Education at Delaware State University for 17 years. He currently teaches courses in introductory Physical and Earth sciences as well as science methods courses. Dr. McIntosh is most interested in the role of college and university faculty in systemic reform. He has pioneered changes in his own science courses and works collaboratively with faculty from other institutions to promote course reform. His work has been presented in the *Journal for College Science Teaching*. Bill is the recent past president of the Society for College Science Teachers.

e-mail: bmcintsh@udel.edu

Eleanor D. Siebert (Ph.D., University of California, Los Angeles) chairs the Department of Physical Sciences and Mathematics and is Professor of Chemistry at Mount St. Mary's College in Los Angeles, CA. She teaches introductory physical science and chemistry to both science majors and non-majors and instrumental analysis and thermodynamics at the upper division level. Her research activities involve studies of phase separation in model biological systems. Dr. Siebert has written many articles and is an author of *Experiments for General Chemistry* and *Foundations for General Chemistry*. She is a charter member of the Society for College Science Teachers and is currently the College Director of the National Science Teachers Association. She is active in the American Chemical Society, currently serving on the Council Committee for Public Relations. She is listed in *Who's Who Among America's Teachers* and in *American Men and Women in Science*.

e-mail: esiebert@msmc.la.edu

Patti Soderberg (M.S., University of Wisconsin-Madison) is currently is the Director of the BioQUEST Curriculum Consortium at Beloit College and is also a doctoral student in science education at the University of Wisconsin-Madison in the Department of Curriculum and Instruction. She has taught at The Blake School in Minneapolis, was a Klingenstein Summer Fellow at Teachers College at Columbia University, and has been involved in K-12 teacher education programs in genetics and biotechnology at the University of Wisconsin-Madison. Her research interests are in problem solving in population genetics.

e-mail: Soderber@beloit.edu

Ethel Stanley (M.S., Wayne State University) is the director of field testing for the BioQUEST Curriculum Consortium at Beloit College, in Wisconsin. She is involved with a number of projects that include working with users of new software, designing and maintaining the organization's web pages, and presenting workshops featuring collaborative investigations in which students develop strategies for research and peer persuasion. Currently a doctoral student in Curriculum and Instruction at Illinois State University, she hopes to facilitate visual learning in field biology by emphasizing the use of visual data sets and collaborative exploration of images. She has taught general biology for non-majors, biodiversity, botany, and field biology as well as developed a biological field methods course for elementary education majors. She is currently active in the Association of Midwest College Biology Teachers (AMCBT) as Chair of the Editorial Board for the Bioscene and in the Botanical Society of America (BSA) as Vice-Chair of the Teaching Section.

e-mail: stanleye@beloit.edu

David J. Stroup (Ph.D., West Virginia University) is Professor of Biology at Francis Marion University in Florence, South Carolina. His scholarly interests are in plant morphology, development of critical thinking skills, and applications of computer augmented instruction to critical thinking development.

e-mail: dstroup@acs3.fmarion.edu

Leona Truchan (Ph.D., Northwestern) is professor of Biology at Alverno College where she has served as chair of the Global Perspectives Ability Department and was a member of the Valuing Ability Department. Currently she serves as a member of the Experiential Learning Committee. She is coordinator of the Science Education Program and has been Dean of the Natural Sciences and Mathematics Division. She is president of the Association of Midwest College Biology Teachers, past-president of the Association of Biology Laboratory Education and former Board Member of the Society for College Science Teachers. Dr. Truchan is a consultant to teachers from K-U in the United States, Canada, Australia, and New Zealand on teaching, learning and assessment and has been principal author and co-participant in numerous grants for improving teaching, learning, and assessment in the sciences.

e-mail: truchan1@execpc.com

Virginia Vaughan (B.A., Pembroke College; B.S., Utica College of Syracuse University) is the managing editor of The BioQUEST Library and the lead programmer for the BioQUEST Curriculum Consortium. She is a co-author of two of the simulations in the BioQUEST Library (*Evolve* and *Isolated Heart Lab*) and has coordinated the publication of the Library for the past three editions. Her current projects include recruiting new software for the next edition of the Library, working with current BioQUEST software developers to revise and update their software, and devising a way to make all the software in the Library compatible with both the Mac and the IBM platforms. She is currently interested in exploring how educational software can be designed to better support an investigative, collaborative, open-ended approach to learning.

email: Vvaughan@hamilton.edu

267

Appendix B

PROFESSIONAL SOCIETIES FOR TEACHERS OF SCIENCE

Here, we have listed several national societies for teachers of science. Keep in mind, too, that most scientific societies in the various disciples also have educational divisions. We have included URLs and e-mail addresses that were available at this writing. There likely will be more sites for these groups in the future. We assume that our readers are well aware of the organizations serving their subject matter areas and have not included them here; nor have we listed state and local organizations.

Being a member of one or more of these groups and reading their journal(s) and attending national conventions carries enormous implications for the professional development of a college science teacher. However, membership can be costly. Keep in mind, though, that most of these groups offer special membership rates for students (including graduate students) and retirees at substantial savings. If these reduced rates are not published, you should ask about them. If you are already affiliated with a college or university, you may want to find out if the school already has, or will consider purchasing, an institutional membership. This generally means that several members of the institution can participate in the organizations activities. Even if the institution is not a member yet, its library may subscribe to the organization's journal. If it does not, you may want to request that they order a subscription (librarians do try to be responsive to patron's interests when planning acquisitions).

American Association for the Advancement of Science (AAAS)
Section Q, Education
1200 New York Ave, NW
Washington, DC 20005
Section Q is a committee within AAAS; it plans programs that focus on issues in education for the AAAS meetings; members of this group serve as liaisons to other sections within AAAS.

American Association of Physics Teachers (AAPT)

1 Physics Ellipse, College Park, MD 20740-3842
E-mail address for information: aapt-memb@aapt.org
Web Site: http://www.aapt.org/
This large, active organization is broadly based. A list of its standing committees will give you some idea of it's diversity. AAPT has committees on: Apparatus, Astronomy, Education, Computers in Physics Education, Graduate Education in Physics, the History and Philosophy of Physics, Instructional Media, International Physics Education, Laboratories, Minorities in Physics, Physics in High Schools, Physics in Pre-High School Education, Physics in Two-Year Colleges, Undergraduate Education, Professional Concerns, Research in Physics Education, Science Education for the Public, Women in Physics.

American Chemical Society, ACS

1155 Sixteenth St., NW, Washington, DC 20036
Phone: (202) 872-4600
WWW ChemCenter

Division of Chemical Education (DivCHED)

Ronald D. Archer, 1997 Chair
Chemistry Department, University of Massachusetts
Amherst, MA 01003-4510
archer@chemistry.umass.edu

The Division of Chemical Education is composed of high school and college/university chemistry teachers. The division holds two meetings annually in conjunction with the meeting of the ACS. Division publications include a newsletter 3 times each year, the *Journal of Chemical Education*; published 10 times each year; JCE: Software and CD's; and coordinates an Examinations Institute. Information on publications at WWW:http://jchemedchem.wisc.edu/

American Geological Institute (AGI)

AGI, a federation of 31 geoscience societies, provides information and education services to its members, promoting a united voice for the geoscience community.
Web Site: http://www.agiweb.org/

Association of Astronomy Educators (AAE)

5103 Burt Street, Omaha, NE 68132
Phone: (402) 556-0082

Association for the Education of Teachers in Science (AETS)

11000 University Parkway, University of West Florida
Pensacola, FL 32514-5753
Web Site: http://wwcareers.com/A/0064.html

The Council for Undergraduate Research (CUR)
University of North Carolina at Asheville, 75 Zillicoa St., Suite 300
Asheville, NC 28801-1049
Phone: (704) 251-6006
CUR has over 3,500 members representing over 850 institutions in seven academic divisions. Serving faculty and administrators at primarily undergraduate institutions in the sciences, CUR encourages the development of research programs; members find CUR's wide range of services have a positive impact on undergraduate research programs and increase member connections with funding agencies and colleagues.

The National Association of Biology Teachers (NABT)
11250 Roger Bacon Drive, #19, Reston, Virginia 22090-5202
Phone: (703) 471-1134/(800) 406-0775
Fax: (703) 435-5582
E-mail address for information: NABTer@aol.com
Web Site: http://www.nabt.org/index.html
This is the largest national association of life science educators. It has more than 8,000 members. Although it focuses primarily on K-12 education, NABT has an active college division.

National Association of Geoscience Teachers (NAGT)
c/o Dr. Robert Christman, Exec. Director
Dept. of Geology—9080, Western Washington University
Bellingham, WA 98225-9080
Phone: (360) 650-3587; Fax: (360) 650-7302
E-mail address for information: xman@henson.cc.wwu.edu
Web site: http://www.agiweb.org/agi/member/nagt96.html

National Earth Science Teachers Association (NESTA)
2000 Florida Avenue, NW, Washington, DC 200009
E-mail address for information: fireton@kosmos.agu.org

National Science Teacher's Association (NSTA)
1840 Wilson Blvd., Arlington, VA 22201-3000
E-mail address for information: publicinfo@nsta.org
Web Site: http://www.nsta.org/
With over 53,000 members this is the largest society of professional science educators in the world. It represents all levels of education, K through graduate school.

The Society for College Science Teachers (SCST)
Michael Donovan, President
Department of Biology, Southern Utah University
Cedar City, UT 84720
E-mail address for information: donovan@suu.edu
Web Site: http://science.clayton.edu/scst/scst.html
The purpose of this organization is to provide a forum for interdisciplinary interaction among teachers of science at all institutions of higher education. It is a divisional affiliate of the National Science Teachers Association. Currently there are approximately 800 members from all of the states and several foreign countries. This book is a project of SCST.

Appendix C

CONNECTING WITH TEACHERS ON THE INTERNET

Unless you make an effort to have it be different, teaching can be a lonely business. How can that be possible? Teachers are working at colleges and universities that are bustling with all sorts of human activities. They are rarely the only faculty member in their discipline. And educational institutions are generally renowned for their collegiality and stimulating intellectual exchange? All of this is true. But yet, when it comes to the actual process of teaching there can be only the most superficial exchanges and a definite sense of isolation for the individual. The reasons for it vary, and I am not sure they are germane to this discussion, but its existence certainly hampers professional growth.

Breaking down the isolating mechanisms and promoting collegiality in teaching at your own institution, or even in your own department, is a start, and you will find some discussion of it in Chapter 22. In Chapter 8, you can read about different approaches to professional development, many of these promote communication between teachers as the means to that end. Talking with colleagues about teaching and sharing experiences within your department, or even across the disciplines at your school, is an important beginning, but there is something else that teachers must do too.

As is the case for individuals, a school has its own institutional teaching perspective that is a part of the institutional culture and is formed from the kinds of students it attracts, the aggregate faculty experience, the institution's mission, and more. Formal professional development programs based only on local resources or informal teachers-helping-teachers communications are limited to a great extent by that institutional culture. One must take the best of what the institution has to offer, of course; but, to maximize our professional growth and to find truly innovative solutions to classroom problems it is really necessary to go beyond the home campus and make contact with our counterparts at other schools.

It is probably safe to say that, while all of us working in this field (institutions as well as individuals) are clever and creative, none of us is as clever and as creative as we can be when we work together. And, re-invention is clearly not one of the more clever things we do. If the cost of rediscovery and reduplicating work is a price we pay for our isolation, it follows that reducing this overhead will lead to greater efficiency in the form of more rapid growth, conserved resources, and recaptured time.

But this is hardly breaking new ground. You will find that the most effective teachers who are working today are almost always well connected with the greater educational community. They draw on the larger network beyond their own campuses to fuel their innovation and stimulate their creativity. They enhance their teaching skills by reading the educational literature, attending conferences, and using the Internet to communicate with their colleagues across the country. The educational literature and conference attendance have been mentioned elsewhere in this volume. Here we will consider ways of making the electronic connection.

Accessing the Internet is becoming increasing facile because virtually all schools across the country are installing the requisite technology and getting online. The 'net is an immense resource for information and communication, but it immediately poses several questions. The first, and the only one there is space here to at least partially address is: *How can college science teachers find one another out there, in cyberspace?*

The two most popular things to look for are Web pages and listservs. Some individuals have their own pages on the World Wide Web (WWW) and so do most colleges and universities. It is probably easier and more productive to search for the institutional Web pages first.

World Wide Web

The University of Texas at Austin maintains a list of American colleges and universities. It includes over 1100 four-year colleges and universities and more than 800 community colleges. Most of those listed have a Web presence. All you have to do is to click on the name of the school and you will fly through cyberspace to its homepage. You can search these lists alphabetically or by state. Find it at:

> http://www.utexas.edu/world/univ/

Mike Conlon, of the University of Florida maintains a list of American schools offering a Bachelor's Degree or higher. This alphabetical list includes more than 1200 schools. The address is:

> http://www.clas.ufl.edu/CLAS/american-universities.html#S

but you can also link to it from the University of Texas's page.

You can obtain a list of community colleges with a Web presence and the address of each Web site from a WWW page maintained by the Maricopa Community College District. The URL is:

> http://www.mcli.dist.maricopa.edu/cc/search.html

At this writing it listed 576 two-year colleges in the U.S., Canada, and Europe and allowed the visitor to search by geographic region and, for schools in the United States, by state. Each of the schools listed at this site has a Web page, and clicking on the name of the college transports you to its WWW address.

When you arrive at a home page there are options to move to related pages. Many schools will have links to their academic departments' pages, campus telephone directories, college bulletins, class schedules, and various special projects that are underway, to mention just a few of the more common options.

Once you reach a college's homepage, finding your counterpart at the other school is a simple matter, and a short e-mail will quickly let you know if you have someone who can supply the sort of information you need, or if they will be able to direct you to someone else on their campus who can.

Correspondence begun this way can produce not only the desired information exchange, but it can also result in collaborative projects that may lead to joint presentations at conferences, the formation of articulation agreements between institutions, and sharing of resources. *The first step is to talk to one another.*

Mailing Lists

Another way of connecting with others who have common interests is to search for mailing lists, also called listservs. Members of mailing lists e-mail their messages to a server, a specialized computer, which sends the message out to all the other members, who then can respond to the original message. The result is an ongoing dialog on specific topics with other people having common interests.

A way to locate mailing lists is to point your Web browser at the following URL:

html//www.tile.net/lists

This Web site is a searchable list of mailing lists. You can do keyword searches to find topics of interest.

For best results, it is important to acquaint yourself with the proper use the Tile search function. There is a help button, and the time it takes to read the instructions comes back to you in searching efficiency. The system uses a Boolean format. You must use *and* or *or* or *and!* (for "and not") between search terms. Strings are not allowed: "cell biology" has to be written as *cell and biology*. Here's a time saver: enter the seach terms *alphabetical and listing* to get a list of the categories of mailing lists. You likely will find your academic area on that list.

Ultimately the search returns the name of the list; its country of origin; where the server is located; an e-mail address for the computer administrator, to whom you will send your commands to subscribe or to unsubscribe, for example; an e-mail address for the human administrator, who will answer your questions; and directions of how to subscribe. Here are a few examples of the output of this Web site.

MODELING
Physics Modeling Workshop
Country: USA

Site: University of Illinois at Chicago, Chicago, IL, USA
Computerized Administrator: listserv@listserv.uic.edu
Human administrator: modeling-request@listserv.uic.edu
　　You can join this group by sending the message "sub MODELING your name" to listserv@listserv.uic.edu

L-ACLRNG
Active and Collaborative Learning
Country: USA
Site: Pennsylvania State University
Computerized Administrator: listserv@psuvm.psu.edu
Human administrator: l-aclrng-request@psuvm.psu.edu
　　You can join this group by sending the message "sub L-ACLRNG your name" to listserv@psuvm.psu.edu

NCPRSE-L
Reform discussion list for Science Education
Country: USA
Site: East Carolina University, Computing and Info Systems, Greenville, NC
Computerized Administrator: listserv@ecuvm.cis.ecu.edu
Human administrator: ncprse-l-request@ecuvm.cis.ecu.edu
　　You can join this group by sending the message "sub NCPRSE-L your name" to listserv@ecuvm.ecu.cis.edu

COMMCOLL
No title defined [discussion of community college issues]
Country: USA
Site: None given [University of Kentucky Community College System]
Computerized Administrator: listserv@lsv.uky.edu
Human administrator: commcoll-request@lsv.uky.edu
　　You can join this group by sending the message "sub COMMCOLL your name" to listserv@lsv.uky.edu

Once you get the information about the lists of interest, you might want to write to the human administrators to verify the kinds of posts that are appropriate for them before you subscribe. Or you can just jump on board and "listen" for a while to find out for yourself.

The listserv (computer administrator) will verify your subscription and send you instructions for communicating with the list as well as the commands you will need to "speak" with it to control mail flow. Be sure to download those instructions and save them for future reference.

Mailing lists can take us well beyond our campus boundaries to interact with colleagues across the country and even around the world without ever getting on an airplane.

And, they are fun.

INDEX

A

abstract ideas, 7-8, 10-12, 14,25,52,120
active learning, **12ff**
administrative, support, 82
adult learners, 8,46
Adventures in Life, 106, 111
age, 7-8,54,62, 86,114, 215, 224,244
Allen, R. D., 35, 88, 119, 261
American Association for the Advancement of Science, 6, 16,147-149
American Association of University Professors, 251
American Chemical Society, 50,196, 201,270
ancillary materials, 207-219
Angelo, T.A., 16
Arons, Arnold, 45
assessment, 49,52,87 , 97, 99,110, **123-134**, 140,
• of students, 30-32, 57-59, 79-80, 95, 167-168,
• of instruction, 87, 241-250, 255
• in laboratory, 194-195
• equity, 156, 229-230
• self, 133, 244, 249
• standards, 58, 129
attendance, class, 104, 140, 169-170, 207, 230
audiovisuals, overhead, 92, 94, 101,120,207, 218

B

Benchmarks for Science Literacy, 6-7, 10, 16
bias, 65-66, 151, 156-158, 214-215
Bionews and Bioviews, 84, 107
BioQuest Curriculum Consortium, 173*ff*
Bloom, Benjamin, 48, 50

Blum, R, 88
Bruffee, Kenneth A., 173*ff*
Bush, George, 53

C

Caprio, M.W., 9, 61, 89,261
cause and effect, relationships, 28
charts, flow, 26
cheating, 168, 224
Chemistry in Context, 46, 50
classroom
• interactive, 89-102
• lecture hall, 161, 166
cognitive, framework, 13
collaboration, 23, 29, 31, 56-57, 93-95, 118, 248
collaborative learning, **21-34**, 192
• problems, 24-27
• managing, 28-29
• grading, 30-32
• activities, 89-102
• computer-enhanced, **173-188**
• groups, 10, 15,27, 90-93, 99, 182-183
collegiality, **251-257**
communication, 47,55-57, 79,82,115,127,134, 139,157,164,190,194,219, 224, 250
community, learners, 153
computer
• learning, 173-188, 190, 195
• electronic information, 61
• Internet, 61, 64, 66, 68, 69, 71, 112,116,128, 131, 165, 168, 254
• program, 162, 170
concept map, 9, 11, 18,24,26,28,128,215
concrete thinker, 7-8, 11-14, 41, 120, 215
constructivism, 9, 12, 17-18, 23, 33, 90-92, 120, 182-183, 192
• collaborative, 23

277

Q 181 .M45 1997 c.1

Methods of effective
teaching and course

DATE DUE